MacArthur's Undercover War

Also by William B. Breuer

An American Saga
Bloody Clash at Sadzot
Captain Cool
They Jumped at Midnight
Drop Zone Sicily
Agony at Anzio
Hitler's Fortress Cherbourg
Death of a Nazi Army
Operation Torch
Storming Hitler's Rhine
Retaking the Philippines
Devil Boats
Operation Dragoon
The Secret War with Germany
Sea Wolf
Hitler's Undercover War
Geronimo!
Hoodwinking Hitler
Race to the Moon
The Great Raid on Cabanatuan

MacArthur's Undercover War

Spies, Saboteurs, Guerrillas, and Secret Missions

William B. Breuer

CASTLE BOOKS

This edition published in 2005 by
CASTLE BOOKS ®
A division of Book Sales, Inc.
114 Northfield Avenue
Edison, NJ 08837

This edition published by arrangement with and permission of
John Wiley & Sons, Inc.
111 River Street
Hoboken, New Jersey 07030

This publication is designed to provide accurate and authoritative
information in regard to the subject matter provided. It is sold with the
understanding that the publisher is not engaged in rendering professional
services. If professional advice or other expert assistance is required, the
services of a competent professional person should be sought.

Library of Congress Cataloging-in-Publication Data:

Breuer, William B.
MacArthur's undercover war : spies, saboteurs, guerrillas, and secret
missions / William B. Breuer
p.   cm.
Includes bibliographical references (p.   ) and index.
1. World War, 1939—1945—Campaigns—Pacific Area. 2.
World War, 1939—1945—Secret Service—United States. 3. World
War—1939—1945—Military intelligence—Pacific Area.   4.
MacArthur, Douglas, 1880-1964. I. MacArthur, Douglas, 1880-1964.
II. Title.

D810.S7B669   1995
940.54'8673—dc20   94-48706

ISBN-13: 978-0-7858-2048-2
ISBN-10: 0-7858-2048-5

Dedicated to
Colonel Barney Oldfield (Ret.),
an American patriot with
a distinguished career as a paratrooper,
Hollywood publicist, broadcast commentator,
newspaper columnist, author, corporate
executive, and philanthropist.
He has walked with presidents
but never lost the common touch.

Battles are not won by arms alone.

—*General Douglas MacArthur*

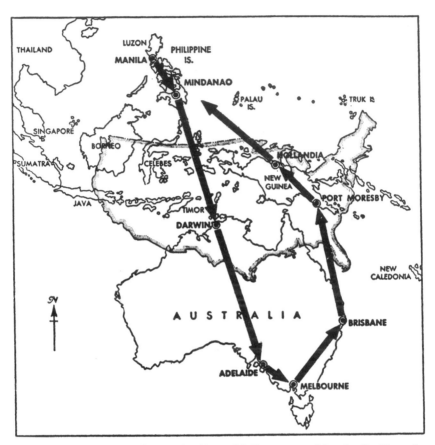

MacArthur's journey from Manila to Melbourne and back. Outline of United States superimposed.

Contents

Maps

Acknowledgments

Sincere appreciation is expressed to a large number of persons who have provided valuable assistance in the creation of this book focusing on a largely unknown but crucial operation in World War II—the Allies' intricate and massive undercover apparatus in the Pacific. Most helpful was U.S. Senator Daniel Inouye of Hawaii, who was seriously wounded while a young officer with the crack Japanese-American 442nd Infantry Regiment in Italy. He took time from his heavy schedule to furnish background information on the activities of Japanese-American soldiers whose efforts played a key role in saving lives in the Pacific.

Vice Admiral John D. Bulkeley (Ret.), American history's most highly decorated warrior, gave insights about his rescue of General Douglas MacArthur from enemy-surrounded Corregidor and of his "kidnapping" of Philippine Commonwealth President Manuel L. Quezon. Mrs. Dorothy Janson, the wife of the Swedish consul in Manila during the war, who risked her life repeatedly by helping American undercover agents and guerrilla leaders, told fascinating details of these clandestine actions.

Colonel Gibson Niles (Ret.) and Colonel Robert S. Sumner (Ret.) told about the top-secret and perilous missions by their outfit, the Alamo Scouts, deep behind enemy positions. Rear Admiral John Harllee (Ret.), a wartime PT-boat squadron commander in the Pacific, provided details about the bold raids by those swift craft. Other information on these "sea cavalry" actions came from Alyce Mary Guthrie, Executive Director of PT Boats, Inc., a ten-thousand-member veterans organization headquartered in Memphis.

Brigadier General George M. Jones (Ret.) told of the recapture of Corregidor, one of the war's boldest operations, by the 503rd Parachute Regimental Combat Team that he led. Likewise, Colonel Edward H. Lahti (Ret.), who was the army's youngest regimental commander in World War II, provided dramatic insights into the bloody battle of Manila, in which nearly one hundred thousand Philippine civilians were murdered by the Japanese. George Doherty, one of the small group of American paratroopers that was the first to land in Tokyo after the surrender, provided fascinating details on that harrowing experience.

Thanks is also expressed to Rumsey Ewing, a former PT-boat skipper; to wartime paratroop battalion commander and noted historian Lieutenant General William P. Yarborough (Ret.); and to Lieutenant General Edward M. Flanagan (Ret.), also a highly knowledgeable historian who was involved as a lieutenant with the 11th Airborne Division in actions in and around Manila during MacArthur's Great Return.

Appreciation is also evinced to those who aided me in research. Among them are Donald M. McKee, who helped enormously in locating participants in the events described in this book: Colonel Lyman H. Hammond, Jr. (Ret.), Director, Douglas MacArthur Memorial, Norfolk, Virginia; Charles Steinhice, reference librarian, Chattanooga Public Library; Richard J. Sommers and his staff, U.S. Army Military History Institute, Carlisle Barracks, Pennsylvania; Ms. Clydie J. Morgan, National Adjutant, American Ex-Prisoners of War; and Dean C. Allard and B. F. Calavante, historians, U.S. Naval Historical Center, Washington, D.C.

My wife, Vivien, was enormously valuable for her diligent research efforts and as coordinator of interviews.

It was my good fortune to have working with me at John Wiley & Sons exceptionally gifted professionals, Senior Editor Hana Umlauf Lane and Associate Managing Editor John K. Cook, and their staff members.

MacArthur's Undercover War

Manila: Hotbed of Intrigue 1

A veil of darkness caressed the sprawling metropolis of Manila as, one by one, furtive figures slipped through a side door of the Triangulo Photography Studio on Rizal Street, named after the Philippine national hero, Dr. José Rizal.[1] Greeting each new arrival was the owner of the studio, Shiko Souy, a Japanese immigrant, who was a popular leader among the many who had come from Dai Nippon (Greater Japan) to make their homes in the city long known as the Pearl of the Orient because of its broad, palm-lined boulevards and magnificent buildings. It was November 28, 1941.

Outgoing and gracious, Souy had established close friendships with prominent Filipino business leaders and high military officers, many of whom had invited him into their homes for social affairs. Actually, Souy was a clever spy for the Imperial Japanese Army. Part of his sleuthing success resulted from the fact that he didn't look or act like the stereotypical spy. Years earlier, Souy had been planted in Manila in preparation for eventual war in the Pacific and an invasion of the Philippines.

Those congregating clandestinely in the photography studio were members of the Legionarios del Trapajo, a militant underground clan of Japanese nationals and turncoat Filipinos. One of the Filipinos was Lorenzo Alvarado, a native of Manila who had spent all of his life there. He had been and was an outspoken critic of the United States, claiming that it had exploited the Philippines and virtually enslaved the people.

When the final conspirator entered the studio, a hush fell over the clique. Thick black drapes covered the windows, thwarting hostile eyes. A single dim light cast eerie shadows about the room. As Shiko Souy, visibly excited and perspiring profusely, stood in front of the gathering, it was evident to the plotters that the master spy had momentous news. Speaking rapidly, he disclosed that one hundred Japanese ships and large

1

numbers of warplanes were at that moment in Formosa, a mountainous island rising from the South China Sea 350 miles north of the Philippines. Thousands of crack Japanese troops would soon board these vessels and invade the Philippines.

Tremendous excitement swept through the room. Lorenzo Alvarado, the turncoat Filipino, joined with the others in subdued calls of *banzai!* When the meeting broke up and the schemers departed, Alvarado rushed to contact his American controller and told him about the alarming disclosure of an imminent Japanese invasion. Alvarado, in fact, had long been an undercover agent for U.S. intelligence.

This shocking information was shuttled up the chain of command of the United States Army Forces in the Far East (USAFFE), but apparently it was pigeonholed before it reached the commander, General Douglas MacArthur.

Shiko Souy, the congenial photography studio proprietor, who reportedly held a major's commission in the Imperial Japanese Army, was only one of the swarm of spies that Tokyo had infiltrated into the Philippines. A year earlier, in late 1940, Major General George Grunert, then the U.S. Army commander in the islands, reported to the War Department in Washington that Japanese immigration was growing at an alarming rate. Most of these "immigrants" were young men of military age—and many of them were known to hold reserve commissions in the Imperial Japanese Army.

These newcomers to the Philippines were industrious and hardworking. They rapidly became shopkeepers, sidewalk photographers, bicycle salesmen, household servants, and tradesmen. Much later, Philippines President Manuel L. Quezon would recall, "I discovered that my gardener was a Japanese major and my masseur a Japanese colonel."[2]

Most Japanese "immigrants" had a camera or two, and they regularly departed from Manila to stroll along the coastline of Luzon, the Philippines' principal island, to snap countless pictures. Thousands of photos of potential invasion beaches flowed into Ichigaya Heights, the nerve center of the Imperial Army in Tokyo. Painstakingly detailed written reports on Luzon defenses (or lack of them) were also shuttled to the Japanese capital as if on a conveyor belt.

While the vast Pacific was teetering on the brink of all-out war between the Empire of Japan and the United States, twenty-three-year-old Richard M. Sakakida, an American citizen, was associating regularly in Manila with Japanese nationals, many of whom U.S. intelligence regarded as secret agents. Born to Japanese parents who had emigrated to the United States territory of Hawaii many years earlier, Sakakida was distrusted by Manilans and many Americans living in the capital, all of whom considered him to be in league with the "enemy."

Actually, Sakakida, a Nisei, as second-generation Japanese-Americans were called, was a bona fide sergeant in the U.S. Army who was a spy for Uncle Sam with the mission of ferreting out Japanese government and military secrets by ingratiating himself with Japanese nationals in Manila.

The chain of events that brought Richard Sakakida to Manila began on March 13, 1941, when he and another young Nisei, Arthur S. Komori, were sworn into the army at Fort Shafter, Hawaii, each with the rank of sergeant. They were assigned to the CIP, which, they were told, stood for Civilian Interpreter Police. Later, they would learn that CIP was the abbreviation for Corps of Intelligence Police, the counterintelligence branch of the U.S. Army.

Komori and Sakakida had been selected to be the first Nisei undercover agents with a specific mission in mind—spying on Japanese nationals in Manila. Major Jack Gilbert, who had enlisted them into the CIP, was known to them from his days as a military instructor at McKinley High School in Honolulu. Sakakida graduated in 1939 and had been cadet colonel in his senior year. Komori had been a star athlete at McKinley, and later earned a degree at the University of Hawaii.

The two new sergeants had been told at first that their duty was to monitor Japanese radio broadcasts and newspapers, translating those items that might be of use to the U.S. military. Within two weeks, however, they were called into the office of a G-2 (intelligence) colonel in Honolulu and briefed on their true assignment. It would be one of extreme danger and could not be disclosed to anyone outside the G-2 office staff. All the two Nisei knew was that they would be assigned to Manila, where they would receive specific instructions.

In early April 1941, Richard Sakakida and Arthur Komori were signed on as civilian crewmen of the U.S. Army transport *Republic*, bound from Pearl Harbor to Manila. Fourteen days later, on April 21, a customs launch came alongside the *Republic* three miles out of Manila and a man in civilian clothes came aboard. A short time later, Sakakida and Komori were summoned to the bridge. There the stranger introduced himself as U.S. Army Captain Nelson Raymond, commander of the CIP in the Philippines.

Captain Raymond handed each Nisei a sealed envelope and told them to read the instructions inside and then to destroy the papers. Also in each envelope was the equivalent of fifty dollars in pesos. Their cover story was that they were civilian seamen who hated the United States and jumped ship to avoid the draft.

After the *Republic* tied up at a Manila dock, Komori and Sakakida slipped over the side in the darkness and walked into the big city. As instructed, Sakakida went to the Nishikawa Hotel and Komori to the Toyo Hotel, both in downtown Manila, where they were to await further instructions. A main contact point was to be a box at the Central Post Office listed under the phony Filipino name Sixto Borja. Twice daily the two Nisei were to check the box to learn what point would be used to rendezvous with American intelligence officers. At the same time, the two Nisei were to use the post office box as a "drop" for their own reports, which would eventually reach General MacArthur at his headquarters at 1 Calle Victoria.

The Nishikawa Hotel was a hangout for prominent Japanese nationals in Manila and proved to be an excellent place to establish contacts, especially after Sakakida trumpeted that he was violently anti-American and had jumped ship to avoid the draft. In subtle ways, he let it be known that he was an admirer of the "new Japan" and her "invincible armed forces," which had been wreaking havoc in China and Manchuria for years.

Arthur Komori also proved to be a fast learner in the cloak-and-dagger business. He, too, let it be known that he was pro-Japanese and considered Emperor Hirohito, whom most Japanese regarded as a god, to be one of his idols. Komori rapidly won the confidence of the Chief of the Japan Tourist Bureau, the Japanese Consul General, and other illustrious Japanese nationals living in Manila.

Komori's degree from the University of Hawaii had been in English, so he was able to obtain a job with Domei, the Japanese news agency. He was even asked to teach a class in English at the Japan Culture Hall. Then Captain Raymond arranged for Sears Roebuck in Manila to place Richard Sakakida on its employee list. Sakakida was instructed to spread word that he worked for Sears Roebuck in Honolulu and that his assignment in Manila was to make certain that all merchandise arrived in the Philippines in good condition. Each morning, he reported for work at 8:00 A.M., went through the motions of carrying out routine functions, then slipped out the side door a half hour later. That schedule permitted him to spend the remainder of the day moving about the city, making contacts, and carrying out undercover assignments.

Meanwhile, Sakakida informed the Japanese owner of the Nishikawa Hotel that his job with Sears Roebuck required only a half day, so the Nisei was given a job as desk clerk. This assignment proved to be an intelligence bonanza, for Sakakida was able to inspect passports of visiting Japanese and shuttle this information to his contact through the post office "drop." Friendly and personable, Sakakida engaged the guests in conversation and drew from many of them detailed information on why they had come to Manila.

One of Sakakida's first covert assignments was to establish a friendship with Clarence Yamagata, legal advisor to the Japanese Consulate in Manila, and elicit data from him. Like Sakakida, Yamagata was a Nisei. Educated at the University of California at Los Angeles, the young lawyer found professional opportunities limited in the United States because of discrimination. So he settled in Manila to practice law and was quickly hired by the Japanese Consulate.

Perhaps because both were Nisei, Sakakida and Yamagata hit it off well from the beginning. Yamagata, who was eleven years older, regarded Sakakida as a younger brother. Although Sakakida liked his new friend, he did not entirely trust him. Yamagata was not only working for the Japanese, but he was also married to a Japanese woman and had three children by her. His family lived in Japan while Yamagata worked in Manila. Secretly, Yamagata was loyal to the United States, however; Sakakida's qualms over Yamagata's loyalty to the United States would prove to be unfounded.

Yamagata often urged Sakakida to call on him any time he needed help, so an opportunity soon surfaced that gave the CIP agent a chance to exploit his diligently nurtured relationship. In an effort to put the brakes on Japan's expanding military aggression in the Far East, President Franklin D. Roosevelt, on July 25, 1941, froze all Japanese assets in the United States and its territories, including the Philippines. This act required Japanese nationals living in those locales to file reports of all bank accounts and other assets.

Within hours, Sakakida recognized that Roosevelt's edict would provide a golden opportunity for the CIP agent to dig out a wealth of intelligence from the Japanese in Manila. He called on Clarence Yamagata, who gave him a crash course on filling out the required forms. Then Sakakida let it be known that he was offering his assistance—for a small fee, so as not to arouse suspicions—to Japanese nationals who were required to file the forms, which were printed in English.

The Philippines

As part of his service, Sakakida told each Japanese client that he would file the forms with the proper U.S. government branch (which he did), so those who called on him for assistance never saw the actual form. When Sakakida asked about a respondent's past and present military service, the client did not know that such questions were not on the form.

When a client seemed hesitant about providing this delicate information, the young Nisei would smile broadly, wink, and suggest that the Japanese respondent lie about his military background. "I'll put down 'none,' " Sakakida would say while going through the motions of writing on the form. Relieved to be off the hook, the Japanese often would tell Sakakida, "off the record," about his true military connection. One man even blurted out that he had been sent to Manila on an undercover mission. Consequently, Sakakida was able to provide Captain Nelson Raymond with a client's rank, branch of service, and where he had been assigned.

Early in December, war jitters in the Philippines heightened. Unidentified aircraft flew high over Clark Field, the United States' largest air base in the Far East, fifty miles north of Manila. A day later, at dawn, a radar operator at Iba Field, forty miles west of Clark, tracked a flight of unidentified planes off the western coast of Luzon. Within a twenty-four-hour period, mystery aircraft were spotted over Lingayen Gulf, 125 miles north of Manila and long recognized by General Douglas MacArthur as the logical locale for a Japanese invasion.

On the night of December 5, a squadron of Colonel Harold H. George's P-40 pursuit planes was on patrol over northern Luzon. In the pale glow of a half-moon, the American pilots sighted a flight of eighteen bombers north of Lingayen Gulf. The P-40s gave chase, but the bombers turned tail and fled north in the direction of Formosa.

Colonel George, who was commander of the U.S. fighter planes in the Philippines, told MacArthur, "They've got all they need to know. Next time they'll come without knocking!"[3]

On December 7, 1941, the Japanese war juggernaut struck without prior warning and with enormous impact at Pearl Harbor.[4] Much of the U.S. Pacific Fleet was caught napping and was destroyed or badly damaged by Japanese carrier planes. A few hours later in the Philippines, Formosa-based aircraft with the Rising Sun emblem on their fuselages came "without knocking," as Colonel George had predicted.

Not for eighteen hours did General MacArthur realize the full extent of the Philippines catastrophe. In one fell swoop, the Japanese had bombed, strafed, and wiped out the key American air bases on Luzon: Clark, Nichols, Nielson, Iba, Vigan, Rosales, La Union, and San Fernando. For all practical purposes, U.S. airpower in the Philippines no longer existed.

Twelve thousand miles from the war-ravaged Philippines on December 8, President Franklin Roosevelt called his secretary, Grace Tully, into his study in the White House in gray, cold Washington and started dictating. "*Yesterday comma December seventh comma nineteen forty-one dash a date which will live in infamy dash . . .*"

Meanwhile, back in Manila, Arthur Komori, the CIP undercover agent, was drinking a toast to the Emperor and to victory in the Pacific with his Japanese friends at the Domei news agency when Philippine policemen charged into the building with pistols drawn. Komori and the others were hustled into buses and taken to Old Bilibid prison, a few miles away.

Komori was worried. Obviously, the local police had no idea that he was a spy for the U.S. Army—and he could not blow his cover by disclosing that fact. So while he awaited developments, Komori spent much of his time trying to draw from his Japanese cellmates information about what assistance they had provided the Imperial High Command in launching the devastating air strikes in the Philippines.

At almost the same time that Komori had been jailed, Richard Sakakida was subjected to a similar fate. A dragnet spread by the U.S. military and Philippine police collected hundreds of Japanese nationals—along with Sakakida. They were confined to the Japanese Club House under heavy guard.

An official at the detention center, Paul Marinas, searched Sakakida and found his fictitious American passport that had been issued to him before he left Hawaii and identified him as a civilian seaman. Marinas immediately concluded that Sakakida was a Japanese spy. Only much later would Sakakida learn that Marinas was also a CIP agent.

A day later, Captain Raymond Nelson covertly notified Marinas that the man suspected of being a Japanese spy was actually an American spy. Raymond slipped word to Sakakida that he was to continue with his undercover role and remain at the detention center; however, the Nisei was allowed to slip out of the compound when he so desired and return later.

On one of these outside excursions, Sakakida returned to his room in the Nishikawa Hotel to pick up his belongings. While he was packing, a squad of Philippine policemen barged in and arrested him as a Japanese spy. An hour later, he was locked in a cell in Old Bilibid prison, where his crony, Arthur Komori, was also confined.

A day later, Captain Raymond sent an officer in civilian clothes to get both CIP agents released. Then, for the first time in nine months, they came out from under cover and put back on their U.S. Army sergeants' uniforms. Richard Sakakida had no way of knowing that his dangerous role as an American master spy was far from over.[5]

These were nerve-racking days for every American and Filipino soldier in the islands. General MacArthur's "air force" consisted of four obsolete, patched-up P-40 fighter planes. Japanese bombers crisscrossed the skies at will, and the Imperial Navy controlled the sea on all sides of the main island of Luzon. At his headquarters on Corregidor, all that MacArthur could do was to wait for the Japanese invasion.

At dawn on December 22, it came—right where MacArthur had predicted it would hit. Veterans of the China war, under Lieutenant General Masaharu Homma, stormed ashore on the broad sandy beaches at Lingayen Gulf and began driving southward toward the Philippine capital.

On Christmas Eve, General Homma's tough, hardy fighting men reached the outskirts of Manila. That night, Douglas MacArthur, his wife, Jean, and their five-year-old son, Arthur, stole out of the city and took a vessel to Corregidor, a fortress island perched in the mouth of Manila Bay. There the commander in chief set up his operational headquarters in Malinta Tunnel, the only point in the Philippines that allowed him radio contact with both Washington and his units scattered throughout the islands.

Meanwhile, according to plan, MacArthur's twenty-five thousand American soldiers and forty-five thousand Filipino troops on Luzon conducted a fighting withdrawal into Bataan, a harsh, forbidding peninsula southwest of Manila. In this green hell, hardly changed from the Stone Age, MacArthur planned to hold until reinforcements arrived from the United States or Hawaii. Neither the commander in chief nor the lowliest private had any way of knowing that the Bataan force had entered a death trap.

After Japanese troops had surged into Manila, Yay Panlillio, a dark-eyed, vivacious Filipina journalist, began collaborating with the conquerors. She went on Japanese-controlled Radio Manila on a regular basis and heaped praise on the new landlords and savaged the "white devils" who, she howled, had exploited the people of the Philippines for decades.

Panlillio infuriated thousands of Manilans, many of whom had known her over the years while she was reporting for a local newspaper. Loyal Filipinos even planned her sudden demise. What the people of the Philippines did not know was that Panlillio was a secret agent for Mac-Arthur and had been asked to remain in Manila to cut a deal with the invaders. It was expected that they would woo her into making propaganda broadcasts, and they did.

As the days passed, Panlillio obediently rattled off the Japanese propaganda line over the radio. Convinced that Panlillio was a Japanese loyalist, her broadcast overseers steadily exercised less supervision of her scripts. So the young Filipina began to slip in prearranged words and phrases that provided key information on the Japanese army in Manila to MacArthur's intelligence teams monitoring her broadcasts.

Suddenly, Panlillio was no longer heard over Radio Manila. Mac-Arthur's intelligence officers were convinced that her subterfuge had been uncovered and that she had met with disaster. Only much later would they learn the true story: Through a confidential source, Panlillio had learned that the Kempei Tai, the dreaded Japanese secret police, were going to arrest her the next day. So she fled into the rugged Zambales Mountains northwest of Manila where she would eventually join a Philippine guerrilla band and continue her fight against the Japanese—this time with a rifle instead of a radio microphone.[6]

At the same time that Yay Panlillio had been broadcasting over Radio Manila, in mid-January 1942, a fierce, no-holds-barred fight was raging on Bataan as the Japanese launched a series of attacks to wipe out Mac-Arthur's troops penned up on the twenty-by-twenty-five-mile peninsula. During the thick of the heavy action, Sergeants Richard Sakakida and Arthur Komori alternated on the front lines. While dodging shells and helping to repel banzai attacks by screaming Japanese, the two Nisei broadcast propaganda to the Japanese over bullhorns and wrote surrender calls, which were hurled by gigantic slingshots behind enemy lines.

On one occasion, Sakakida's translation of a captured document resulted in an ambush by American tanks and prevented the Japanese from making an amphibious landing behind MacArthur's lines.

Hungry, exhausted, disease-racked, and with no hope of relief, the outnumbered and outgunned Americans and Filipinos, who now called themselves the Battling Bastards of Bataan, fought on.

Kidnapping a President 2

In his tiny office deep in Malinta Tunnel on Corregidor, General Douglas MacArthur was reading a decoded message that had just arrived from the War Department in Washington. Signed by U.S. Army Chief of Staff George C. Marshall, the communication alerted America's most famous general that President Franklin Roosevelt might order him to leave Corregidor and go to Melbourne, Australia, three thousand miles to the south. It was 12:03 P.M. on February 23, 1942, seventy-five days since powerful Japanese forces had invaded the Philippines.

MacArthur was jolted by the signal from Washington. The thrust of the message seemed to provide proof of what the general and his embattled men on Bataan had suspected for weeks: Roosevelt and his Joint Chiefs of Staff had written off the Philippines, sacrificing the American and Filipino troops in the islands, along with 17 million natives, on the altar of global expediency in order to buy time for a woefully unprepared United States to rearm and build combat-ready forces.

Indeed, a crucial decision had been reached in Washington: America's first priority would be the defeat of Nazi Germany (which had declared war against the United States two days after Pearl Harbor), then the full brunt of Uncle Sam's military power would be unleashed against the Japanese. That crucial secret was kept from the commander most affected—Douglas MacArthur.

MacArthur made no reply to General Marshall's message. Six days later, he received a radio communication from President Roosevelt: MacArthur was to "proceed to Australia and assume command of all troops [there]."[1]

MacArthur was skewered on the horns of a dilemma. If he disobeyed President Roosevelt, he could be court-martialed. If he followed the order, he would be accused of deserting his trapped men on Bataan. That night, the anguished general dictated his resignation from the U.S. Army and told his staff that he would cross over to Bataan and fight to the end as a rifleman.

MacArthur's staff was horrified and urged him to tear up the resignation. Could he better serve his country, they asked, as a dead infantry private or as a live general? Aides reminded him that the best hope for salvaging the grim situation in the Philippines was to go to Australia, take command of the army that Roosevelt and Marshall had implied was awaiting him, and lead it back in time to rescue the Battling Bastards of Bataan.

A week later, a second radio message from President Roosevelt prodded the reluctant general. "Situation in Australia indicates desirability of your early arrival."[2] Again aides pleaded with MacArthur to try to escape. They were aware that an American turncoat who called herself Tokyo Rose had been boasting over Japanese radio that MacArthur would be captured on Corregidor and hanged in Tokyo as a war criminal.

Seventy-two more hours passed. Finally, the general agreed to leave for Australia. Going with him would be his wife, the couple's young son, the boy's Filipina nanny, Ah Cheu, and fourteen staff officers and one enlisted man. Left behind would be twenty U.S. generals. The Bataan and Corregidor forces would be turned over to a longtime friend of MacArthur's, Major General Jonathan M. "Skinny" Wainwright, a gaunt old cavalryman.

MacArthur decided to break through the Japanese naval and air blockade of Corregidor in four patched-up PT boats, which were led by thirty-year-old Lieutenant John D. Bulkeley. The navy skipper had already become a household name on the homefront because of his widely publicized, slashing PT-boat attacks on Japanese warships, freighters, and troop-carrying barges.

Plans called for MacArthur and his party to be carried in the PT boats to the large Philippine island of Mindanao, 620 miles to the south. There, three four-engine B-17 Flying Fortress bombers flying up from Australia were to pick up the Corregidor refugees.

A few days before departure time, the scrappy John Bulkeley had told MacArthur that the long dash to Mindanao would be "a piece of cake," but the boat-squadron commander knew that it would take a near-miracle to pull off the desperate venture. The torpedo boats would travel mainly in darkness. As the seventy-seven-foot craft knifed through the uncharted waters, the hulls could be ripped open by jagged coral, hurling occupants into the inky, shark-infested waters.

None of the PT boats was equipped with a pelorus (a navigational instrument), so Bulkeley would have to set a course by the use of a simple compass, dead reckoning, and the stars—techniques used by the ancient mariners. The crews and passengers aboard the mahogany-hulled plywood boats would be perched on powder kegs. The deck of each craft would be crowded with twenty steel drums, each holding fifty gallons of high-octane gasoline. An enemy's incendiary bullet could ignite the fuel fumes in a drum and instantly turn a boat into a raging inferno.

Powerful Packard engines on the PT boats were meant to be changed every seven hundred hours of use, but after three months of heavy duty at sea without adequate maintenance, the squadron had already quadrupled the engines' normal life span. And due to their being clogged with carbon, the engines could not gain full speed, so some Japanese warships might be able to overtake the PT boats en route.

On the afternoon MacArthur was scheduled to depart, he called in General Wainwright. Throwing an arm around his old friend's shoulders, MacArthur said in an emotional tone, "Skinny, I'll be back with as much as I can as soon as I can!"

"I know you will," Wainwright replied.[3]

At sundown on March 11, the four decrepit PT boats stole out of Manila Bay, and John Bulkeley set a course for Mindanao. A short time later, the Americans spotted huge bonfires on the shores of the Japanese-held Apo Islands—the historic signal that a night escape through a blockade was in progress.

As the craft plunged through the sea, the passengers were thrown around by the rough waters. During the night, there were frequent alarms when Japanese warships were sighted. On these occasions, the engines were cut off, and the PT boats lay dead in the water with those on board praying that the tiny flotilla would not be detected.

Thirty-three hours along the way, another peril arose. Storm devils began shrieking over the Mindanao Sea. Heaving, angry waves thundered over the bows of the boats, pitching the occupants about like rubber toys in a child's bathtub.

All of the landlubbers were violently sick. A brigadier general, draped over a torpedo tube, refused the offer of a young sailor to help him below, away from the torrential blasts of water and wind. "No, no!" moaned the man. "Let me die here!"

Lying on a bunk, General MacArthur was so sick that he constantly gnashed his teeth. His wife Jean was crouched on the dirty floor next to him, chafing his hands to improve circulation. She, too, was ill, having vomited several times.[4]

Dawn broke, the storm subsided, and the waters calmed. Those on the boats were elated when, at 6:30 A.M, a lookout spotted the contours of Cape Cagayan on Mindanao—the destination. After thirty-five grueling hours, on the often angry sea, navigating by primitive means and dodging enemy warships, John Bulkeley had hit the target right on the nose.

At 7:02 A.M., the PT boats tied up at a rickety dock. Glancing at his watch, Bulkeley quipped, "Damn! We're two minutes late!"[5]

Douglas MacArthur helped his wife step from PT-41. Then he walked over to the bearded, red-eyed, exhausted Bulkeley, shook his hand warmly, and said emotionally, "Johnny, you've taken me out of the jaws of death—and I won't forget it!"[6]

MacArthur and his entourage were driven five miles inland to the Del Monte pineapple plantation, where the guest lodge and clubhouse had been set aside for them to await the B-17s from Australia. That afternoon, the general, through a secret source, received a shocking report. Feisty, diminutive Manuel Quezon, president of the Philippine Commonwealth, who earlier had left Corregidor by submarine for the island of Negros, was wavering in his loyalty to the United States and on the verge of defecting to the Japanese. Such an eventuality would be an enormous propaganda bonanza for Japan and might cause millions of Filipinos to accept Japanese control of the islands.

When the Japanese invaded his country, President Quezon had been convinced that Franklin Roosevelt, whom he considered to be an old and trusted friend, would rush massive reinforcements to the embattled Philippines and MacArthur would soon drive the invaders back into the sea. When not a single soldier, airplane, or warship arrived, Quezon suspected the truth: "Old friend" Roosevelt had abandoned the Philippines. Consequently, the commonwealth president had grown bitter.

Before leaving Corregidor, Quezon heard a broadcast over Radio Tokyo in which the Japanese strongman, General Hideki Tojo, "promised" to grant the Philippines full independence in the near future. Tojo's announcement deeply impressed the bewildered Quezon. His bitterness at Roosevelt grew. His loyalty to the United States wavered.

Quezon heatedly exclaimed to Carlos P. Romulo, a trusted aide, "We must try to save ourselves, and to hell with America. . . . The fight between the United States and Japan is not our fight."[7]

Now, General MacArthur, on Mindanao, sent an officer to locate Lieutenant John Bulkeley, who was at the Cagayan pier patching up his decrepit PT-41. Rushing to Del Monte, Bulkeley, who had not slept in forty hours, found nearly everyone but Douglas and Jean MacArthur gripped by jitters. Word that the American general had arrived on Mindanao had reached the ears of the Japanese, and they were reported to be moving troops northward from Davao, in southern Mindanao, to kill or capture MacArthur.

Bulkeley met the general on the porch of the clubhouse and had never seen the usually calm MacArthur so agitated. Jaws were clenched, face flushed. Without preliminaries, the general told Bulkeley he had a top secret mission for him: "Hop over to Negros [one hundred miles northwest of Mindanao], find Quezon, and bring him and his whole tribe back here."[8]

Clearly angry, MacArthur added, "I don't care how you get him here—just do it. We're sending Quezon to Australia to form a Philippine government in exile, whether he likes it or not!"

Bulkeley was puzzled by the order, having been unaware of the high-level machinations behind the scenes. Wasn't President Quezon supposed to be a staunch American ally? But if the general wanted Quezon brought to the Del Monte plantation, he would get him there— by whatever means was required.

His briefing concluded, MacArthur sent for Don Andres Soriano, a Filipino who was said to be a former aide to President Quezon. "He will serve as your guide in the rescue operation," the general said to Bulkeley. *Rescue operation?* To Bulkeley, it looked like a kidnapping.

Bulkeley, by gut reaction, took a dislike to Soriano and was uncertain of his true loyalty. He made a mental note to keep a watchful eye on his guide during the mission. If Bulkeley failed to survive due to Soriano's treachery, then he'd make certain that Soriano didn't come back either.

Shortly after dark, Bulkeley cast off in PT-41, with Ensign George Cox as the skipper. Before America entered the war, Cox had volunteered as an ambulance driver for the French army in 1940 and had been awarded the Croix de Guerre medal for gallantry. Also going along was PT-35, skippered by Ensign Anthony B. Akers, a lanky, soft-spoken Texan. Plunging through the heavy swells on the blackest of nights, the two-boat flotilla set a course for Negros. An hour later, lookouts discerned the dim outline of a Japanese destroyer, and the PT boats hid behind a tiny island until the enemy ship had disappeared.

The little port of Zamboquita on Negros was deathly hushed when John Bulkeley's boats edged toward shore on muffled engines. No one on board had charts, but when the water was found to be extremely shallow, Bulkeley decided to have his boats lie to offshore and wade in, rather than to risk getting the craft shot up in an ambush. According to information given by General MacArthur (who apparently had a spy planted in Manuel Quezon's entourage), the Philippine president was holed up in a house in blacked-out Zamboquita.

Clutching a tommy gun in one hand, Bulkeley began striding through the surf. With him were Soriano and two heavily armed GI crewmen. Before departing the boat, Bulkeley had taken the two sailors aside and told them to shoot Soriano if the party ran into an ambush.

Reaching the dock, Bulkeley and the others walked rapidly in the direction of Quezon's house and ran into a Filipino constable who said the president had left earlier that day for an undisclosed locale. The policeman added that Quezon had instructed him to tell any Americans who might arrive that he was not interested in leaving Negros.

"Where did President Quezon go?" Bulkeley asked sharply.

"I'm not supposed to tell you," the constable replied.

Cocking his tommy gun and shoving the muzzle against the Filipino's stomach, Bulkeley roared, "The hell you can't—now start talking!"⁹

Badly shaken and trembling, the constable blurted out that Quezon had gone to Bais, a village about twenty-five miles up the coast. Bulkeley and the others hurried back to their boats and raced to Bais. There Tony Akers was directed to patrol the shoreline in his PT-35, while Bulkeley went ashore and searched for the elusive president of the Philippines.

Bulkeley and his landing party came upon a local resident who said that Quezon was in a house a few miles inland. So the skipper "borrowed" a pair of ancient automobiles, and he and Andres Soriano roared off into the night. At a *nipa* hut (one made of palm thatches) perched on the side of a hill, Soriano called to Quezon. Two minutes ticked past. Not a sound from the hut. The guide shouted again. Moments later, a light glowed inside, and the president appeared in the doorway, a small, lonely figure clad in nightclothes.

Bulkeley and Soriano went inside. Quezon, coughing spasmodically from the tuberculosis that racked him, was ill at ease and his hands were trembling. Part of Quezon's uneasiness may have resulted from his first look at John Bulkeley in the dim glow of a kerosene lantern: The navy officer resembled a reincarnated pirate. He wore no uniform, having lost all of his clothing when his barracks in Manila was bombed in the first day of the war. His boots were mud-caked, and his unruly black beard and longish hair tied around his head with a bandanna gave him a menacing appearance. (Bulkeley's razor and other gear also had been destroyed in the bombing.) Embellishing that sinister look, Bulkeley clutched a tommy gun, carried a pistol on each hip, and had a nasty-looking trench knife in his belt.

John Bulkeley wasted no time in idle chatter. If he was going to get Quezon, his family, and a large entourage across the one hundred miles of open sea before daylight in order to avoid Japanese warships and airplanes, he had no time to lose. It was now 2:30 A.M.

As soon as Bulkeley informed the president that he had come to take him to MacArthur on Mindanao, Quezon dug in his heels and said he wasn't going. Without mentioning that MacArthur felt Quezon planned to go over to the enemy, Bulkeley reminded the president of widespread treachery by the Japanese government and military in the Far East, inferring that they would turn on Quezon and lock him up—or execute him.

A few minutes later, Bulkeley glanced at his watch. Fifteen minutes had gone by. There was not another moment to be lost. "Well, Mr. President, are you ready to come with us?" Bulkeley asked sternly, glaring menacingly at his quarry. Quezon began shaking even harder. Finally, in a soft voice, he replied, "I am ready to go."

Quezon's family, as well as officials in an adjoining house, were rousted from their beds and herded into the two automobiles. Jammed into them were Bulkeley, Soriano, Quezon and his wife, son, and two daughters, Vice President Sergio Osmeña, a general, and two cabinet officers. With a raucous revving of engines and thick clouds of exhaust smoke, the old cars lurched forward for another wild dash across the dark countryside.

Reaching the rickety Bais dock, Bulkeley learned that Tony Akers' patrolling PT boat had struck a submerged object, gouging a gaping hole in her bow, and had to be beached. Moments later, as if by magic, seven more of Quezon's cabinet suddenly appeared at the pier. So, too, did huge amounts of luggage, along with seven bulging mail sacks filled with U.S. currency. Depending on the denomination of the bills, Bulkeley calculated that there were 12 to 15 million dollars.

Bulkeley glanced at his watch: It was 3:05 A.M. The dock was in utter chaos. The Filipinos were arguing excitedly over who would sit where on the boat and which pieces of luggage would get favored positions.

"All right!" Bulkeley shouted over the hubbub, "Everyone get aboard—and leave those damned suitcases on the dock!"

There would be no room for the baggage. Only the money sacks were put aboard. The PT boat would be crammed with its own crew, along with Quezon's good-sized group and Ensign Akers and his men from the beached PT-35.

Grumbling, the Filipinos began scrambling aboard. All but Manuel Quezon. He told Bulkeley, "I've changed my mind—I'm not going."

A shouting match erupted. "The hell you're not going!" Bulkeley bellowed. Quezon climbed into the boat.

PT-41 cast off. A half hour out to sea, a violent storm erupted, pitching the craft about and threatening to capsize it. Within minutes, nearly all of the Filipinos were ill and vomiting. But Bulkeley had more pressing concerns: He was keeping a sharp eye open for the seven Japanese destroyers that reportedly were prowling the sea between Negros and Cape Cagayan on Mindanao.

Now an alarming new specter reared its head. A heavy wave had snapped the shear pins of two torpedoes, causing the engine of one of them to start while still in the tube with its nose in the water. This activated the firing mechanism so that a sharp slap by a wave could detonate the torpedo, blowing boat and passengers to smithereens.

Lieutenant Bulkeley and torpedomen James Light and John Houlihan began working feverishly at the delicate task of forcing the armed torpedo out of the tube and into the water. The bucking of the boat threatened to wash the three men overboard, but they finally succeeded in dislodging the ticking time bomb.[10]

As if Mother Nature were rewarding the three men for their courage and resourcefulness, the angry winds ceased howling and the sea calmed. PT-41 and its human cargo were halfway to Mindanao.

Minutes later, President Quezon came up to Bulkeley and said he wanted to go back to Negros. "Go right ahead," the skipper replied. "But you're going to have a hell of a long swim!"[11]

At 6:00 A.M., the PT boat tied up at the Mindanao pier. Brigadier General William F. Sharp, commander of the ill-equipped U.S. troops on Mindanao, had an honor guard and a band to greet President Quezon, America's loyal friend, as he climbed onto the dock.

Watching the beaming Manuel Quezon being feted by the U.S. Army contingent on the dock, John Bulkeley joked to Ensign Akers, "I wonder when the statute of limitations for kidnapping expires?"[12]

Bulkeley knew that his "gut reaction" about Don Andres Soriano had been wrong. "Soriano's loyalty was exceeded only by his intense desire to help make our mission successful," he told Akers.

Later that day, General MacArthur sent for Bulkeley and congratulated him on locating and bringing in the Philippine president. "Johnny, I've got another mission for you," the commander in chief added. "I want you to take a hard look at the beaches at Cotabato where the river flows into the sea [on Mindanao]. Then send me a report in Australia."[13]

Holding the belief that an army awaited him in the land Down Under, MacArthur anticipated an early return to the Philippines with an initial landing in the Cotabato region, Bulkeley deduced.

Seventy-two hours had gone by since Douglas MacArthur reached Mindanao, and still the B-17s from Australia failed to arrive. Tension racked nearly all of the Corregidor refugees other than the general and his wife. Slammed doors caused people to jump. Japanese warplanes periodically buzzed the clubhouse, and it was conjectured that they were reconnoitering for the enemy ground force closing in through the jungles from the south.

Against this background of jitters, on the third night, Captain Allison Ind, an intelligence officer on MacArthur's staff, strolled into the nearby fields to enjoy the fresh night air and gain relief from the smoke-filled rooms he had inhabited for many hours. Suddenly, he halted. Discernible in the distance and moving toward him were two shadowy figures. Ind quietly pulled his .45-caliber pistol from its holster and took aim at the taller figure. Then he recognized Douglas MacArthur, who was taking a walk with Jean.

Lowering his weapon, the horrified Ind gasped, "General, I nearly shot you!"

MacArthur chuckled and replied, "Well, Ind, we'd better decide who's going to escort whom back to the compound!"[14]

Meanwhile, many of the officers forced to remain at the Del Monte plantation for four days were angry at Lieutenant General George H. Brett, the U.S. Army Air Corps chief in Australia, whom they blamed for the exasperating delay. Unbeknownst to MacArthur and his aides, there was but a handful of B-17s in all of Australia, a continent almost as large as the United States.

Finally, General Brett managed to scrounge three serviceable B-17s from Vice Admiral Herbert F. Leary, the U.S. Navy commander in

Australia. A few hours later, the three planes lifted off for Mindanao, but one developed engine trouble and had to return to its base.[15]

Shortly before midnight, the two B-17s, after a seven-hour flight, approached the Del Monte airstrip, and the runway was quickly illuminated by primitive means—a flare at each end.

Soon, the evacuation party scrambled onto the two aircraft. Since one plane had aborted, the passengers had to be packed in like sardines. Jean MacArthur lay on the cold metal floor. Major Sidney Huff, MacArthur's aide, sat in the bombardier's seat. Two officers were wedged together over the bomb bay. MacArthur took over the radio operator's seat.

As the first Flying Fortress, piloted by Lieutenant Frank B. Bostrom, started down the short runway, hoping to get airborne before reaching the flare at the end, the engine began to splutter. No one took comfort in reflecting that mechanics had spent an hour repairing a defective supercharger after the planes had arrived at Del Monte. Bostrom peeked at MacArthur and saw no change of expression. Moments later, the coughing engine caught and the B-17 lifted off. The second plane followed.

Thirty minutes later, the bombers were engulfed by a violent storm that tossed the occupants about and triggered an epidemic of airsickness. When winging over the Indies, Timor, and northern New Guinea—strongholds of the expanding Japanese empire—the pilots had to make sharp, evasive turns, because enemy eyes no doubt were scanning the skies.

At daybreak, Japanese Zeros, swift, highly maneuverable fighter planes, rose to search for the B-17 intruders, but Bostrom and the other pilot managed to elude them. Then, those on board cast silent sighs of relief—off in the distance, they saw the coast of northern Australia shimmering in the morning haze. Moments later, Bostrom received an alarming radio report. Darwin, where the planes were going to land, was under heavy attack by Japanese warplanes.

Fuel was running low on the B-17s. Just as Bostrom began toying with the notion that he would have to crash-land—always a perilous endeavor—with America's most famous general on board, a radio message diverted the flight to Batchelor Field, an airstrip fifty miles from Darwin.

Hopping down from the bomber after landing, General MacArthur spotted an American officer, called him over, and inquired about the progress of the buildup to reconquer the Philippines. Bewildered, the officer hemmed and hawed. Finally, he stammered, "Sir, as far as I know there are very few troops in the entire country."

Now it was MacArthur's turn to look bewildered. Turning to his chief of staff, Major General Richard K. Sutherland, MacArthur declared, "Surely, he is wrong!"[16]

Most of the remainder of the fifteen hundred miles to Melbourne, on the southeastern coast, was in a special train arranged by the beleaguered General Brett. The "special train" was a relic from the past. It consisted of a tiny, wheezing locomotive, two dilapidated coaches with hard wooden benches, and a bright red caboose. On this ancient conveyance, the MacArthur party would have to ride over one thousand torrid miles to Adelaide, where they would board a speedy, modern train provided by the Australian government for the remainder of the trip to Melbourne.

On the third day of the rail trip, Colonel Richard J. Marshall, Mac-Arthur's deputy chief of staff, came aboard at a hamlet just north of Adelaide. Marshall had escaped from Corregidor with MacArthur and had flown from Batchelor Field to Melbourne to get a handle on the situation there.

Without preamble, Marshall gave the general the heaviest shock of his long career: The army that MacArthur and his staff thought was waiting in Australia did not exist. The four Australian infantry divisions were halfway around the world, fighting the Germans in the North African deserts. In fact, there were only thirty-two thousand Allied troops in all of Australia, and most of them were noncombat types. There were fewer than one hundred serviceable aircraft, and not a single tank was in all the land. Neither was there any naval force. A short time earlier, Admiral Leary's fleet had been destroyed in the Battle of the Java Sea.

For perhaps the only time in his life, MacArthur was plunged into gloom. And to trusted aides, he spoke bitterly of President Roosevelt, who, he was convinced, had lied and "tricked" him into leaving Corregidor.

Eleven thousand miles from Australia on March 18, a blaring headline in the *New York Times* electrified its readers:

MacARTHUR IN AUSTRALIA
Move Hailed as Foreshadowing Turn of the Tide

MacArthur indeed was Down Under. But any "turn of the tide" was wishful thinking on the part of newsmen far removed from reality. Actually, two powerful Japanese thrusts were bearing down on Australia, and MacArthur, with all of his acknowledged military brilliance, might be unable to keep the undefended nation from being invaded and overrun.

Thumbs Down on Wild Bill's OSS **3**

O n the beautiful, sun-drenched morning of March 21, 1942, a bois-terous, excited throng of six thousand citizens assembled at the Spencer Street Station in Melbourne, Australia's second largest city and the capital of the state of Victoria. An honor guard of 360 U.S. soldiers, all clad in white helmets and white gloves, stood by. The crowd had come to greet an American general, Douglas MacArthur, who was as popular in the land Down Under as he was in his own country.

Most of the Aussies felt that they would be welcoming a Messiah, who was coming to save their country from the Japanese juggernaut that had plunged southward from Tokyo, swept around the stubborn defend-ers in the Philippines, and now was barreling hell-bent for New Guinea, the world's second largest island, which was only three hundred miles across the Coral Sea from northern Australia.

It appeared to panicky Australians that the Tokyo warlords had tar-geted Brisbane, Sydney, Canberra, and Melbourne, the east coast cities where most of the nation's 9 million citizens lived, for early capture. And the average Aussie would have been much more alarmed had he or she been privy to a top government secret: All twelve thousand miles of the coastline of a continent the size of the United States were undefended.

Suddenly, a shout rang out from the crowd at the Spencer Street Station. "Here *he* comes!" It was 9:52 A.M. Moments later, the Adelaide Express rolled to a halt. Bedlam erupted. Men and women jostled, shoved, and pushed, trying to get a closer glimpse of the Messiah. Sixty Victoria constables strained mightily to hold back the human avalanche that threatened to engulf the train.

Minutes passed, but there was no sign of Douglas MacArthur. Al-ways the showman, the four-star general was lounging in a plush chair in his private parlor car until the "stage" was set for his debut in Melbourne.

23

Finally, a mighty roar as MacArthur, wearing a bush jacket and trade-mark gold-encrusted cap, emerged and stood on the Adelaide Express's observation platform. Fifty newsmen from several Allied countries tried to elbow their way forward.

Stepping down from the platform, MacArthur strode to an Austra-lian Broadcasting Company microphone. Aides noticed that the exuber-ant welcome had lifted the general's spirits. In his stentorian tones, Mac-Arthur began to speak: "The President of the United States ordered me to break through [the Japanese sea and air blockade of Corregidor] . . . for the purpose, as I understand it, of organizing an offensive against Japan, a primary objective of which is the relief of the Philippines. I came through . . . and *I shall return.*"[1]

Raucous cheers from six thousand throats echoed across Melbourne.

When welcoming ceremonies had been concluded, MacArthur, Jean, little Arthur, and the boy's nanny, Ah Cheu, climbed into a limou-sine for a drive to the Menzies Hotel, which would be home for the family. A motorcycle escort had been provided; however, through a mix-up, it had already departed. "That figures!" the general grumbled.[2]

For the remainder of the day, MacArthur relaxed in his suite at the Menzies, and the next morning, he was driven to his new headquarters on the eighth floor of a bank building at 121 Collins Street. Conferring with members of what was known as the Bataan Gang (the key staff members who had come with him from Corregidor), MacArthur discov-ered that he was commander of nothing. Expecting a directive spelling out his new title and forces assigned to him to be waiting, MacArthur was told that not a peep had been heard from on high in Washington.

Several days passed. Still no word from the Joint Chiefs of Staff. One week. Two weeks. MacArthur railed to his staff that it had been his "understanding" that he would be Supreme Commander of all Allied forces in the Pacific.

Unbeknownst to the frustrated general and his Bataan Gang, guer-rilla warfare had erupted in Washington over which service—army or navy—would carry the ball in the Pacific. Crusty Admiral Ernest J. King, who had recently been appointed Chief of Naval Operations, argued vehemently that because the conflict against Japan would be largely conducted on the seas, it would be foolish to name an army officer—that is, Douglas MacArthur—as overall commander. King, a hulking, often vitriolic man, swore that he had no intention of risking his precious aircraft carriers and other capital ships in MacArthur's hands.

King put forth a candidate for Allied Supreme Commander in the Pacific—white-haired, unassuming Admiral Chester Nimitz, who had taken command of the U.S. Pacific Fleet ten days after Uncle Sam was bombed into global war at Pearl Harbor. Outside of navy professionals, the capable Nimitz was virtually unknown, and his rank was junior to MacArthur. For his part, General George Marshall had no intention of entrusting large numbers of army troops that would eventually reach the Pacific to an admiral, meaning Nimitz.

While the army and navy brass were skirmishing in Washington, back in the Philippines Lieutenant John Bulkeley took his remaining three PT boats northward across the Mindanao Sea to Cebu. Shortly after sundown on April 8, coastwatchers reported two Japanese destroyers and a cruiser steaming toward the southern tip of Cebu. Bulkeley in PT-41 and Lieutenants George Cox and Robert Kelly, skippering the other two boats, charged out to tangle with the enemy vessels.

A bitter clash erupted in the blackness. There were not three but six Japanese ships. Darting about, the PT boats sent several torpedoes into the enemy vessels but in turn were heavily damaged by the combined firepower on ships thirty times the size of the pesky PT boats. By dawn, two of the American craft had been destroyed. Then, General William Sharp, the U.S. Army commander on Mindanao, explaining that there were no more torpedoes, commandeered Bulkeley's PT-41 and ordered it hauled to Lake Lanao, fifteen miles inland, and to be used to prevent Japanese floatplanes from landing on the water there.

Before lifting off from Mindanao for Australia, General MacArthur had asked Bulkeley to "take a hard look at the beaches" near the town of Cotabato where a river flows into the sea on Mindanao. After the loss of all his PT boats, John Bulkeley and many of his crewmen took to the hills to fight as guerrillas and promptly headed for the Cotabato region. There Bulkeley organized a small group of native guerrillas, dressed them like fishermen, and had them paddle about the mouth of the river in *bancas* (small boats). The "fishermen" took soundings in bays and inlets by the primitive means of lowering strings tied to rocks; they recorded their findings on crudely sketched maps.

Bulkeley collected this information and then located a clandestine radio over which the operator sent a message to MacArthur's headquarters in Melbourne. "Cotabato beaches no good for large-scale landings."[3]

Brooding in Melbourne, MacArthur's thoughts seldom strayed from the Philippines and his desperate men left behind on Bataan and Corregidor. When the telephone rang in his Collins Street headquarters, the receptionist answered, "Hello, this is Bataan." An airplane that was scraped up for the general's use was named *Bataan*. And when his wife, Jean, christened a new Australian destroyer, at MacArthur's request, it was called *Bataan*.[4]

Aides had noticed of late that the patrician Douglas MacArthur seemed withdrawn, given to long periods of silence and meditation. Uncharacteristically, he was sharp with many high-ranking officers, especially those in the U.S. Navy and Army Air Corps, the two branches he felt had betrayed him by not coming to his aid in the Philippines after the Japanese invasion.

At sixty-two, MacArthur looked twenty years younger. His dark hair had receded and his piercing blue eyes either mesmerized those he was seeking to woo or scared the hell out of those who had gained his displeasure. He walked with a brisk step and carried his paunch, concealed by broad pleats on his trousers, like a military secret.

Each morning, throngs of Aussies gathered outside the Menzies Hotel to see the general climb into his waiting car for the ride to his headquarters, a few blocks away. Then, and on most other occasions, he always looked as though he had just emerged from a tonsorial parlor, and his uniforms were crisp and neatly pressed at all times.

MacArthur's subtle air of aloofness and what some considered to be his stage props—the gold-encrusted cap, thirteen rows of "fruit salad" (ribbons representing decorations), and a walking cane—resulted in a few high-ranking U.S. officers regarding him as arrogant. However, junior officers idolized him, and they sought to imitate his every move and gesture. The general never played cards or swapped jokes or barracks tales, and he seldom drank. Each morning before climbing out of bed, he read passages from the Bible.

While MacArthur awaited word from Washington, a bloody curtain was lowered on the bitter tragedy in the Philippines. Weakened by tropical diseases and suffering hunger pangs for many weeks, the Americans and their Filipino comrades were rapidly losing their capacity to resist. Hemmed in on Bataan, armed with ancient weapons, and firing shells that failed to explode, the men who called themselves the Battling Bastards of Bataan began to eat mule, dog, horse, cat, lizard, monkey, and iguana meat. Many gnawed on tree roots, bark, and leaves. On April 10, 1942, the beleaguered Bataan force surrendered. In Melbourne, Douglas

MacArthur was in his office when he heard the tragic news. An aide happened to walk in and noticed that tears welled in the general's eyes.[5]

Meanwhile, Sergeants Richard Sakakida and Arthur Komori, who had been key undercover agents in Manila, had been sent from Bataan to Corregidor, where they were assigned to help decipher intercepted Japanese radio messages. Raymond Nelson, their boss, who had just been promoted to major, also brought Clarence Yamagata, the Nisei who had been working for the Japanese Consulate, to Corregidor. Although a civilian, Yamagata helped in deciphering intercepted Japanese messages.

With the fall of Corregidor seeming to be inevitable after the Bataan surrender, General MacArthur's headquarters in Australia ordered Sakakida and Komori to be evacuated to Australia. They were to take one of the last flights off the embattled fortress. Linguists and interpreters were crucially needed in Australia for MacArthur's return to the Philippines.

Yamagata would be left behind, a fact that haunted Sakakida. The conquerors would not deal lightly with the Nisei who had been employed by the Japanese Consulate and had a wife and three children in Japan. So Sakakida contacted an aide to General Wainwright and requested that Yamagata be assigned his reserved seat on the imminent flight.

MacArthur's headquarters approved the change, and when the light aircraft lifted off from Kinley Field, the airstrip on Corregidor, Komori and Yamagata were two of the three passengers on board. At Panay Island, the three passengers climbed into a twin-engine B-25 bomber. After a refueling stop at the Del Monte plantation on Mindanao, where fifty-gallon drums of fuel were put aboard, the Corregidor refugees flew on to Australia and eventually reached Melbourne.

On reporting to a headquarters outside the city, Sergeant Komori discovered, to his dismay, that he was not such an important gear in the Allied war machine as his flight to Australia seemed to indicate. The only American soldier Down Under with actual combat experience in interrogating Japanese prisoners on the front lines was put to work driving a truck.

On April 18, more than four months after the United States went to war against the empire of Japan, President Roosevelt and the Washington brass resolved the bitter dispute over who would command in the Pacific—by compromise. Violating military doctrine, the Joint Chiefs created *two* theaters of operation. MacArthur, based in Australia, was appointed Supreme Commander of the Southwest Pacific Area, and Admiral Chester Nimitz, whose headquarters was in Hawaii, five thousand miles east of the Philippines, was designated commander of the Pacific Ocean Area.

With the fall of Bataan, the American and Filipino garrison on Fortress Corregidor, two and a half miles offshore from the peninsula, braced for the inevitable thunderclap. It came on May 4, when the Japanese artillery saturated the tiny island with sixteen thousand shells and hundreds of bombs in one day, and an amphibious force stormed ashore. Heavy fighting ensued, but the situation was hopeless for the defenders. On May 6, a white flag was raised over the bastion.

General Skinny Wainwright, the U.S. commander in the Philippines, insisted that only Corregidor was capitulating. But Japanese threats to massacre the sixty-five thousand Americans and Filipinos who were taken when Bataan fell left Wainwright with no alternative. He radioed his troops on the other islands to lay down their arms.

By June 1942, Japan had conquered the Philippines, Singapore, Hong Kong, the Dutch East Indies, Malaya, Borneo, the Bismarck Islands, Siam, Sumatra, the Gilberts, the Celebes, Timor, Wake, Guam, much of the Solomons, and half of New Guinea. Japanese bombers were pounding the northern Australian port of Darwin. Dai Nippon now radiated for five thousand miles from Tokyo in nearly every direction, and Emperor Hirohito, the diminutive, mild-mannered father of six, reigned over one-seventh of Planet Earth.

The stunning operations left Japan's 70 million citizens in a state of euphoria. *Hakko-ichiu* (bring the eight corners of the world under one roof) had become the national slogan. Clearly there was nothing to halt the rampaging Rising Sun from barging into Australia and then on eastward in the direction of the United States.

In Washington, gloom was thick. Shocked by the speed and finesse of the Japanese blitzkrieg, which dwarfed Adolf Hitler's vaunted conquests in Europe, the generals and admirals predicted that it would require ten years to be in a position to invade Dai Nippon—provided the American public was willing to accept horrendous casualties.

Secretly, President Roosevelt and his military advisors were prepared to write off Australia, which was regarded as having no direct strategic value. If the huge landmass was swamped by the Japanese tidal wave, Hawaii would be the lone base for launching an eventual counter-offensive in the Pacific.

In Canberra, the capital, Australian Prime Minister John Curtin and his military chiefs had designated what they called the Brisbane Line, which ran east-west along the tropic of Capricorn a short distance above Brisbane. Nearly all of the vast regions in the north and west would be abandoned to the Japanese. Plans called for blowing up power plants, destroying coastal docks, wrecking military installations, and putting the torch to anything that could be of value to the invaders.

Meanwhile, in Tokyo, where the heady aroma of widespread victory was in the air, a squabble erupted at Imperial General Headquarters between Admiral Isoroku Yamamoto, the commander of the Combined Imperial Fleet, and General Hideki Tojo, the army leader who had seized the post of premier shortly before the outbreak of hostilities in the Pacific. Yamamoto, who had been educated and learned to play poker at Harvard, had been the architect of the attack on Pearl Harbor and was a national hero in Japan. Now he proposed landing an initial force of five divisions on the eastern, heavily populated coast of Australia. After the big cities were captured, he would turn Japan's armed forces against Hawaii, and from there they would charge on eastward and invade California between Los Angeles and San Francisco.

Yamamoto's chief antagonist, Hideki Tojo, was nicknamed "the Razor" because of his sharp intellect. A short man barely five feet three, his unkempt mustache and circular, oversized horn-rimmed glasses gave him an owlish appearance, which belied his ambition, drive, and utter ruthlessness. Although Tojo agreed with Yamamoto on Australia's being the next major objective, he and his army leaders were convinced that the admiral's scheme to invade Hawaii, five thousand miles east of the Philippines, and the ensuing leap to the California coast, another three thousand miles away, bordered on the reckless at this time.

As the Washington brass had done in settling their dispute over who would command in the Pacific, the warring factions in Imperial General Headquarters resolved their squabble by compromise. New Guinea, the Solomons, and other islands in an arc around northern Australia would be invaded and used as bases to seize the land Down Under. Yamamoto was satisfied. Once Australia was conquered, Tojo, he felt, would agree to far bolder operations—such as the capture of Hawaii and the invasion of California.

Consequently, Operation Mo was created. It called for Vice Admiral Takeo Takagi, whose naval armada had destroyed U.S. Admiral Herbert Leary's flotilla in the Java Sea a few weeks earlier, to capture Port Moresby at the eastern end of primitive, godforsaken New Guinea.

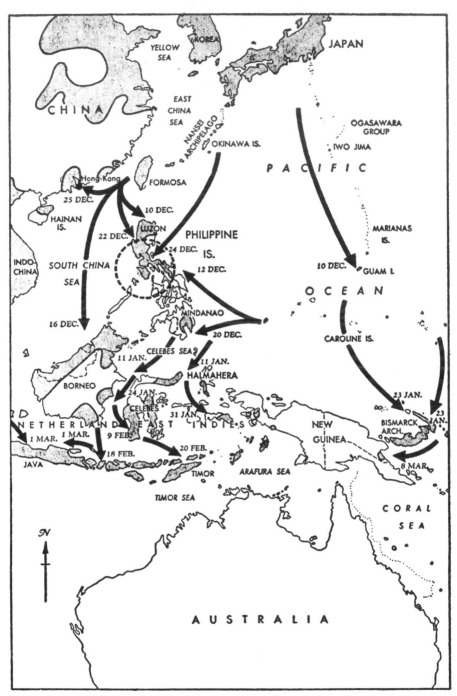

Japanese blitzkrieg in the Pacific

Moresby was the only Allied enclave north of Australia, and it was held by only a few hundred "Diggers," as Aussie soldiers called themselves. Once Moresby had been taken, the entire fifteen-hundred-mile-long island would fall like an overripe apple.

Then, using Moresby as a springboard, Japanese forces would seize Fiji, Samoa, and New Caledonia, U.S. bases east of Australia, thereby severing the ocean lifeline between America and the land Down Under. These maneuvers would leave eastern Australia wide open to landings by five Japanese divisions.

Unknown to the Japanese, the American army and navy had a secret weapon in the Pacific: a chain of intelligence radio monitoring posts that ringed the Japanese empire from Alaska to MacArthur's headquarters in Australia. These secluded posts were key components of Operation Magic, the cover name given to safeguard the source of the high-grade intelligence gained by American cryptologists who had been eavesdropping on coded Japanese radio messages. Months earlier, the secret Japanese naval code had been broken by an obscure, unheralded U.S. Navy commander, Joseph J. Rochefort.

A former enlisted man, Rochefort had combined a thorough grasp of the Japanese language with a natural aptitude for his work in breaking the naval code, an effort that had required an enormous memory for details and a knowledge of Japanese naval operations and ships acquired through years of study. Now, across thousands of trackless miles of the Pacific, hundreds of enemy messages were being plucked out of the air, decoded, and rushed to designated American commanders.

On May 3, 1942, Admiral Takagi's amphibious force sailed from Rabaul, a Japanese stronghold in northern New Britain. Destination: Port Moresby, six hundred miles to the southwest as the crow flies. Magic's intercepts detected Takagi's departure, and Task Force 17, under scrappy U.S. Rear Admiral Frank Jack Fletcher, was rushed toward Moresby to meet the enemy armada. Fletcher linked up with an Australian task force commanded by Rear Admiral J. G. Crace.

Southeast of Port Moresby, the Japanese and the Allied armadas collided. No one on either side knew that naval history was being made. For the first time, two fleets fought from over the horizon without being in sight of one another. Each tried to destroy the other by bombs and aerial torpedoes loosed by warplanes taking off from aircraft carriers. Both sides inflicted heavy damage as the savage engagement raged for three days. Finally, Admiral Takagi's force broke off the fight and headed back to Rabaul.

Australia was safe from invasion—at least for the present. However, Tojo and Yamamoto would try again, MacArthur was convinced.

Meanwhile, significant numbers of Allied troops were landing Down Under nearly every day. To the cheers of large dockside crowds, Australian brigades, veterans of bitter fighting in the North African desert and in Greece, swung down gangplanks and began jungle training. Transports carrying the U.S. 41st Infantry Division tied up at Port Adelaide, and ten days later, the U.S. 32nd Infantry Division docked at the same place.

MacArthur continued to press Washington for more fighters and bombers, even though on paper his air branch had mushroomed to 250 Royal Australian Air Force planes and 517 U.S. aircraft. However, most of these were being repaired, cannibalized, or overhauled, so there were only 220 combat planes of all types.[6]

Elsewhere, Prime Minister Curtin and his advisors felt that these new troop formations should dig in along the Brisbane Line and prepare for the Japanese invasion. MacArthur, who had been awarded a chestful of high decorations for valor as a thirty-seven-year-old colonel and brigadier general in World War I, had other ideas: He vowed to take the offensive.

A lesser stalwart than the Supreme Commander would have been awe-struck by the gargantuan size of the Southwest Pacific Area. So vast were the distances, a map of the United States could be superimposed over one of Australia, then a second map of the United States could sit on top of that one, and finally a chart of Canada could fit above the two United States maps—and all that oceanic area, with its countless islands, seas, and atolls, would be MacArthur's theater of operations.

On July 20, the Supreme Commander moved his headquarters from Melbourne to Brisbane, twelve hundred miles closer to the oncoming Japanese. There the general, his family, and the Bataan Gang took over picturesque Lennon's Hotel. A day later, MacArthur was at his desk on the eighth floor of the AMP Building, which had been occupied by an insurance firm whose executives and employees had fled southward.

Since the outbreak of the shooting war in the Pacific, MacArthur had been grossly handicapped by an almost total lack of combat intelligence.

"You can't fight 'em if you can't see 'em!" the general was fond of saying.

The Supreme Commander felt that one of his most pressing needs was reliable tactical intelligence on the Japanese—what, when, where, and how they were moving. Washington recommended that he utilize the

Office of Strategic Services (OSS), a clandestine outfit that had been founded from scratch a year earlier by its leader, a dynamic Irishman and World War I hero, Colonel William J. "Wild Bill" Donovan. Prior to the establishment of the OSS, at a time when war clouds had been gathering over the Pacific, the United States had been the only major country without a global intelligence organization.[7]

Months earlier, MacArthur had soured on the OSS. Reports had reached him from confidants in Washington that the gung-ho Donovan, who had been awarded the Congressional Medal of Honor while leading the famed 69th Infantry Regiment in France twenty-four years before, was looked on by army brass in the capital as a "Hollywood comic sleuth" who was "as confidential as a foghorn" in his "rousing game of cops and robbers."[8]

Many of Bill Donovan's schemes for subversive warfare did not sit well with MacArthur, especially since a few of the suggested operations poached on the Supreme Commander's preserve, the southwest Pacific. One scheme was especially bizarre. Donovan, in January 1942, came up with the grandiose idea of announcing to the world that the Japanese planned to attack Singapore, a British bastion at the southern tip of the Malay Peninsula. When the enemy failed to do so, Donovan declared, Washington could proclaim that this "failure" was the "turning point" of the war in the Pacific.

Donovan had submitted the Singapore ploy to President Roosevelt, an old friend to whom the OSS chief had direct access. Roosevelt shuttled the idea to army Chief of Staff George Marshall, who replied in diplomatic terms. The entire western Pacific was so open to Japanese assaults that it "would be best" not to openly invite the Tokyo warlords to strike at any particular locale.[9]

A week later, a Japanese force hit Singapore. In a lightning operation that lasted only a little more than two weeks, the "impregnable" fortress fell. Nine thousand British servicemen had been killed, 130,000 captured—a monumental Allied disaster.

At the same time, the military brass in Washington (and Douglas MacArthur, as well) turned thumbs down on another of Wild Bill Donovan's schemes. The OSS boss proposed using "a man" he had in Manila to establish a "stay-behind" spy operation in the Philippines once the Japanese had overrun the islands.[10]

Like most American military professionals, General MacArthur had a conservative political bent, so he also viewed the fledgling OSS with a jaundiced eye because of a galaxy of liberal intellectuals whom Bill Donovan had recruited into his cloak-and-dagger operation and inserted in key policy-making slots in Washington. Chief among them was angular Robert Sherwood, noted playwright and formerly a speechwriter for President Roosevelt. Sherwood had been awarded three Pulitzer prizes for drama: *Idiot's Delight, Abe Lincoln in Illinois,* and *There Shall Be No Night.* His plays usually set forth his liberal political views.

Sherwood headed up the Foreign Information Service, the propaganda branch of the OSS, and he hired a few other playwrights of similar political leanings to work with him. When MacArthur learned through the army grapevine that much of Sherwood's propaganda being beamed into Nazi-held Europe was far to the left of American mainstream thinking, the death knell had sounded for the OSS in the southwest Pacific.

Even had the Supreme Commander chosen to accept the OSS into his theater of operations, it was doubtful if the clandestine agency was yet prepared to be of much value to the war effort in the early months of 1942. When Bill Donovan had asked President Roosevelt what he considered to be the most crucial intelligence just before shooting erupted in the Pacific, Roosevelt had replied, "Japanese intentions."

So Donovan collared Kenneth Landon, then a professor of philosophy at Earlham College in Indiana, and rushed him to Washington. Landon, whose wife, Margaret, wrote *Anna and the King of Siam,* had been recommended to Donovan by the Council of American Learned Societies and Donovan confidants at Yale, Harvard, and Princeton. When Landon arrived at OSS headquarters, Donovan promptly briefed him on the vital need for information about Japanese intentions in the western Pacific.

Handed a key by Wild Bill and cautioned not to lose it, Landon opened a cabinet labeled "Southeastern Asia Intelligence." The first three drawers were empty. In the fourth drawer, there was a lone envelope marked "Top Secret." After several minutes of debating with himself over his authority to open and read such crucial, top secret intelligence, he finally slit open the envelope. Inside were two magazine articles—both of which Landon had written.[11]

Less than a year after Professor Landon had found his Far East Intelligence cupboard almost bare, a top-ranking OSS executive had flown to Brisbane to try to get permission for Donovan's eager "cowboys" (as they called OSS agents working in the field) to run subversive and psychological warfare operations in MacArthur's theater. Although the Supreme Commander received Donovan's emissary with typical cordiality, the bottom-line reply was a resounding "No."

There remained a desperate need for means to gain needed intelligence and to conduct unorthodox warfare if MacArthur were to travel the bumpy road to Tokyo and hold his casualties to a minimum. So he decided to create his own cloak-and-dagger organization.

4 A Clandestine Agency Is Born

When the Australian winter season was a damp, raw reality in June 1942, Douglas MacArthur conceived a doctrine to follow along the ocean-and-jungle road to Tokyo, five thousand miles to the north. Instead of launching frontal attacks on Japanese strongholds, he would leapfrog over them, leaving the bypassed garrisons to wither and die on the vine. A former star baseball player at West Point, the general borrowed an old term for his new strategy: "hit-'em-where-they-ain't."[1]

Now, the Supreme Commander called in his chief intelligence officer (G-2), Colonel Charles Willoughby (later promoted to Major General). Shrewd, incisive, and demanding, Willoughby was born Karl Weidenbach in Germany, and he spoke with a thick Teutonic accent. Known to some underlings as the "Prussian Drillmaster" and to others as "Sir Charles," he was a tough professional, skilled in his trade. Speaking with his customary crisp tone, MacArthur told Willoughby that he wanted him to form a large undercover warfare apparatus to help pave the road to Tokyo.

Between Australia and the Philippines, MacArthur wanted hundreds of spies on the ground in Japanese-occupied territories and elsewhere behind enemy lines. There should be elite, commando-type units to conduct hit-and-run raids, keeping the enemy jittery and off balance. Groups trained in silent killing and sabotage would blow up factories, ships, airfields, power plants, arsenals, warehouses, people—anything and anyone valuable to the Japanese. Mixed with these action outfits would be a widespread propaganda operation, a crucial ingredient in modern warfare, to give hope to populations under the Japanese yoke and to demoralize enemy soldiers.

On July 2, Captain Allison Ind, who had nearly shot General MacArthur at the Del Monte plantation on Mindanao, was summoned by his immediate boss, Colonel Van S. Merle-Smith, a member of a prominent New York family and Willoughby's deputy G-2. Speaking in conspiratorial whispers, he briefed Ind on MacArthur's plan for a single undercover warfare agency to be called the Allied Intelligence Bureau (AIB).

There were several small, unorthodox warfare and intelligence outfits already in existence to form a foundation for the AIB. These would be greatly expanded and provided with adequate, modern tools of their trades. Each of these units would have a needed degree of autonomy, but they would be given central direction by the AIB.

Within a week, Merle-Smith and Ind drew up a directive spelling out the function of the AIB: "Obtain and report information on the Southwest Pacific Area. . . . Weaken the enemy by sabotage and destruction of morale. . . . Render aid and assistance to local efforts [guerrillas] in enemy-occupied territories."[2] Appointed AIB controller was Colonel G. C. Roberts, the director of intelligence for the Australian army. A man of enormous energy, integrity, and skill, Roberts would supervise and coordinate day-to-day operations. Captain Ind was named deputy controller and finance officer.

Although Colonel Roberts was a consummate professional, his designation as controller had been largely dictated by diplomacy in order to get the full cooperation of Australian government and military leaders. With an American, Allison Ind, in charge of the AIB pocketbook, MacArthur held indirect control of clandestine schemes. Without Ind's approval, any proposed operation by a component of the AIB would be stillborn from financial anemia.

On July 6, 1942, without fanfare, the super-secret AIB was born. It had only one truly trained and effective component—a unique Australian spy network consisting of coastwatchers holed up on remote islands in a 2,500-mile-long arc that covered the land, sea, and air approaches to northern Australia.

With unusual foresight, the Australian government had organized the coastwatcher network in September 1939, more than two years before the Japanese juggernaut began rolling inexorably southward to threaten the land Down Under. Directed by Captain R. B. M. Long, chief of intelligence for the Royal Australian Navy, junior officers had fanned out into some of the world's most primitive islands to recruit jungle-wise gold miners, copra traders and planters, missionaries, telegraph operators, and administrative officials.

Each coastwatcher was intimately acquainted with his region and knew, if war were to break out, which natives would be friendly to

Caucasians and which would be hostile. If "the enemy" (that is, Japan) were to overrun their locales, the spies were expected to remain in place and report ground, sea, and air movements by radio to the secret coast-watcher headquarters in Townsville, on the northeast coast of Australia.

As soon as the Japanese struck in the Pacific, Captain Long, an energetic and capable officer, promptly began expanding his covert organization, which represented Australia's first line of defense. Lieutenant Commander Eric A. Feldt, a soft-spoken, action-oriented officer and Long's number two man, directed the crash expansion.

Feldt supplied the code name for the jungle-spy organization: Ferdinand, after the famous bull in a book by Munro Leaf. The label was most appropriate. The fictitious bull did not like fighting but preferred to sit quietly under the shade of a tree and smell the flowers—that is, until he was stung, and then Ferdinand became a force to be reckoned with.

Ferdinand operatives had to be especially dedicated to their cause. Never numbering more than a few hundred men, the spy organization was top secret and its existence would never be revealed during the entire war. Hunted down by the Japanese and occasionally betrayed by treacherous natives, these lonely sentries endured almost ceaseless, nerve-racking adventures.

The coastwatchers' communications device, called teleradios, had been developed by Australian scientists especially for Ferdinand. These small instruments would resist jungle mildew, torrid heat, and the crude handling of communications amateurs and could be transported by hand in emergencies.

None of the coastwatchers was under any illusion as to his fate should he be captured by the Japanese. As civilians, the Ferdinand operatives had no right, under international law, to transmit intelligence. So if caught, the coastwatcher would be executed as a spy—after undergoing agonizing torture in an effort to get him to disclose details of his work.

Although the Australian navy could not order a civilian to remain behind once the Japanese tidal wave had overrun his island, most of the Ferdinand operatives chose to stay in place. From their painstakingly camouflaged vantage points on beaches, ridges, and mountaintops, they passed tension-filled days scanning the horizon for signs of Japanese activity.

While Japanese counterintelligence found it almost impossible to detect the coastwatchers' hideouts from the air, they often did intercept the spies' radio signals through the use of direction-finding equipment to pinpoint the source. Japanese patrols fanned out over the suspected region, forcing the Ferdinand agents to flee to hideouts where caches of supplies had been concealed earlier. At one fallback position in a cave in the Solomons, there were 110 cases of food, 93 bags of rice, 200 cases of kerosene (for illumination), and 50 cases of whiskey (which had been stolen earlier from the Japanese).

Although the coastwatchers grumbled about the occasional intrusion of outsiders they called "boarders," the jungle spies did their best to make them feel at home. Nick Waddell, a coastwatcher in the Solomons, kept a "guest register," as he loftily called it, and formed the Rubber Rafters Association, a club composed of rescued Allied airmen. Each Rubber Rafter was presented with a crudely lettered certificate and required to pledge that he would get drunk annually on the anniversary of his rescue after the war.

New Zealander Donald G. Kennedy was more than just a Ferdinand coastwatcher: He was a recruiter, a trainer, and a guerrilla leader. Although his life was in danger almost constantly, he lived a more comfortable existence than did most jungle spies in a plantation house abandoned by executives of a copra firm at Segi Point in southern New Georgia. In a nearby little bay, Kennedy kept a schooner and, on occasion, he and a small native crew sallied forth to fight pitched battles with Japanese patrol boats.

One of Kennedy's early recruits was Geoffrey Kuper, the son of a German planter and a native woman. Although Germany was an ally of Japan, Kuper proved to be one of Ferdinand's best operatives. Once Kennedy had schooled him on the techniques of jungle spying and fighting, Kuper was sent off to the village of Tatamba on Santa Isabel in the central Solomons. With Kuper was a radio, a scavenged motor cruiser, and his native wife of three weeks.

As time went by, Kuper and the local agents he recruited rescued twenty-eight Allied airmen and mounted numerous hit-and-run raids against Japanese camps and patrols. In one of their boldest attacks, twenty-six Japanese soldiers were ambushed and killed on a nearby island.

Although New Georgia was held tightly by the Japanese, Don Kennedy managed to maintain a force of local warriors who remained loyal to the Allies when most natives on the island were drifting over to the Japanese occupiers.

Another coastwatcher, Cornelius Page, who had been born in Sydney, was managing a copra plantation on Simberi, a tiny island east of New Guinea, when war broke out in the Pacific. When asked by Commander Feldt to become a Ferdinand operative, he leaped at the chance. It was an ideal situation for the personable young man: He could remain on the island he loved while living with his beautiful native girlfriend, Ansin Bulu, and serve his country at the same time.

Middle-aged Jack Talmage, also an Aussie, had lived for twenty-two years on an adjoining plantation. Like Page, he knew the region well and was highly respected by the natives. He also joined with his neighbor as a coastwatcher.

Working on yet another Simberi plantation was Eric "Sailor" Herterich, a German who had married a native woman years earlier. Sailor— no one knew where he had acquired the nickname—was regarded by other Europeans as being shiftless, lazy, and lacking in character. Over the years, Herterich had chosen not to disclose that he was of German nationality, but, with the Japanese bearing down on Simberi from the north, he began to trumpet his birth status around the island. Japan was an ally of Nazi Germany, he repeatedly reminded the natives in their dialect, so when the Japanese invaded Simberi, he would become master of the island.

Cornelius Page soon heard of the German's boasting, so he launched a mini-propaganda blitz of his own.

The Japanese won't dare come, he told natives with a conviction he did not truly feel. If they do come, he added, the Allies would soon kick them out.

Although bewildered by the conflicting claims, the Simberi natives gradually climbed onto Sailor Herterich's bandwagon. So Page and his sidekick, Jack Talmage, would be isolated if the Japanese landed on the island.

Page became furious when a group of natives from a nearby island stole onto Simberi under cover of darkness and looted his plantation. There was no doubt in the Australian's mind about who had instigated the raid: Sailor Herterich, who now was flying a Nazi flag on his property.

Then, one day in March 1942, Japanese troops came ashore on Simberi, and Page and Talmage were forced to flee to a previously prepared hideout. It became apparent that escape was hopeless unless they could be rescued by sea. They radioed their predicament to Townsville, and word was sent back that a submarine would be dispatched to retrieve the two spies at a designated point on the coast.

For three nights, the two Australians, along with Page's native girlfriend, Ansin Bulu, crouched along a dark, quiet beach, directing the agreed signals from a flashlight, always in danger of discovery by the

Japanese or the hostile population. The submarine never came. Page and Talmage would later learn by radio that the underwater craft had developed major mechanical trouble and had to return to port. When Ferdinand officials tried to secure a second submarine, they were told that the few underwater vessels available to the southwest Pacific were engaged in more important missions.

A day later, Townsville received a desperate message from beleaguered Cornelius Page: A special contingent of Japanese soldiers and natives was going to use hunting dogs to track down the two spies. No more was heard from Simberi.

Ansin Bulu was captured first. She was taken to Kavieng, a Japanese base on the northern tip of nearby New Ireland, where she was tortured for a week. She kept repeating a lie: Page and Talmage had left Simberi several days earlier. Her suffering was in vain. On June 16, the two Ferdinand operatives were betrayed by a native for the equivalent of two U.S. dollars. They were captured, grilled brutally, and beheaded.[3]

A few hundred miles north of Simberi in the spring of 1942, the Japanese were rapidly converting Rabaul, at the northeastern tip of New Britain, into a mighty bastion from where future operations aimed at the capture of Australia could be directed, reinforced, and supplied. Rabaul's wide and deep harbor served as an anchorage for Japanese warships and transports and, almost nightly, convoys departed to carry materials and troops to forces pushing southward.

Within a few weeks, the Japanese built many large warehouses that bulged with shells, torpedoes, and small arms ammunition. Four new airfields around the town served as bases for swarms of Zeke and Zero fighter planes and Mitsubishi bombers. Guarding the huge military complex were some sixty thousand Japanese troops.

When war broke out, Rabaul had twice as many Caucasians living there as natives. Only four obsolete Australian fighter planes and a battalion of ill-equipped Aussie soldiers defended the town, which was rapidly overrun by the Rising Sun tidal wave. Caucasian and Chinese civilians fled to surrounding jungles.

A few months later, on July 2, Douglas MacArthur received an amazing directive, one that reflected Washington's ignorance over the true desperate situation in the Southwest Pacific Area. With the Japanese powerhouse still driving southward with little to impede its progress, MacArthur was ordered to recapture New Britain, which included the Rabaul stronghold.

Complicating matters was the fact that the Supreme Commander was void of intelligence about enemy troop dispositions and facilities in the Rabaul region. So the AIB was called on to sneak an agent into the area to obtain military information and to determine the natives' reaction to white intruders into their bailiwick. Learning of the espionage mission, Malcolm H. Wright, a dark-haired, personable lieutenant in the Australian navy, pleaded for the assignment and was accepted. Wright had been an employee of the colonial government in New Guinea before the war, so he was conversant with the ways of natives in the islands.

After being thoroughly briefed on his incursion, Wright climbed into the ancient U.S. submarine, dubbed merely S-42, in the Brisbane River, and the underwater craft was soon knifing northward through the Coral Sea. Destination: Adler Bay, less than forty miles from the Rabaul stronghold. Lying on his bunk that night, the lieutenant was bathed in perspiration. It was the confined quarters, he told himself. Then Wright came to grips with reality: He was just plain scared as hell.

After a voyage of nearly a week, during which the old tub ran on the surface at night and beneath it during the day, the S-42 slipped underwater into Adler Bay. When darkness blanketed the region, the submarine surfaced. Standing on deck, Lieutenant Wright and the craft's skipper, speaking in whispers, repeated the time and place for the return pickup. Then the spy, burdened with a rifle, a trench knife, a flashlight, and assorted survival gear, climbed into a rubber dinghy and began paddling.

Within minutes, the tricky tides off New Britain and an angry wind gripped his frail raft and spun it around in circles. Wright tried not to panic. A fleeting thought told him to return to the submarine—but the S-42 had rapidly departed. Furiously, he kept stroking the paddle; hopefully he was heading toward shore. Along with being encumbered by the blackness, a thick mist nearly blinded Wright. He kept battling the angry sea.

Suddenly, a swell lifted the dinghy and pitched it forward. Wright realized that he had come down on the beach—hard. Shaking the cobwebs from his head, he collected his rifle and other gear and concealed his raft. Then he moved inland for perhaps fifty yards, slumped to the ground, and fell into a deep sleep.

Awakening after daybreak, Wright peeked though tall grass to get his bearings. Off in the distance, he saw a native village of palm huts. Walking toward the flimsy structures, he reflected that within minutes he would know for certain if the natives were friendly to Caucasians, a key facet of his espionage mission. As he neared the hamlet, an old man, clearly the native chief, appeared, walking toward the newcomer. When the two men were within a few yards of one another, they stopped. For long moments they stared, then Wright broke into a smile. With great relief, he saw the old chief return the smile.

With this mutual display of friendship, the entire population streamed out of the huts to greet the visitor. The head man then escorted his guest to a hut, where they talked at length. In pidgin English, the native related all that he knew about the troops and defenses at Rabaul.

Wright learned from his host that a large number of Chinese men and women, who had to flee when the Japanese captured Rabaul, were living in a collection of huts and tents a short distance up the coast. So early the next morning, the spy bid farewell to the old chief and headed for the new Chinatown. Reaching the village, Wright was accosted by some fifteen Chinese men, some armed and most decidedly hostile.

One Chinese, who had been educated in Melbourne, spoke flawless English, and he minced no words as to how he and his companions felt about Australians: They were the culprits who had abandoned the Chinese in Rabaul and let the Japanese steal their homes and businesses. Then the man turned and spoke at length in Chinese to his sullen companions.

"My friends do not like you any more than I do," the English-speaking Chinese told Wright. "They think we ought to turn you over to the Japanese and see how well you get along with them."

Struggling to remain calm, the Australian said that a large Allied force was being built up in the southwest Pacific to recover the lands captured by the Japanese, but the Allies could not succeed unless they obtained information about Rabaul. When Rabaul was recaptured, Mac-Arthur would restore the properties that had been stolen from them, Wright told the group.

Now a second Chinese began speaking in English, and he indicated that he had been in Rabaul recently. Wright began questioning him, but the first Chinese, who seemed to be the leader, barked a sharp order and the man lapsed into silence.

Now Wright was convinced that the Chinese band was going to hand him over to the Japanese, who no doubt would execute him as a spy. So he took the only course open to him. Turning his back on the group, he began walking toward the nearby jungle, fighting off an overpowering urge to look back. At each step, he expected a bullet in the back, but no effort was made to stop him.

Traveling through the jungle all night, Wright reached the native village that he had left earlier. There he remained for three days. Twenty-four hours before he was to rendezvous with the submarine, the Australian had a surprise visitor—the second English-speaking Chinese who had told him about being in Rabaul. For whatever his reason, perhaps anger over the stinging way his leader had cut him off when he had tried to speak to Wright in their earlier encounter, the man talked for nearly two hours. Although he had been prohibited from entering restricted areas in the Rabaul region, he was able to provide valuable intelligence. He told about Japanese troop positions, the approximate number of warplanes and types based at each of the four airfields, and the kinds of ships that used the bay as an anchorage.

On the following night, Malcolm Wright, clutching tightly to a container holding the voluminous notes he had jotted down during his interrogation of the Chinese, climbed into submarine S-42. A week later, the information he had collected from the enemy's front yard at Rabaul was turned over to AIB specialists for analysis.

Meanwhile on July 20, shortly after MacArthur's arrival in Brisbane, he learned through Magic that a large Japanese convoy was preparing to sail from the stronghold of Rabaul. His intuition told him that the flotilla was bound for Buna and Gona, villages on the northeastern tail of New Guinea and 110 air miles above Port Moresby, the only Allied enclave north of Australia.

MacArthur ordered a force to be scraped up to occupy Buna and Gona, which were held by neither side. But the Japanese convoy got there first and disembarked Major General Tomitaro Horii's fourteen thousand soldiers. Burdened with machine guns, mortars, shells, ammunition, rifles, and small artillery pieces, Horii's men began a grueling climb southward over the towering Owen Stanley Mountains. Their objective was Port Moresby, a springboard to Australia.

After four weeks of agonizing struggle, the Japanese had crossed the series of 13,000-foot-high peaks and reached the straw-hut village of Ioribaiwa, only twenty miles from virtually undefended Moresby.

All the while, Douglas MacArthur was pacing back and forth as his staff looked on in silence. They knew pacing was the general's habit when mulling over a major decision. Suddenly, he spun around and said in a voice trembling with emotion, "I'll defend Australia in New Guinea!"[4]

New Guinea? MacArthur's aides were stunned. With a strong enemy force driving on Moresby, the 1,500-mile-long island was a lost cause, they were convinced. MacArthur calmed their concerns. "If you didn't expect it," he stressed, "then neither will the Japs."

Now MacArthur was confronted by the ugly logistical facts. There were three infantry divisions in Australia to send to Moresby, but with the Japanese navy roaming the sea lanes, he feared a disaster might ensue should his troops be sent in ships.

Then, Major General George C. Kenney, who was attending his first staff conference as MacArthur's new air chief, leaped to his feet. Short, tough, and gregarious, the fifty-two-year-old Kenney blurted, "Hell, I can land 26,000 soldiers on Moresby's five airfields, keep them supplied, and provide them with all the equipment they need to drive the bastards back to Buna!"[5]

Amidst the pessimism engulfing his staff, MacArthur was delighted. Throwing an affectionate arm around Kenney, he enthused, "This fellow has given me a new and powerful brandy! I like the stuff!"[6]

Within hours, Kenney's planes, each loaded with some twenty foot soldiers, began a shuttle service to Moresby, and in two weeks a substantial Allied force (mainly Aussies) was slugging it out with Tomitaro Horii's warriors only a few miles from the port. On September 19, Horii issued orders to fall back to the north coast, retracing the narrow trail over the treacherous Owen Stanleys.

Only a few hundred exhausted, starving men eventually stumbled into Buna. Ten thousand Japanese had been lost in the all-out effort to seize Port Moresby. Among the casualties was General Horii, who drowned while trying to cross a raging mountain river.

Top secret Magic again had saved the Allies from disaster.

5 Sneaking Back into the Philippines

Two months after the Philippines surrendered, Douglas MacArthur continued to believe that the war there had never really ended. Hundreds, perhaps thousands, of American and Filipino soldiers had fled into the mountains on numerous islands and were eager to strike back at the conquerors, he was convinced. Yet there had been nothing but a haunting silence from that troubled country.

Suddenly, the quiet was broken. On July 10, 1942, a secret monitoring post on the Japanese-controlled island of Java picked up a weak radio signal from the Philippines addressed to MacArthur and passed it along to the AIB in Australia. The message said, "Detachments of Fil-American forces—we have not surrendered—are actively raiding towns of Pangasinan and Dagupan [central Luzon]. Radio censorship by Jap very rigid resulting in almost complete ignorance of Filipinos of the true and correct status of the war. As remedy we disseminate information and words of encouragement through our pamphlet, *Bataan Fortnightly*, copies of which are distributed in several provinces, including Manila."

The signal went on to declare, "Jap penalty for possession of this pamphlet and other counter-propaganda is death. . . . Our people, nevertheless, are undaunted and continue to seek correct information. Your victorious return is the nightly subject of prayers in every Filipino home."[1]

Signing the message was Lieutenant Colonel Guillermo Nakar, who had been a battalion commander of the 14th Infantry Regiment, which was fighting in northern Luzon when Bataan and Corregidor fell.

Possibly no other message of the war gave such a boost to the morale of Douglas MacArthur than did this one. Now he knew that the resistance to the Japanese conquerors was continuing long after the Philippines had been overrun. It confirmed his faith in his fighting men who had avoided capture. He knew that he had a potential powerful force in place behind Japanese lines, and all that was needed was to organize and arm it.

A month passed. Then, on August 7, an ominous warning came from Colonel Nakar. "Intelligence report reveals that enemy has detected the existence of our radio station, possibly by geometric process, and detailed a large force to look for us."[2]

Nakar continued his message by giving long and detailed instructions for codes and deceptive timing to mislead the Japanese, a calm recitation of security precautions by one under imminent danger of capture. For weeks following this report, quiet followed. Colonel Nakar, it would be learned much later, had been captured during that period of time by the enemy force and beheaded.

There followed another long period of silence from the Philippines. Then, a listening post in northern Australia picked up a faint signal from Major Macario Peralta, Jr., who had fought with the 61st Division on the island of Panay, in the central Philippines. Peralta reported that he had taken command of guerrilla forces in the Visayan Islands (Panay and several other landmasses in the region). He had some eight thousand men under his control, he advised MacArthur.

Peralta's message continued, "[We] control all Panay interior and west coast. Civilians and officials ninety-nine percent loyal. Supplies could be dropped [by aircraft] away from towns, and subs could make coast anywhere more than twenty miles distant from [larger towns]."

In Brisbane, Douglas MacArthur was jubilant and replied immediately, "Your action in reorganizing Philippine army units is deserving of the highest commendation and has aroused high enthusiasm among all of us here. You will continue to exercise command. Primary mission is to maintain your organization and secure maximum amount of information. [Combat] activities should be postponed until ordered from here. Premature action of this kind will only bring heavy retaliation upon innocent people."[3]

In his typical fashion, the Supreme Commander concluded his message with words of encouragement, "The enemy is now under heavy pressure and victory will come. We cannot predict the date of our return to the Philippines, but we are coming."

Peralta, whose life was endangered each time he radioed a message from within the midst of the Japanese, replied tersely: "Mission assigned us will be accomplished. Humblest soldier has blind faith in you."[4]

The flow of messages from the Philippines steadily increased. A radio flash was picked up from north Luzon. Signing it was Captain

Ralph B. Praeger, who had been a company commander in the crack 26th Cavalry at the time of the surrender. "If I may be permitted," he said in part, "I can organize 5,000 able-bodied trainees, ROTC's, and [other soldiers] provided we would be furnished with arms and ammunition."

MacArthur replied that he would send help as soon as possible, for he considered the guerrilla actions to be of the utmost importance.

As the result of the exchange of radio signals with Captain Praeger, the Supreme Commander learned that Lieutenant Colonels Martin Moses and Arthur Noble, both from the Philippine 11th Division, had escaped from Bataan and were directing guerrillas. The two officers radioed that they had "unified command over approximately 6,000 guerrilla troops in provinces north of Manila."

Next, Mindanao, the southernmost island, was heard from. Wendell W. Fertig, a civilian engineer who had escaped from Luzon just prior to the capitulation, radioed that he had "taken command of a strong force [of guerrillas]" on the island and that they had "complete civilian support."[5]

These radio contacts, and others like them from other guerrilla leaders in the Philippines, convinced MacArthur that this spark of determined resistance could be fanned into a roaring conflagration by the time of his Great Return.

Japanese propaganda termed the guerrillas "bandits," and they were hunted ceaselessly. Unless MacArthur gave official recognition to the ragged, often starving, lightly armed irregulars and formed them into a semblance of a cohesive military organization, they might eventually lose hope and fall prey to Japanese propaganda. Instead of resisting the conquerors, they might yield to the dictates of survival.

So in early December 1942, Douglas MacArthur instructed Charles Willoughby to organize a commando-like force that would be the first to penetrate the Japanese-controlled Philippines from outside. Its mission was to get a handle on the true guerrilla situation in the islands. The AIB launched a frantic search for the right man to lead a party (code-named Planet) into the Philippines. It could not be a Caucasian, for he would be too easily detected.

In order to find this leader of extraordinary skills, courage, daring, and resourcefulness, AIB officials turned to Captain John McMicking, who had escaped from Corregidor on one of John Bulkeley's PT boats that carried MacArthur to Mindanao. Son of a wealthy Spanish-Filipino family, McMicking had been born in Manila, had traveled extensively throughout the Philippines over the years, and had contacts on many of the seven thousand islands. Before the war, he had worked with Willoughby in putting together a large number of civilian communications workers who would go underground and form a clandestine radio network for sending messages to MacArthur's headquarters.

Captain McMicking had the ideal candidate in mind: an energetic, cerebral young Filipino named Jesus Villamor. He was the son of a prominent Manila jurist, and in the first award ceremony of the war, General MacArthur had decorated U.S. Air Corps Captain Villamor for bravery. Villamor, the citation read, had led a handful of obsolete P-36 fighters and took on a flight of at least fifty-four Japanese bombers and fighter planes. One bomber had been shot down before Villamor and his fellow pilots had been forced to break off the hopeless duel.

John McMicking hurried to an airfield outside Sydney where he contacted Jesus Villamor. They greeted one another enthusiastically, for they had long been friends, as had been their families. Then, McMicking asked evenly, "Jesus, how'd you like to go back to the islands?"

McMicking gave his friend a rundown on the Planet party that he was to lead back to the Philippines. Villamor eagerly accepted.

In the meantime, at the direction of MacArthur, the AIB greatly expanded the mission of Planet. Now Villamor and his men were charged with establishing a net for military intelligence and secret services throughout the islands: organize a chain of radio communications, both within the Philippines and to Darwin in northern Australia; locate and contact influential persons known to be loyal; and develop an organization for covert subversive actions and sabotage.

Undaunted by this awesome challenge, Jesus Villamor (now promoted to major) reported to a secret training camp outside Brisbane. His first task was to recruit and screen numerous candidates for what was described to them, with much justification, as a highly dangerous mission that would play a crucial role in the war against Japan.

Within a week, Villamor had selected six men, and they began a rigorous training course, one that required physical strength and endurance. The Planet men learned judo and how to kill silently with a trench knife. They learned how to operate small boats, read maps, and sketch in the field. There were lessons in Morse code and cipher systems.

Their demanding taskmaster was a husky Australian, Captain Allan Davidson, with whom the Planet men soon developed a love/hate relationship. Davidson never let up. He made them chop wood and plow land until their fingernails were cracked and broken and their hands grimy with dirt. This was done in support of their cover stories should they be captured, that they were simple, hard-working farmers who had come down from the hills out of curiosity to see what progress was being made in the Japanese empire's trumpeted Greater East Asia Co-Prosperity Sphere.

Finally, Villamor and his men were decked out in typical, tattered work clothes and given shoes that did not fit. In the Philippines at this time, few farmers had shoes that fit. As a result of the improper footgear, the Planet men's feet became calloused—just as Captain Davidson wanted. If they were detained by the Japanese, calloused feet could save their lives.

There were problems to be overcome in this first official penetration of the Philippines. One was how could seven single-spaced typed pages written in a cipher system for a guerrilla leader on Mindanao and another one on the island of Panay be smuggled in when the Planet men would be wearing only light, short-sleeved shirts, shorts, and straw hats? That vexing question was solved when the pages were microfilmed and the thin slivers of celluloid were placed inside hollowed-out teeth by an Australian dentist sworn to secrecy.

After three weeks of training, Planet's departure neared. As part of the tight security lid on the expedition, Major Villamor was lied to about the exact date. Then, one day in late December, the men were instructed to don old dungarees and told that they were going to load a submarine berthed in the Brisbane River. Much grumbling ensued. As they climbed into a truck, they saw that its bed was filled with the gear that they themselves had placed into watertight containers only a week earlier.

In daylight, the Planet men worked like genuine stevedores, making a large number of trips in and out of the submarine *Gudgeon*, each time lugging the containers. The blue dungarees were a hedge to allay the suspicions of any hostile eyes. Unlike regular stevedores, none of the men emerged when the *Gudgeon* prepared to cast off.

From the moment the submarine set a course for the open sea, the six Planet men assumed new "cover" lives and new identities. Jesus Villamor, known at the AIB by the code W-10, became Ramon Hernandez. His second in command, Rudolfo C. Ignacio, became Carl Noble and J-20 at the AIB. Emillo Quinto, the radio operator, was now Juanito del Rosario; Delfin Cortes Yu Hico's new name was Juan de Jesus; Patricio Jorge became Vicente Reyes, and Dominador Malic was now Delmacio Canto Macilag. All six had military backgrounds, but from this point, after changing into their new "work clothes," they were dirt farmers.

On a starry night during the first week of January 1943, the *Gudgeon* lay to off the southern coast of Negros, an island in the central Philippines. Through the periscope, the submarine's skipper spotted lights on shore. So a night later, the *Gudgeon* edged up to an alternate landing site several miles away. This time, the coast seemed to be clear: Only blackness reflected in the periscope.

Now the submarine surfaced and the Planet men prepared to lower three rafts. Two would carry three men each, and the third, containing quinine, vitamins, medical supplies, cigarettes, and candy for the guerrillas, would be towed. Then it was discovered that one raft was torn and could not be inflated. Villamor made a snap decision: The guerrilla supplies would have to be left in the *Gudgeon*.

Soon the six men shoved off in the two rafts. With them were their weapons, a radio, codes, and money. When halfway to shore, Villamor discerned a haunting specter: the dim silhouette of a nearby *banca*, a native canoe with outriggers. Who were the three dark figures in the *banca*—Filipinos or Japanese? The Planet men were gripped by tension. "Keep paddling!" Villamor whispered.

Villamor's nimble mind tumbled back and forth. What to do about this unexpected situation? If he and his men riddled the *banca* with gunfire, the sound would alert any Japanese for a mile inland. It appeared that those in the banca had spotted the two rafts, for the unidentified craft began moving swiftly away and was soon swallowed up by the night.

Villamor and his men remained silent, but each knew that those in the *banca* could spread the alarm that intruders were coming ashore. It was too late to turn back. Minutes later, the rubber rafts crunched onto the sandy beach. After burying their rafts, the party began stealing inland through the black and ominous jungle. The calls of exotic birds accelerated their tension.

During the last few hours of darkness, the Planet men settled down for a short sleep. After dawn, they resumed their arduous trek along a narrow trail through the thick vegetation. Suddenly, a nearby shout. "Halt!" The marchers froze. Crouched in the brush were at least three men. Villamor was aware that rifle barrels were aimed in his direction.

Hoping that these were Filipinos, Dominador Malic called out in a local dialect, "We are friends!" If these were Japanese, a torrent of bullets would erupt. Long moments of silence. Then, a voice from the concealed strangers said, "You come with us." Villamor and the others felt a twinge of relief to learn that those holding them at bay were not Japanese, but they could be Filipinos collaborating with the conquerors.

After marching for about a half-mile with their hands clasped behind heads as ordered, the Planet men, escorted by their captors, reached a barrio (village). There, Villamor was taken inside a palm and bamboo hut where he came face to face with an unsmiling old man named Madamba, who was the village chief. Suspicion was thick enough to cut with a knife. Neither man trusted the other.

Moments later, several armed Filipinos gathered around Madamba, and much talk ensued. Villamor felt that the natives were discussing whether or not to kill the intruders. Then, the old chief rose from his chair and stood before Villamor, closely examining the major's facial features. Speaking in a dialect that the Planet leader understood, Madamba said that it was a high honor to play host to the famous Jesus Villamor, national hero of the Philippines.

Villamor breathed a deep sigh of relief: The old chief and his warriors were not collaborators with the Japanese as he had believed, but rather they were patriotic Filipinos who despised their country's occupiers. Judging from the wild celebration touched off by Madamba's identifying the Planet leader, the old chief had first been convinced that Villamor and his party were spies sent by the Japanese to locate their village.

Villamor would learn, much to his astonishment, that the old chief discerned his true identity from a photograph of the major that had appeared in the *Manila Tribune* when he was being decorated by General MacArthur. This newspaper photo, now yellow with age, had long been pinned on the wall of Madamba's home as a beacon of hope in these dark days for the Philippines.

During the next two days, Villamor held long talks with Madamba and he placed much credence on the counsel of the chief. The Planet leader, Madamba declared, was far too well known to move about freely. His newspaper photograph was in countless barrios in the islands, and he might not be so lucky next time if he were recognized. And if the natives recognized him, no doubt the Kempei Tai would do likewise.

Villamor realized that the older man spoke the truth, but he could not, at this time, hole up in a village and abandon his plan for the penetration of Manila to form the heart of his espionage network. Bidding Madamba and the others a fond farewell, the Planet team headed through the jungle to establish headquarters at a locale not revealed to the old chief and his warriors, one of whom could conceivably be a traitor.

Two weeks later, Villamor was standing on a rickety little dock on the island of Panay, some two hundred miles south of Manila. He waved goodbye to the three-man crew of a decrepit thirty-foot boat that, huffing and wheezing, was heading northward to Luzon with a load of vegetables destined for Manila.

Returning Villamor's wave was an old friend named Jose Casteñada, who was also a guerrilla. If the seemingly innocent cargo were to be closely inspected, it would result in the crew's arrest and beheading. On board were corn, coconuts, potatoes, beans, and pineapples, but they had been split open and tiny radio parts—hundreds of them—delicately inserted. The ingenious scheme to smuggle a radio into tightly guarded Manila had been conceived by Villamor.

Casteñada's leaking little boat passed several Japanese patrol craft and reached southern Luzon, where the vegetables were loaded into three small carts. Then, the three Planet men began pushing the two-wheeled vehicles along dusty back roads toward Manila. A few hours later, they rounded a bend and stumbled into a Japanese roadblock. Backing away was impossible. The three Filipinos would have to brazen it out. Images of the chopping block at notorious Fort Santiago prison filled their minds. Casteñada hastily recited a Hail Mary and hoped his quivering hands would not betray him.

Five sullen Japanese soldiers with rifles slung over their shoulders painstakingly searched the ragged peddlers and then picked up vegetables at random and began examining them. Although gripped by fear, Casteñada summoned up the strength to protest indignantly, "These vegetables are for the dining rooms of the Imperial Japanese Army officers. If we are late in getting there, you will be to blame!"

The Japanese soldiers glared menacingly at Casteñada and then waved the cart convoy onward. Eventually, the three men reached Manila after having been halted for inspection two more times. Casteñada knew that he had a good thing going for him, so at each roadblock he cautioned the Japanese that his vegetables were destined for Imperial Army officers; the carts were allowed to continue almost at once.

Near exhaustion from their long pushing, Casteñada and his two companions headed into the heart of Manila to the ancient Walled City known as Intramuros. Built by the Spaniards in the sixteenth century, with walls that were nearly forty feet thick and fifteen feet high in places, Intramuros was an imposing locale. Along with many closely built houses, a Kempei Tai station, and the dreaded Fort Santiago prison (where hundreds of Philippine men and women had been tortured and executed), was the residence of Frank Jones, whose father was an American and whose mother was a Filipina.

Jones was apparently regarded as a Filipino by the Japanese, for he was left unmolested since the occupation of Manila. Actually, Jones was an AIB spy. So was his sister, Helen Jones, whose house north of Manila was a temporary haven for undercover agents on the run from the Kempei Tai.

Under the concealment of night, Casteñada and his two companions trundled their carts up to Frank Jones' home, where the vegetables were taken inside, pried open, and the tiny radio parts extracted. Casteñada, a skilled radio operator, tediously assembled the wireless set, and the clandestine radio was soon in operation, virtually under the noses of the Kempei Tai, which had a post just down the street.[6]

Steadily, the AIB infiltrated spies into Manila. Most of them were equipped with Australian transceivers that were comparable in size to the average household breadbox. These were superb pieces of equipment and were easy to carry as well as to hide. But radioed reports from Manila carried for only 150 to 200 miles, making it impossible to contact secret AIB posts elsewhere in the Philippines or Australia. This serious communications shortcoming had to be resolved, so it was decided to establish a "forwarding station" on Mindoro, an island south of Manila. Mindoro then could relay secret messages to a powerful guerrilla radio station on Mindanao, a few hundred miles farther to the south, which would shuttle the reports on to the AIB in Brisbane.

So the AIB tapped one of its keenest Manila agents, Rodolfo Ignacio, for the perilous task of smuggling a transceiver to the Mindoro site selected for the forwarding station. The resourceful Ignacio, who had been a lieutenant in the Philippine army, had no difficulty in sneaking the electronic set to another Filipino, Major Ricardo L. Benedicto, an AIB operative holed up on Mindoro.

His mission accomplished, Ignacio, wearing the work clothes of a Filipino farmer, began walking toward the Mindoro coast for a rendezvous with a submarine. While strolling through a barrio, he was approached by a smiling man who obviously recognized him. Likewise, Ignacio knew the other: It was his cousin, who was not aware of Rodolfo's cloak-and-dagger connection.

Rushing up to Ignacio and throwing his arms around him, the cousin cried out in joy, "Rodolfo! Rodolfo!"

Ignacio felt a twinge of alarm over this display of affection, for there could be Kempei Tai informers in the village.

"But there must be some mistake," Ignacio declared while backing off from the other's embrace. "I have never laid eyes on you before. Please excuse me."

As Ignacio walked onward, resisting an impulse to look back over his shoulder, his cousin, no doubt, was mesmerized by the incredible resemblance of this passing stranger to the cousin he had known so long.

6 Ferdinand's Pistol-Packing Padre

Diminutive Father Emery de Klerk, a Dutch priest, was one of the few Caucasians living on Guadalcanal, a large island in the Solomons chain, northeast of Australia. Father de Klerk belonged to the Marist order of Catholic missionaries, whose motto was notably appropriate for the island on which they served—*Ignoti et quasi occulti* (hidden and unknown).

The island the priest had called home for several years was infested with giant rats, cannibals, poisonous snakes, and frogs as large as footballs. It was a land of stinking swamps, towering mountains, and tropical diseases. No European in his right mind would choose to live on Guadalcanal, but Father de Klerk's mission was to save souls, so he had adapted to the hostile environment and converted a flock of some one thousand natives.

Suddenly, in the spring of 1942, the tranquil life on Guadalcanal changed dramatically: A large force of Japanese soldiers, complete with bulldozers, steamrollers, and other heavy equipment, came ashore and began constructing an airfield a short distance inland from the beach.

On July 10, several days after the men of the Rising Sun went ashore on Guadalcanal, a large Japanese sampan, packed with dome-helmeted troops, headed into the anchorage of Tangarare, Father de Klerk's mission. After telling the children to scatter into the jungle and say their Rosary, the priest put on his black cassock and headed for the beach. Soon, four Japanese officers and a large landing party of tough-looking soldiers waded ashore, and their leader introduced himself as Captain Ishimoto.

It soon became evident to Ishimoto that de Klerk would be an ardent collaborator. The little priest, always beaming graciously, cozied up to the newcomers and spoke glowingly of Japan's plan for establishing the

Greater East Asia Co-Prosperity Sphere throughout the Pacific. For their part, the Japanese were apparently delighted that at least one Caucasian embraced the concept of "Asia for Asians."

If de Klerk and the other missionaries obeyed Japanese law and didn't try to contact the Allies, they would be allowed to stay in Tangarare, Captain Ishimoto declared.

"Well, we're certainly not spies and we take no interest in politics," the padre replied.[1] Actually, the thirty-six-year-old priest was one of Commander Eric Feldt's Ferdinand coastwatchers.

Then, Ishimoto ordered his men to search the compound for weapons. A short time before the Japanese party came ashore, de Klerk had hidden a rifle and a shotgun and deliberately left a pistol in plain sight, feeling that the Japanese would not believe him if he said he had no weapons. Now the priest assured Ishimoto that there was nothing but a pistol. As the Japanese soldiers began their search, de Klerk spotted two new shotgun shells lying in plain sight on a table in the first building they inspected and nearly fainted from fright. By now it was growing dark, however, and he managed to scoop up the shells and conceal them in his cassock—praying that the Japanese did not frisk him before they departed.

Satisfied that there was only a pistol that de Klerk used for protection against wild animals, Captain Ishimoto asked if there were any more whites on Guadalcanal. Certainly not, the priest responded. Only hours earlier, he had concealed three white European nuns in a secret hiding place near the compound. Nor did he mention, of course, that his Ferdinand contact on the western end of the island was an Australian, F. Ashton "Snowy" Rhoades, who had been manager of the Burns Philp copra plantation there.

Ishimoto then wanted to know if the Dutch "collaborator" could provide him with a workforce of five hundred natives. Impossible, the cleric answered. There weren't that many healthy natives in the entire region; however, de Klerk pointed out, he could provide the Japanese with perhaps 150 native workers—if Ishimoto was willing to accept lepers and those with advanced tuberculosis.

When the long conference concluded, Father de Klerk, as a gesture of respect, ordered his native men to carry the four Japanese officers through the surf to their sampan. Wearing broad smiles and talking in their Gari dialect (which the Japanese did not understand), the natives went about their chore. As Ishimoto thanked de Klerk's men for their courtesy, the natives smiled even more broadly, bowed, and cheerfully replied in Gari: "You all smell like parrot shit!"[2]

Father de Klerk's conscience was clear over the litany of lies he had told. On occasion, the good shepherd had to look after his flock and take a large stick to the wolf invading his fold.

Meanwhile, Magic had been eavesdropping, and intercepts advised the Joint Chiefs of Staff in Washington that General Tojo was constructing the Guadalcanal airfield in order to launch swarms of warplanes against the convoys from the United States that were the lifeline to besieged Australia. To head off this deeply alarming threat, a decision was made to capture Guadalcanal and nearby Tulagi island.

In Tokyo, the Imperial General Headquarters remained smugly confident of total victory. It held to the belief that the United States could not mount an offensive in the Pacific for many months as a result of the carnage inflicted on the American fleet at Pearl Harbor and Uncle Sam's woeful unpreparedness for war.

This false sense of security was not shared by Lieutenant Commander Haruki Itoh of the Naval Intelligence Center in the capital. Late in July, his electronic monitors picked up two new Allied call signs in the southwest Pacific. Because both of these stations operated on the same circuit and both communicated directly with Pearl Harbor, Itoh concluded that either could be a headquarters for a new Allied task force.

Commander Itoh promptly urged monitoring posts in the southwest Pacific to try to pinpoint the locale of the Allied task forces, and on August 1 his radio direction finders discovered that one station was at Noumea, New Caledonia, and the other near Melbourne. The first, Itoh deduced accurately, was the headquarters of Vice Admiral Robert L. Ghormley, U.S. naval commander in the South Pacific.

As a result of these electronic intercepts, Commander Itoh and his staff sent an urgent warning that the Allies were forming a task force at Noumea and were about to launch an attack against the Solomons. Nonsense, replied Imperial General Headquarters. It would be six months or longer before the Americans could conduct offensive operations.

Early in August, an American invasion fleet of eighty-two ships sailed from Noumea (just as Commander Itoh had predicted) and headed for the Solomon Islands. Five days later, on August 7, ten thousand men of the U.S. 1st Marine Division, under Major General Alexander A. "Archie" Vandegrift, hit the beaches on Guadalcanal and Tulagi. By sundown the next day, the Marines, whose average age was nineteen, had seized Tulagi and secured their major objective, the nearly completed airfield on Guadalcanal.

During the early hours on Guadalcanal, it appeared to General Vandegrift that the enemy had fled. But they had pulled back inland to reorganize, and a long, bloody slugfest would rage on the ninety-two-mile-long island.

Three weeks after the Americans landed on Guadalcanal, three Marist priests, four white nuns, twenty-four black nuns, and sixty schoolchildren stumbled into Father Emery de Klerk's mission with frightening tales of Japanese butchery against civilians. Among the newcomers was Bishop Jean Marie Aubin, who, like most of the Catholic missionaries, had hoped to maintain a sort of Christian neutrality in the bloody struggle on the island. But it was difficult to be neutral when friends were being brutalized and killed.

Two days later, a report spread that the Japanese were closing in on Tangarare, and the panicky newcomers got ready to resume running. Father de Klerk, a persuasive man, talked them out of it: He had lookouts all along the coast, so if the Japanese were coming, he would give them ample warning. His pleas fell on deaf ears. Finally, the padre said that he would make a personal reconnaissance. Reluctantly, the refugees agreed to await his return.

Emery de Klerk, a man of God, first called on Bishop Aubin. He was going to carry a pistol and a rifle—could he use them if he ran onto the Japanese? The bishop gave his approval—that would be self defense.

Then de Klerk said, "This is war. If they see me first, they'll shoot to kill."

So if he saw the Japanese first, should he let them wipe him and his men out? "No," Aubin replied, "you must protect yourself by shooting first."[3]

A week later, the padre and his small patrol of natives returned. They had not spotted a single Japanese. The refugees issued sighs of relief. Forty-eight hours later, panic broke out again after native scouts reported that Japanese patrols were prowling the island some ten miles away. Through Snowy Rhoades' radio, de Klerk arranged for the ketch *Ramada*, which had belonged to the resident commissioner, to pick up the refugees. Everybody packed their meager belongings except de Klerk, who told no one that he intended to remain.

When the *Ramada* arrived, the spunky priest slipped off into the jungle, while the refugees scrambled aboard the vessel. On a hill a half-mile from Tangarare, he watched the *Ramada* sail away, then he returned to the compound. There he was greeted with loud cheers by his flock of one thousand natives.

Meanwhile, Lieutenant Dale M. Leslie, a lanky Marine pilot, was on a routine mission when he was ambushed by a Zero over Guadalcanal. With his cockpit on fire, Leslie bailed out and splashed down six hundred yards from shore. Despite his ordeal, he managed to swim to the beach and headed inland—where he promptly ran into a Japanese patrol coming down a path toward him. Dashing a few yards into the jungle, Leslie lay flat while the enemy formation passed by. Exhausted, he fell into a deep sleep.

At dawn, the Marine pilot began edging his way down the southwest coast of Guadalcanal, and for eleven days he lived on coconuts and dodged Japanese patrols. Then, on October 10, he spotted a canoe near an enemy camp. Fashioning a makeshift paddle, he crawled under a log to await nightfall. An hour later, Leslie, hearing a rustling sound, peered at a Japanese soldier staring down at him. The Marine sprang to his feet and both men dashed off—in opposite directions.

A couple of hours later, Leslie stole back to the beach where the canoe was tied. Again he sought a hiding place until darkness, this one under a fallen coconut palm tree that lay so that its roots and the dirt clinging to them made a cave of sorts. He wriggled in there and waited.

Within minutes, Leslie had a curious sensation that someone was near. Then sand began trickling down on him. Gingerly peeking out of his space, he felt a surge of fright—a Japanese soldier was sitting on the fallen palm only inches above him, casually eating his supper. Like a turtle when danger is at hand, the Marine pulled back his head.

Hardly daring to breathe, Leslie was soon aware of a new peril: The palm tree began sagging under the weight of the Japanese soldier, and, eventually, it caved in on the Marine. Then Dame Fate smiled on the concealed American—the enemy soldier apparently got so uncomfortable that he moved to another fallen log to finish his meal.

Eventually, a veil of night blanketed Guadalcanal. Leslie, weakened from his coconut diet, began stealing toward the canoe, paddle in hand. On both sides, he could see the dim silhouettes of Japanese soldiers cavorting and chattering along the shore to both sides of him. Just as he slipped into the canoe and began paddling, the enemy soldiers saw him and began shouting, but because they had come to the beach to frolic, they were naked and unarmed.

For three more nights, the Marine lieutenant paddled along the shore, hoping to contact Americans or friendly natives. Nearing the end of his tether, he beached his canoe, walked inland, and collapsed. Instead of dying alone and rotting in the jungle, Leslie was discovered by a friendly tribe. They carried him to their village and fed him vegetables for several days until he had partially regained his strength. A native, who spoke in pidgin English, told him that a white priest lived a short distance away. The next day, the natives, with Leslie on an improvised litter, entered Father de Klerk's compound.

Leslie, it developed, was the second Marine pilot in the priest's charge. A few days earlier, natives had brought in another downed aviator, Lieutenant Douglas Grow. Then the padre sent a native runner through Japanese positions to contact the 1st Marine Division. A day later, the ketch *Ramada* suddenly appeared and took Dale Leslie and Doug Grow back to their comrades. Had it not been for Emery de Klerk and other Ferdinand jungle spies, no doubt the two pilots would have perished.

A few days later, two U.S. planes circled low over de Klerk's compound and dropped a message wrapped around a flashlight battery. It was from General Vandegrift's intelligence officer and asked for the priest's assistance on future operations.

"If you accept, stand in open and wave your arms," the note stated. Father de Klerk walked to an open space and vigorously flapped his arms. Wagging their wings in acknowledgment, the aircraft flew away.

Two planes were back that afternoon, dropping a much longer message. Vandegrift wanted to know if de Klerk could supply guides and pack carriers for a looming Marine landing on the south side of Guadalcanal. Again the priest waved his arms as an affirmative signal. So the padre would remain as priest, doctor, and shepherd of his flock, and, at the same time, he became a sort of "field marshal of the southern Guadalcanal army." Perhaps some one hundred of his best native males were armed with rifles parachuted from planes, and a communications network of runners was established.

On November 19, a plane dropped a message to de Klerk: Could he provide guides for a patrol of twenty Marines to be landed on the following night? Once again de Klerk responded that indeed he could and that he would go along on the operation. With a pistol on one hip and a rifle slung over a shoulder, the priest led the Marine patrol on an eleven-day reconnaissance mission deep behind Japanese positions.

When the priest returned to Tangarare, he learned that the U.S. Army had replaced the Marines on the island and that a new commander, Major General Alexander M. Patch, had supplied the base with rifles, ammunition, and a large number of hand grenades. Patch even gave the compound a code name: Pineapple. And messages sent to Father de Klerk referred to him as the "base commander."[4]

While the savage fighting continued on Guadalcanal, on Japanese-occupied Bougainville, the largest and westernmost island of the Solomons chain, another Ferdinand jungle spy, an Australian named Paul Mason, was holed up along the eastern coast and observing heavy Japanese ship and air movements in the wake of the Guadalcanal invasion by Archie Vandegrift's Marines. His was a lonely, dangerous existence. Louis Antoine de Bougainville, a French explorer, had discovered the primitive island in 1768, and there had been no civilized progress since that time. Cannibals and headhunters roamed inland.

Mason, who was the manager of a plantation at Kieta, was a small, middle-aged, mild-mannered man who peered nearsightedly through thick-lensed glasses. But his appearance was misleading: His strength and stamina were equal to those of much younger, larger men. He knew jungle-covered Bougainville thoroughly, for he had lived there for twenty-six years.

Within forty-eight hours of the invasion of Guadalcanal, five hundred miles southeast of Bougainville, Mason radioed a crucial message: A flight of twenty-seven Mitsubishi bombers, flying from Rabaul, had just passed over and were heading in the direction of the Marine landing beaches. The warning gave the U.S. invasion fleet and soldiers on Guadalcanal nearly ninety precious minutes in which to prepare for the Japanese bombers, thereby saving many lives.

A series of later warnings made Mason's call letters (STO) familiar to every radio operator on U.S. ships lying off Guadalcanal and to army communications men at Henderson Field, a prime Mitsubishi target. Then, a few weeks later, STO ceased sending messages. Unbeknownst to anyone on Guadalcanal or at Ferdinand headquarters in Townsville, Paul Mason was running for his life. He had been betrayed to the Japanese by a tribesman in return for a few trinkets.

Chasing the Australian was a band of Japanese soldiers led by a captain named Tashira, who had spent many prewar years on Bougainville and knew the island almost as well as did his prey. A few days before Christmas 1942, Tashira and his men trapped Paul Mason and a small group of guerrillas in the mountains of southern Bougainville. Cocksure that he was about to capture the Australian "bandit," Captain Tashira sent a message to the suspected hideout of Mason: "Come in and eat Christmas dinner with us. If you don't, we'll shoot you on sight."

Mason ignored the ultimatum. But hours later, a Japanese patrol approached while he and an elderly friend huddled over a cold Christmas meal. Mason fled into the nearby jungle and escaped through a hail of bullets. Left behind was his radio and most of his supplies. His friend was too infirm to go along, and he was captured, beaten up, and beheaded.

Mason and the few men who had escaped with him spent the next thirty days hacking their way through jungles and arduously scaling towering mountains along slimy, narrow paths; they finally made contact with Jack Reed, another Ferdinand operative, on the northwestern tip of Bougainville. Reed also had a few guerrillas in his camp, and the two groups joined ranks. In the weeks ahead, the middle-aged Mason and Jack Reed waged a secret war, ambushing Japanese patrols and raiding outposts. Soon Mason and Reed had prices on their heads.

At about the same time that the two Ferdinand operatives were torment-ing the Japanese on Bougainville, Father Emery de Klerk and other European missionaries on Guadalcanal had come under suspicion. The little priest apparently was not all that he made himself out to be, the Japanese concluded. Caucasian clergymen and nuns were rounded up and hurled into crude stockades, but de Klerk escaped the dragnet.

Aware that he had been unmasked, the priest went into hiding and launched his private guerrilla war. Wearing khaki shorts and shirt, with his ecclesiastical white collar on backward, de Klerk armed himself with a Colt .45 and led bands of his native flock in bold forays against isolated Japanese outposts. Soon, he was badly wanted by the frustrated enemy. But try as they did, they would never catch up with the peripatetic pistol-packing padre.[5]

Meanwhile in Australia in the fall of 1942, a unit of the AIB, known as Secret Intelligence Australia (SIA), had become alarmed over reports that Japanese propaganda was making an enormous impact on the mil-lions of natives in the lands and territories overrun since war broke out seven months earlier. "Asia for Asians," was the theme. "Drive the white devils out!"

SIA's function was to deal with subversion, not only in Australia, but also in lands conquered by the Japanese. However, when Dutch and

Australian operatives were sent to penetrate Borneo, Netherlands East Indies, and other islands above Australia, they were never heard from again.

Borneo, the world's third largest island (behind Greenland and New Guinea) was of special significance to SIA. MacArthur's intelligence believed that thousands of British soldiers captured at Singapore early in the war were being held prisoners there. And Borneo's rich oil fields were feeding General Tojo's thirsty war machine. There also was much concern in Brisbane about the fate of stranded European civilian administrators, oil company families, and missionaries. Not a peep had been heard about them.

Collaborators among the Borneo population were out in force when the Japanese invaders had arrived, and much of the country welcomed the newcomers as liberators and also as the fulfillment of an ancient prophecy. According to widely accepted lore, Djojobojo, a Borneo king in the fourteenth century, had predicted that his country would suffer centuries of subjugation under a Caucasian race and then would be freed by Asian people from the north. The Japanese were believed to be those people.

Even before the war, Japanese propagandists took aim at winning over leaders among Borneo's predominantly Islamic population. Tojo's slick experts had been shipping in thousands of leaflets and booklets emphasizing the similarities between Shinto ("the way of the gods"), Japan's main religion, and Islam. Because Emperor Hirohito was thought by most Japanese to be a direct descendant of the sun goddess, the highest of the Shinto deities, the propagandists spoke loudly of Hirohito's possible conversion to the Islamic faith. No doubt such a conversion would have been startling news to the emperor.

Shortly after the Japanese occupied the big island, they opened a Religious Affairs Office in order to continue wooing the Moslem population and its Islamic leaders. Seeking a solution to keeping the huge numbers of Borneo Moslems from succumbing to Japanese propaganda and going over to the side of the invaders, SIA officials in Melbourne contacted the Raja of Sarawak, a Britisher named Sir Charles Vyner Brooks, who had escaped from Borneo to Australia just ahead of the Rising Sun occupation.

For decades prior to the war, the political organization of the large island had comic-opera aspects. In the oil-rich northern region, British colonial enterprises had carved out four enclaves, one of which was the sultanate of Sarawak, run by a series of "white rajas." Most of the southern portion of Borneo had been held by the Dutch, who operated major oil pumping and refining centers along the east coast. The vast interior of the island, ribbed with spiny mountain ranges and thick with impenetrable jungles, belonged only to aboriginal tribes, who were living as their ancestors had in the Stone Age.

Now in Brisbane, the Raja of Sarawak immediately advised SIA officials that if cooperation was expected from him, the SIA first would have to help him with a major problem. He let it be known that he was in a quandary over what to do with his three lively, attractive daughters, who, along with his wife, had escaped with him. The young women, the raja indicated, had started to "run wild" since the family arrived in Australia, and he feared that they would get into "embarrassing difficulties." One daughter was dating a professional wrestler, another a saloon singer, who, the raja was convinced, was a narcotics addict. If SIA would arrange for air transportation to Los Angeles, California, for his three offspring, he would try to help with the problem of Japanese racial propaganda. A few days later, the daughters were winging to the United States on a bomber that was making a routine flight.[6]

With the raja in Australia was the former minister of his Borneo fiefdom, a Scotsman who had converted to Muhammadanism. A shrewd old man, he wore the green turban of a bonafide hajji, one who had made the holy journey to Mecca and thereafter would be held in the highest esteem by other Moslems. The hajji provided a gold mine of information on the Islamic world. SIA learned from him that Islam had an effective and highly organized missionary service abroad with spiritual headquarters in Cairo, Egypt. Moslem priests often wandered around Morro villages in the islands above the northern rim of Australia, the hajji pointed out.

Listening to his minister's recital, the raja of Sarawak came up with a scheme for infiltrating SIA agents into the targeted territories: Why not use itinerant Moslem priests whom the natives would respect and not likely betray? That sounded good to the SIA men, who promptly began rounding up green-turbaned Moslem priests in Australia. Many balked, some out of fear, others because they felt it was wrong to combine the work of their religion with war-oriented tasks.

Despite their initial reluctance to become AIB spies, several Moslem priests eventually agreed to be infiltrated into assigned locales heavy with Moslem populations. Not only were they highly effective in neutralizing the Japanese racial propaganda, but they also sent back much useful intelligence. A few of the hajjis vanished in the months ahead, however, never to be heard from again. Either they had been caught by the Japanese and executed, or they had simply dropped out of the espionage business.[7]

The Great Manila Bay Silver Heist 7

While the AIB was sneaking hajjis into enemy-occupied Borneo and adjacent islands, Japanese authorities in Manila became upset over a flood of genuine silver pesos that was circulating in stores in the city. If the source of the silver deluge was not discovered and the influx halted, it could corrupt the entire system of Japanese occupation currency in the Philippines.

What the conquerors did not know was that a few American prisoners were conducting their own private undercover war in Manila Bay, right under the noses of the Japanese and at great peril to themselves.

The chain of events resulting in the silver flood in Manila began in April 1942 when it had become clear to U.S. commanders that defeat in the Philippines was inevitable. A decision was made to save the commonwealth's treasury—the equivalent of $8.5 million in silver pesos, which were packed in wooden boxes in a steel vault on Corregidor.

American army officers drew two lines at a point in the water near the curved tail of Corregidor. There the water was deep and turbulent enough to discourage Japanese salvage.

U.S. Navy Lieutenant Commander George Harrison, who was in charge of harbor craft at Mariveles at the southern tip of Bataan, rounded up twelve navy enlisted men, most of whom were sea divers. Sworn to secrecy, they were told that the silver would have to be dumped quickly and at night to keep the Japanese from finding out about the cash cache.

Workers lugged the heavy boxes, each holding six thousand pesos, onto a pair of flat-topped barges, which were towed to the dump site. There the cargo was pushed into the sea. It was a tedious and backbreaking task, requiring numerous trips and ten nights to move the 420 tons of silver.

When the job was done, George Harrison warned his divers to keep their mouths shut about the secret operation.

"If you're captured, don't even tell the Japs that you're divers," he told them.[1]

A few weeks later, Corregidor fell, and the divers were among those captured. In mid-July, the commandant at Cabanatuan, a putrid, disease-ridden POW camp sixty miles north of Manila, sent for Bosun's Mate First Class Morris "Moe" Solomon. Known to the American POWs as Baggy Pants, the colonel said, "We know you're a diver. Manila harbor is filled with sunken ships, and it must be cleared for traffic."

Solomon hid his suspicions. Clearly, a stool pigeon among the GI prisoners had told the Japanese that he was a sea diver. His hunch was confirmed when the colonel then singled out P. L. "Slim" Mann, Virgil L. "Jughead" Sauers, Wallace A. "Punchy" Barton, and two other veteran divers. Before departing for Manila, the divers sought out their former skipper, Lieutenant Commander Frank Davis.

"You know what the bastards really want," Davis declared. "Don't let them get it!"[2]

"It" was the fortune in silver lying on the bottom of Manila Bay.

Rapidly, the divers conceived a scheme to thwart the Japanese. If they were sent below, they would have to bring up some silver or be shot, so the recovery project would be stretched out for as long as possible. All the while, the divers would steal as much of the silver as they could and smuggle it into Manila.

Captain Oshio Takiuti, a young, personable man from a wealthy Japanese family, greeted the divers at the North Dock on Corregidor. Speaking fluent English, he told the captives that they would be assigned a sixty-foot boat on which to live. It turned out to be a bucket of bolts tied at the dock. This had been home for six Filipinos whose job it had been to tend to a few native divers who had already brought up eighteen boxes of silver. The inexperienced Filipino divers had stayed down too long, came up too fast, and died in agony of the "bends."

Now it was clear to the Americans that they were expected to take the places of the dead Filipino divers. That night, a strategy session was held on the boat. Inasmuch as eighteen boxes already had been brought up, it proved that the rest of the loot could also be recovered. So they agreed it would be necessary to invent excuses for the slowness of their diving efforts.

At the crack of dawn, the Americans were hustled onto a small fishing boat and taken to the point along Corregidor's tail where there was a flat diving barge anchored directly over the spot where the Philippine national treasury had been dumped. Now the sham that they were to clear sunken ships was brought to a screeching halt. The divers were ordered to go into action.

Jughead Sauers made the first dive, inching his way down a heavy rope that had been anchored to the bottom. Suddenly, he saw before him on the ocean floor a large stack of wooden boxes, neatly concentrated on top and beside one another. If the Japanese knew that the cache was so close together, they would realize experienced divers could bring up the entire load in a matter of a couple of weeks. That hardly coincided with the Americans' scheme to drag out the recovery operation for months.

Sauers' nimble mind told him it would be best to send up a few boxes right away to show the divers' reliability, for the Japanese knew the cache was directly under the barge. So Sauers wrapped the lifting cable around one box, gave three tugs (the signal to haul up the loot), and minutes later he was on the barge.

Now it was Moe Solomon's turn, and he sent up a box. The Japanese officers on board were delighted. Then Punchy Barton made a dive, landed directly on a stack of boxes, but returned to the surface twenty minutes later.

"Couldn't find a damned thing," he told the disappointed Japanese. "Jughead and Moe must have brought up everything that was down there."[3]

That night on the bucket of bolts, the Americans resumed their plotting. The two boxes they had brought up were waterlogged and threatening to break open. So they would assist Mother Nature. When diving resumed, they would loosen the ends of the boxes so that the heavy bags of silver would spill out on the way up. Then the divers would steal the loose bags.

Now the plot thickened. Moe Solomon hacked up a few pairs of trousers and sewed the pants legs into bags with drawstrings and a cord to tie around the diver's waist. The bag would hang under his diving underwear and be invisible to the Japanese. Now the six Filipinos tending to the divers' needs were sworn to secrecy and brought into the scheme. Once on the bottom of the bay, the diver would fill his secret bag with silver, and after he surfaced and came aboard, the Filipinos, whose job it was to help remove his diving gear, would take the silver and conceal it under a pile of raincoats stashed in a corner on deck.

All this was perilous business. Should the double-cross be discovered, the Americans and the Filipinos would be killed at once.

It was Slim Mann's time to dive first. He concealed beneath his diving underwear a short metal bar with a pointed end for breaking open the boxes. On the bay floor, he pried at one end of a box until it came loose. Then he tugged on the lifting cable three times. Halfway to the surface, the box broke open and bags of silver fluttered down.

Feeling the weight removed, the Filipinos on deck dropped the cable again. Mann attached a second box. It, too, broke open. Then Mann hid the metal bar on the bay floor for future use and surfaced. On board, the Japanese were furious.

"This is going to be one hell of a job," Mann declared with the proper mixture of disgust and anger. "Those damned boxes are so rotten that they fall apart as soon as you pick one up!"[4]

The Japanese were mildly suspicious, pointing out that the two boxes recovered the previous day were solid.

"We were lucky," Mann replied. "You could see that those boxes were rotten, too."

Punch Barton went down next. To appease the Japanese, he sent up an intact box. The next box, after being given "the treatment," came apart, and Barton stuffed the loose bags into the sack he had hidden under his diving underwear.

During the next two weeks, the Americans hid some $10,000 worth of silver pesos in the bilge of the boat on which they were living. They were disappointed: The Japanese take was $50,000. The Americans vowed that the percentage would be reversed. In the near future, the bilge was bulging with silver pesos.

Now came the task of distributing their loot. The Filipino tenders were brought into the act, since they were allowed to visit their families in Manila. There the Filipinos located some Chinese money changers who were elated to exchange Dai Nippon's occupation currency for genuine silver pesos—no questions asked—at a black market rate that undercut the Japanese yen. Eventually, so much silver got into circulation in Manila that the rate of exchange fell to thirty to one and few wanted any part of the Japanese occupation currency.

After the divers labored on in the weeks ahead, a savage typhoon ripped into Corregidor. Most of the Japanese sought shelter in Malinta Tunnel while the storm smashed the diving barge into smithereens. Miraculously, the old bucket of bolts in which the Americans' stolen silver was stashed survived the typhoon.

When the turbulence moved on, the Japanese formed working parties of American prisoners to circulate around Corregidor cleaning up the destruction. Since the cleanup parties were lightly guarded and the Japanese could not tell a diver from the other POWs, two or three divers at a time would drift into a group, pretend to be working, then slip concealed bags of silver to the astounded POWs. Soon thousands of silver pesos were being used on Corregidor to buy "luxuries"—such as food and medicine—from guards on the take.

One morning, the affable Captain Takiuti paid a surprise visit to the bucket of bolts. Together with a sour-faced man, whom the Americans were convinced belonged to the Kempei Tai, Takiuti poked into nooks and crannies, looked under straw mattresses, and kneeled to see under the stove. Watching, the divers felt their hearts skip beats. Clearly, the Japanese knew of the pilfery that had been taking place and they were searching for the loot.

Now Captain Takiuti moved through the cabin and stood directly on a ragged carpet that concealed the trapdoor to the bilge where the stolen silver was hidden. The divers thought they were goners. After standing silently for several moments, Takiuti walked away and left the boat. The Americans resumed breathing.

After the departure, the divers conjectured about Takiuti's actions. He knew that there was a trapdoor under the rug—even if the Kempei Tai did not—for he had seen it numerous times. If the two Japanese had been seeking silver pesos, an obvious place to search would be below the trapdoor. Then the Americans reached agreement: Captain Takiuti didn't really want to find the silver. Had he done so, he would have lost enormous face.[5]

That theory may have been valid. It was officially reported to Tokyo that the reason so much silver was circulating in Manila was that the typhoon had washed large numbers of boxes ashore where the genuine pesos had been grabbed by Manilans.[6]

In the meantime, the savage struggle for Guadalcanal and its key airfield continued to rage. In mid-January 1943, Admiral Bull Halsey was notified that Secretary of the Navy Frank Knox, a former newspaper publisher, and Admiral Chester Nimitz were on their way to Guadalcanal and would reach the island of Espiritu Santo, an American base 550 miles southeast of Guadalcanal, for an overnight stop. Halsey left immediately to meet the visiting firemen (as U.S. servicemen called brass on junkets to battle areas). It soon became evident that the Japanese also were gifted in cracking secret codes.

That night, Knox, Nimitz, and Halsey had just settled into their bunks aboard the aircraft tender *Curtiss* when the eerie whine of falling bombs pierced the hushed night. Moments later, explosions in the water rocked the vessel, but no hits were scored. As there had not been an air raid on Espiritu Santo in several weeks, Halsey and the visitors conjectured about an information leak.

On the following night, the two visiting firemen and Halsey were on hot, stinking Guadalcanal. At 10:30 P.M., they were in an exhausted sleep in small huts when the ground around them was rocked by bomb blasts. Japanese bombers, their engines sounding like washing machines in need of repair, were circling overhead.

With the first *wham!* Frank Knox (no spring chicken), Rear Admiral John S. "Slew" McCain, and Bull Halsey leaped from their cots, dashed outside, and barreled into foxholes to spend the remainder of the night, half-naked, as bombs continued to drop periodically from the sky. Now there was no doubt that Japanese code-busters had intercepted messages detailing the itinerary of the Secretary of the Navy and Admiral Nimitz.

All the while, Nimitz slept on in his dry, relatively comfortable cot, explaining after daybreak why he had not raced for water-filled foxholes with the others: He was afraid of mosquitoes.

Halsey and the traveling dignitaries were not the only ones on Guadalcanal convinced that a leak had disclosed their presence. When their plane took off from Henderson Field later that day, an American communications officer in the night's heavily bombed area started to send out a routine departure signal when a shaken comrade quipped, "Do me a favor, will you? Send the message in Japanese. I want the Jap bastards to know for sure that the high-priced help has left here!"

Three weeks after Secretary of the Navy Knox departed from embattled Guadalcanal, Jack Reed, the Ferdinand jungle spy on the northeastern coast of Bougainville, reported on the night of February 6 that a large enemy naval force, including twenty destroyers, had sailed from the Japanese base on Bougainville. Neither the Ferdinand operative nor Magic suspected that General Tojo had thrown in the towel on embattled Guadalcanal. Yet on this night and the following one, the eleven thousand emaciated and starving Japanese soldiers remaining on Guadalcanal were evacuated. Precisely six months after Archie Vandegrift's Marines had come ashore, a ghostly silence fell over the blood-drenched island.[7]

Two weeks after the Japanese pullout from Guadalcanal, General MacArthur's electronic snoopers intercepted a Japanese battle order. A flotilla of eight transports, crammed with 6,912 soldiers and escorted by eight destroyers, was preparing to depart from Rabaul, a Japanese stronghold on New Britain, to reinforce garrisons at Lae and Salamaua, on the northern coast of New Guinea. A few days later, American scout planes took off from Port Moresby and spotted the convoy plowing through the Bismarck Sea off Lae.

After dawn on March 3, swarms of American and Australian fighter planes and bombers took off from Moresby airfields, winged northward over the Owen Stanley Range, and pounced on the Japanese flotilla. Hours later, when the smoke of battle had cleared, seven of the eight transports and four of the eight destroyers had been sunk or so badly damaged that their crews had to abandon them.

Now the Bismarck Sea was dotted with hundreds of Japanese soldiers and sailors clinging to life rafts and rubber boats or swimming frantically. Allied pilots raced up and down, strafing and sinking everything in sight. Then, for the next few days, ten PT boats, under U.S. Lieutenant Commander Barry K. Atkins, dashed about sinking the troop-filled rafts. To the Americans, it was a gut-wrenching task, but it had to be done. In the Pacific, the Japanese had set the ground rules: dog-eat-dog, no quarter asked, none given.[8]

Capturing the floating Japanese soldiers was out of the question. They had been imbued with the Bushido philosophy that surrender was disgraceful and that they should resist to the death, thereby giving their lives for the emperor. If captured, they would often seek revenge on their captors. A Japanese sailor, who had been plucked from an almost certain watery grave by the crew of a PT boat (for later interrogation), grabbed a gun and killed a bluejacket in the act of giving this enemy a cup of warming coffee.[9]

Meanwhile, a lifeboat from the Bismarck Sea encounter was found abandoned on the beach at Goodenough Island, a few miles off New Guinea's tail. In the craft were many Japanese documents, which were rushed to the Allied Translator and Interpreter Service (ATIS), a component of the AIB. Cloaked in secrecy at Indooroopilly, a few miles outside Brisbane, the ATIS was headed by Colonel Sid Mashbir, a brilliant linguist and administrator who had been a language student in Tokyo.

Most of Mashbir's good-sized staff were Nisei soldiers, whose job it was to translate and interpret captured diaries, maps, orders, and other documents that might disclose Japanese plans and problems. It was a tedious and difficult task: The Nisei were dealing with one of the world's most unfathomable languages that grossly complicated cryptanalysis.

Back in the United States, army intelligence officers had a difficult time locating Japanese-language experts. Only about one hundred persons in the entire country were proficient in *both* English and Japanese. Four thousand Nisei soldiers disclosed that less than ten percent of them could even speak or write a smattering of their parents' native tongue. So the most promising Nisei linguists were assigned to take exhaustive courses in Japanese at the U.S. Army Defense Language Institute in San Francisco. After graduation, they were rushed to Indooroopilly.

Now, with the documents in hand from the lifeboat at Goodenough Island, Colonel Mashbir put his entire staff to work translating. It was a time-consuming, mind-numbing task. When completed, the pages translated into English filled fourteen filing cabinets.

English language translations were rushed to General MacArthur, Admiral Chester Nimitz in Hawaii, and the Joint Chiefs in Washington. The documentation proved to be the kind of intelligence bonanza that military commanders only dream about—the Japanese Army List, a roster of forty thousand officers from General Hideki Tojo, the commander-in-chief, down to company commanders and platoon leaders, as well as to which units they belonged.

Later, intelligence culled by Magic, by Ferdinand operatives, and by AIB spies established the location of many Japanese units. MacArthur would now have a prodigious advantage in planning and executing "hit-'em-where-they-ain't" operations.

Ten thousand miles from New Guinea, on June 7, the *Chicago Tribune* put into jeopardy the super-secret that had made possible the Bismarck Sea victory and other naval and ground battles in the Pacific—the fact that the United States had broken the Japanese naval code. This irresponsible disclosure, which eventually could have cost the lives of thousands of Americans, carried no byline, but it had been sent from the Pacific by correspondent Stanley Johnston.

The *Tribune* story came on the heels of the smashing American victory at the Battle of Midway, in which the Imperial Navy lost four aircraft carriers. The strength of the Japanese fleet at Midway was well known in American naval circles several days before the battle began, Johnston's article said. The navy, upon learning of "the gathering of the powerful Japanese units soon after they put forth from their bases," had guessed that Midway Island might be the target. It then described the four Japanese carriers of the strike force and the four cruisers escorting the army units that were to invade Midway.[10]

From Port Moresby to Pearl Harbor to Washington, shock waves reverberated around the high councils of command. The public release of such detailed and accurate information would surely result in Tokyo's changing its naval code. But the fears proved to be groundless: The Imperial Navy, convinced that its code was unbreakable, attributed its defeat at Midway to bad luck and overconfidence.

Meanwhile, in Tokyo, Prime Minister Hideki Tojo was shaken to learn that four aircraft carriers had been lost in a single battle.

"The news must not leak out," he told aides. "Keep it a complete secret."

A day later, Tojo had an audience with Emperor Hirohito, who customarily was apprised of the performance of his fighting forces. However, Tojo did not say a word about the naval disaster at Midway.

Tojo's orders to conceal the crushing defeat were carried out. Survivors of the sunken ships were isolated. Then, on June 10, Imperial General Headquarters finally announced that Japan had "secured supreme power in the Pacific" and that the war "has been determined in one battle."

That night, tens of thousands of people staged a flag procession and lantern parade in downtown Tokyo to celebrate the great Imperial Navy "victory" at Midway.

8 A Spectacular Prison Break

E arly in the sunlit morning of February 11, 1943, Sergeant Richard Sakakida of the U.S. Army was led from Bilibid Prison, the hellhole in Manila, by armed guards to be taken to the office of Colonel Hashiri Nishiharu, chief judge advocate (legal officer) of the Japanese Fourteenth Army. Suspected of being an American spy, Sakakida would soon learn his fate—a grim prospect, indeed.

Sakakida had been in Bilibid since Corregidor fell in May 1942. Just before the fortress capitulated, Major Nelson Raymond, his mentor, gave him his final instructions for going undercover once again. Before the Japanese took the defenders prisoners, he was to get rid of his uniform and surrender as a civilian. If the opportunity presented itself later, Sakakida was to resume his role as a spy for MacArthur in Manila.[1]

For six interminable months after his capture, Sakakida had been brutally interrogated by the Japanese military police after being locked up in Bilibid. The captive insisted that he was an anti-American, draft-dodging civilian who had jumped ship in Manila a year earlier. Once the war had broken out, he insisted, the U.S. Army threatened him and his family and forced him to work for the Americans.

A short time after his incarceration, Sakakida received an enormous jolt: A Japanese soldier was brought into the room and pointed an accusing finger at the captive.

"You are a sergeant in the United States Army!" the man shouted. Sakakida had interrogated him on Bataan while wearing a sergeant's uniform, he declared.

Sakakida tried to maintain his composure. It was a case of mistaken identity, he insisted. Actually, he remembered grilling this particular soldier, who had been freed after Bataan surrendered.

When the Nisei clung to his cover story that he was actually an employee of Sears Roebuck in Manila, he was dragged repeatedly to a dingy torture chamber. Lit cigarettes caused hideous burns on sensitive parts of his body. His hands were tied behind his back and his body lifted by a rope until his shoulders were dislocated. While suspended, he was suddenly dropped, halting just short of the stone floor and sustaining excruciating pain.

As the weeks passed and the torture continued, Sakakida knew that he had to stick to his cover story. If he were to confess his true role, he would be signing his own death warrant. His greatest fear was that the Japanese would uncover military records left behind on Corregidor, possibly the recommendation that he be awarded a battlefield commission as a second lieutenant.

Making matters even worse for the Nisei, the Japanese, under existing law, considered all persons of Japanese ancestry, no matter in which country they lived, to be citizens of Dai Nippon. His interrogators regarded him as either a traitor to Japan or an American spy against the empire. Either way, the Nisei appeared to be doomed.

Keen-witted and resourceful, despite the savagery that had been and was being inflicted on him, Sakakida urged his tormentors to check the citizenship records of the Japanese Home Ministry in Tokyo, aware that his mother, a few years earlier in Hawaii, had changed his dual citizenship to that of a U.S. citizen only.

Governmental bureaucracy wheels grind slowly, and it seemed a lifetime to the Nisei before word came back from Tokyo: Sakakida had been registered with the Japanese consul in Honolulu at the time of his birth (as was the custom of Japanese residents at that time), but his citizenship had been voided by his mother in August 1941 (while the sergeant was working as an American undercover agent in Manila).

Based on this crucial information, treason charges were dropped by the Japanese Fourteenth Army headquarters, but the spy charge was still hanging over his head. Slowly, the days and nights of torment slipped past for Sakakida as he awaited his eventual fate. Meanwhile, he stuck to his cover story that he was simply a civilian employee of Sears Roebuck who had been caught up in a quagmire of wartime confusion and mistaken identity.

Finally, nine months after being captured, the Nisei was being escorted from Old Bilibid Prison to Fourteenth Army headquarters and a confrontation with Colonel Nishiharu. Sakakida was well aware that the penalty for espionage was beheading—and a remote, unmarked grave where his parents would never find his remains after the war.

It became clear that Nishiharu had thoroughly reviewed Sakakida's explanation as to how he had managed to be captured as a civilian on Corregidor. The colonel announced that spying charges were being dropped against the Nisei but that they were being replaced by a charge of disturbing the peace and order of the Japanese forces in the Philippines—an allegation that could be interpreted in a variety of ways. It could even result in the prisoner being beheaded.

Standing impassively before the Japanese colonel, who had a reputation within the army for being a stern, hard-nose taskmaster, Sakakida heard his "sentence" on the latest charge against him: He would work in Nishiharu's judge advocate's office, make tea for the staff, crank the mimeograph machine, sweep the floor, and perform whatever other menial tasks were assigned to him. When not on official duty, Sakakida would serve as houseboy in the colonel's comfortable home.

Sakakida tried to conceal his enormous relief: He had escaped the executioner's sword by clinging tenaciously to his cover story. Now he found himself in an incredible situation: an American spy, who was a bona fide sergeant in the U.S. Army and who had been recommended for a commission as a second lieutenant, taking up duties in the nerve center of the Japanese armed forces in the Philippines.[2]

Richard Sakakida left the judge advocate's office a free man, and the next morning he reported for work. Overnight, he had developed yet another worrisome concern: When General MacArthur returned to the Philippines, would the Nisei be charged by the Americans with treason for being a Japanese spy?

A few days later, while Sakakida was hustling up tea and going out for cigarettes for the Japanese staff, his convoluting saga took a new twist. Surreptitiously, he was approached by agents of the Bocho Han, the Japanese army counterintelligence branch, in an effort to recruit him to work undercover for them. His mission would be to ferret out any efforts by Filipino patriots to organize espionage rings in Manila.

Sakakida purposely displayed coolness to the offer, even though the thought of working closely with the Bocho Han, whose function was to uncover American agents such as him, delighted the Nisei. When he continued to show no enthusiasm in order not to seem too eager and raise suspicions, the Bocho Han did not pursue the matter.[3]

Although an energetic and dedicated worker in the judge advocate's office, the Nisei was still not trusted by some of the Japanese officers on the legal staff. They periodically tried devious schemes for tricking him into unmasking himself as a member of the U.S. Army. On one occasion, a captain, who had graduated from Harvard University, handed him a .45 pistol of the type commonly issued by the U.S. Army and ordered him to clean it. If Sakakida disassembled the weapon, it would be a clear admission that he was an American soldier.

Sakakida was an expert with this weapon; if necessary, he could have taken it apart and reassembled it while blindfolded, a skill taught to American soldiers. Realizing the subterfuge, Sakakida carefully wiped the handgun with an oily rag and then asked the Japanese officer to have someone take it apart so that he could clean the rest of it.

On a regular basis, Colonel Nishiharu received a shipment of captured American liquor and cigarettes. He always consumed the booze long before the next shipment of goods was due, but he did not smoke. So Sakakida, the houseboy, relieved the judge advocate of most of his cartons of Lucky Strikes and Chesterfields. One day, Nishiharu returned home unexpectedly and caught Sakakida red-handed pilfering the cigarettes.

Nishiharu erupted in anger, roundly cursing his houseboy for his thievery and banishing him from the house. However, the Nisei would continue with his duties in Fourteenth Army headquarters, and he was assigned to live in the English Club, which had been converted into an army barracks. Being billeted in the English Club proved to be a blessing for the undercover agent, for the arrangement provided him with far more free time than he had had while serving as a servant in Colonel Nishiharu's house.

Although the Japanese lieutenant in charge of the English Club was a strict disciplinarian and took roll calls at 6:30 A.M. and 10:30 P.M., Sakakida had much time to sneak out of the building after the last bed check and rendezvous with Filipino underground members in the city. He always returned to the barracks in time for the early morning roll call.

While cranking a mimeograph machine in the judge advocate's office one day, Sakakida casually looked up as an attractive young Filipina came into the room. He immediately recognized her as the wife of Ernest Tupas, who had served with him during the heavy fighting on Bataan in early 1942. Sakakida felt a surge of fear: If Mrs. Tupas gave any sign of recognizing him, he was a goner.

Sakakida breathed easier when the woman walked on past without giving any telltale sign of recognition. After she left the headquarters, he learned that she had been seeking permission to visit her husband, who was a prisoner in Manila's Muntinglupa Prison, a hellhole where five hundred Filipino "bandits" (guerrillas) were confined.

Mrs. Tupas had been turned down in her effort to gain a pass to visit her husband, but she returned a second and a third time. On the last call, Sakakida managed to talk with her alone for fleeting seconds and identified himself as a former comrade of Tupas on Bataan. The woman was suspicious of the man in a Japanese army uniform: Was this a devious scheme to trap her into some sort of admission of wrongdoing?

Finally, the persuasive Nisei won her over when he slipped her a Muntinglupa visitor's pass he had stolen in the judge advocate's office and signed with forged signatures. Still, Mrs. Tupas was fearful: After all, this *was* a fraudulent document. Not to worry, Sakakida assured her: Turncoat Filipino guards at Muntinglupa Prison could not read Japanese. And because the pass appeared to be authentic, they would permit her to enter the old stone enclosure.

Twenty-four hours later, Mrs. Tupas held a joyous reunion with her husband, who was only a physical shadow of his former robust self after months of maltreatment. She had no trouble getting into Muntinglupa, as Sakakida had predicted: The Filipino guards studied her phony pass, not understanding a word of it, then waved her on through.[4]

In the days ahead, Sakakida stole more visitor's passes, filled them out in Japanese, and got them in the hands of many other wives of Muntinglupa prisoners. Consequently, a stream of wives passed through the gates to have emotional visits with their spouses.

Now Sakakida's nimble brain concocted a venture of enormous magnitude—and peril. He would organize a prison break to free the five hundred guerrillas from Muntinglupa, a daunting task. Using his contact with Mrs. Tupas, he arranged for members of the Filipino underground in Manila to reconnoiter outside of the massive structure. Disguised as street peddlers, telephone repair workers, and door-to-door salesmen, the underground warriors discovered how many guards there were, where each was posted, and the time of day or night each would be relieved.

Through this clandestine reconnoitering, Sakakida learned that four or five Japanese soldiers came to the prison to conduct a security check. With clockwork regularity, the patrol arrived between midnight and 2:00 A.M.

In preparation for the breakout, Sakakida, through a clever ploy, managed to get Ernest Tupas assigned to the prison electrical shop where the switches were located. Tupas would play a crucial role in the venture.

Early on the designated night, Sakakida put on a Japanese lieutenant's uniform, which he had "borrowed" from the unsuspecting owner. At the same time, four Filipino guerrillas with him donned authentic Japanese enlisted men's garb. An hour later, the five impostors strode up to the massive gate of Muntinglupa Prison. As the impostors neared, the two Filipino guards made their customary—and required—deep bows to the five "Japanese." As the guards straightened up, they found a pair of pistol barrels stuck right between their eyes.

Moments later, in the delicately timed operation, Ernest Tupas, in the electrical shop, threw the switches, and the entire prison was plunged into darkness. Now some thirty armed Filipino guerrillas, who had been lurking nearby in the shadows, charged through the open gate and overpowered all of the Filipino guards inside.

In the hectic minutes that followed, five hundred prisoners fled helter-skelter out of the prison and soon were swallowed up by the night in the sprawling city. Most of them fled to the mountains north of Manila, where they were organized into a guerrilla force under Ernest Tupas.[5]

Minutes after the last guerrilla had raced away from Muntinglupa, Sakakida shucked his Japanese lieutenant's uniform and slipped back into the English Club in time for the 6:30 A.M. roll call. An hour later, he arrived for duty at Fourteenth Army headquarters, which was abuzz about the escape of the "five hundred bandits." A few junior officers put their heads together and selected Sakakida, the office handyman, to break the shocking news to Colonel Nishiharu when he arrived at 9:00 A.M.

Standing before the grim Nishiharu, the Nisei was delighted, but feigned distress, to inform the colonel of the spectacular breakout. There may have been treachery involved, Sakakida hinted, for it was reported that a Japanese officer and four enlisted men had confronted the guards at the front gate.

Sakakida struggled to control his glee when Nishiharu exploded in wrath. The colonel demanded an immediate investigation. For weeks, the Kempei Tai and the Bocho Han frantically tried to identify and apprehend the mastermind behind the prison plot. Never would they learn that the mastermind was providing the latest details of the investigation to Colonel Nishiharu each day.

A few weeks after the guerrillas were freed, Richard Sakakida was transferred from the judge advocate's office to Fourteenth Army intelligence. In the meantime, the Nisei, through native runners, usually teenagers, established contact with Ernest Tupas' guerrilla band in the mountains. This development permitted Sakakida to send regular intelligence reports to Tupas, who would, in turn, relay them to General MacArthur's headquarters by radio or submarine.

Sakakida focused on shipping schedules, information he pilfered from reports that came into the intelligence office. After the details reached MacArthur's naval officers, U.S. submarines often intercepted and created havoc among ship convoys hauling troops and supplies to the far-flung Japanese military outposts in the southwest Pacific.

The Cat with Nine Lives 9

American spies and guerrillas operating in the southwest Pacific were especially vulnerable to detection and death, as their Caucasian features set them off from the native populations. In early 1943, one of those constantly on the run with a hefty dead-or-alive bonus on his head was U.S. Navy Commander Charles A. "Chick" Parsons, who was known at the AIB by the code Q-10. A nonconformist, Parsons had lived in the Philippines for many years prior to the war. In his capacity as an executive of a shipping company, he had traveled the intricate patterns of the archipelago on hundreds of occasions and knew its topography, and people, as had few white men.

When the Japanese military machine thundered into Manila on New Year's Eve 1941, Parsons, his Filipina wife, Katsy, and their three children were trapped. Characteristically poised, Parsons burned his reserve officer's naval uniform and papers. Then, he hurried about the task of passing himself off as a Panamanian. For several years, he had served as honorary consul of Panama until a full-time professional could be sent to the islands, and he still had the seals and stamps of his post. Now a big sign was placed on his gate, "Panamanian Consul," and a Panamanian flag was removed from its dusty resting place and unfurled in front of his house. If the Japanese were to take him into custody, Parsons would declare diplomatic immunity as a neutral and demand passage out of the Philippines for himself and his family. He knew that only genuine career consuls were entitled to diplomatic immunity, but he was banking that the Japanese commander would not know that fact.

Parsons' preparations had been completed just in time, for the Japanese were thoroughly combing Manila street by street. When it came time for the Parsons family, Chick brazened it out, even being accorded a subtle deference by his interrogators. However, two weeks later, the "honorary consul" was seized by the dreaded Kempei Tai, the Japanese secret police, and hurled into a dungeon in Fort Santiago Prison, from which few emerged alive.

In the gloomy, wet, underground chamber, Parsons never lost heart. To the contrary, he constantly harangued his captors for jailing a neutral-country diplomat and shouted that they would be in big trouble with their superiors in Tokyo unless he was released promptly. A deaf ear was turned to his demands.

Eventually, Parsons managed to smuggle a note to an outside contact, Helge Janson, a Swedish honorary consul, whose status the Japanese had accepted. An American, Janson was the wife of the genuine Swedish consul. Turning a blind eye to his own neutral status, Janson's husband sent a secret message through Stockholm to Panama, whose president protested to Tokyo: Explain how the Japanese government recognized the honorary consul status of Helge Janson, but not the one of Charles Parsons, who represented the neutral Republic of Panama.

Suddenly, after several months in Fort Santiago, Parsons was released, and he and his family were provided air transportation to Hong Kong. From there, they caught a ship to the United States. Helge Janson's courage and resourcefulness had saved Parsons, and possibly his wife, from internment or possible execution.[1]

Even before the Parsons family arrived in California, the AIB in Brisbane learned of the episode from Peter Grimm, who had been the boss of and friend to Parsons on Luzon. Grimm was now a colonel in the Army Transportation Corps in Brisbane. An immediate request was put in for Parsons' services, and General MacArthur himself took action to see that he was brought to the southwest Pacific as rapidly as possible. Parsons was promoted to lieutenant commander and rushed to Brisbane for assignment by the AIB.

A stocky swashbuckling type, Chick arrived while the AIB was preparing Fifty Party, code name for an operation to sneak supplies, weapons, and ammunition to guerrillas on Mindanao, in the marginal hope that the large island could serve as a base for Douglas MacArthur's return to the Philippines.

On Mindanao, a large, rugged, trackless island, the Japanese occupied towns along the coast, and they ventured inland only on occasion to raid suspected guerrilla hideouts and arms caches. Leading the Mindanao guerrillas was an American, Wendell W. Fertig, who had bestowed upon himself the rank of general. A civilian engineer, Fertig, who was considered to be as brilliant as he was eccentric, had been a mining consultant in the Philippines for many years and fled Luzon shortly after Corregidor fell.

Meanwhile, at the AIB supply depot in Brisbane, Chick Parsons was strolling around amid feverish activity in which the cargo to be taken to Mindanao was being placed in waterproof containers. Suddenly, he spotted an old friend from Manila days, Charlie Smith, who had been a mining engineer and now held the rank of major in the U.S. Army. Both men confessed that neither had expected to see the other alive again.

Smith, like his pal Parsons, was a venturesome type, one possessing courage and ingenuity. When the Japanese steamroller overran the small island of Masbate in the middle Philippines, Smith and a close friend, tall, angular Jordan Hamner, overcame heavy odds and navigated a small boat sixteen hundred miles to northern Australia. Fried almost black by the scorching sun, Smith and Hamner collapsed on a remote beach near Darwin, where they were found by passersby and rushed to a hospital for emergency treatment. Then they were flown to Brisbane, where the AIB took them in tow.

Charlie Smith and Jordan Hamner needed no coaxing by AIB officials: They immediately volunteered to go back to the Philippines as spies. Smith, it was decided, would be in charge of Fifty Party, while Hamner would go in later and establish a network of sub-spies on the small islands in the direction of Borneo, southwest of the Philippines. Each infiltration party would include a few Moro tribesmen, who, like Hamner and Smith, had risked death at the hands of the Japanese or hostile seas by sailing two small boats to Australia.

As Parsons and Smith meandered around the Brisbane supply depot, they were astonished by the large and diversified shipment being prepared for "General" Fertig's guerrillas: radio transmitters, receivers, batteries, tools, wire, and spares. There were rifles, pistols, tommy guns, ammunition, and grenades. In other buildings, there were large bundles being put in waterproof tins: drugs, surgical kits, vaccines. Each container was marked with a red cross. Countless other items were being crammed into the tins: socks, shirts, trousers, underwear, chocolate bars, sewing kits, soap, cartons of cigarettes, newspapers and magazines.

Also, in one container were the two metal silver leaves and commission of a lieutenant colonel in the U.S. Army for Wendell Fertig, whom Douglas MacArthur had "demoted" from his self-appointed rank of general.

"There are no generals in the Philippines guerrilla army," the Supreme Commander had radioed Fertig earlier.[2]

In the first week of March 1943, Fifty Party was ready to be launched. However, there was one major deficiency: money. That item was as important to keeping the guerrillas in action as were food, medicine, and weapons. A hurried check with Washington disclosed that a huge shipment of Philippine pesos for the Mindanao operation had been shipped by a special air transport. As a security measure to ward off sticky fingers, the small fortune's container was labeled "Finance Forms."

Near panic erupted. Where was the money shipment? Colonel Allison Ind, the South Dakotan who served as the AIB's deputy director and finance officer, and an aide climbed into a car and drove through a black and stormy night to Amberley Field, thirty miles from Brisbane. Dismounting, Ind and the other officer groped along the rain-soaked tarmac in the blackout and stumbled onto a waterlogged package. It had been dumped at that spot the previous night by an exhausted air crew before taxiing off in their plane for a hot meal and a warm bed. Obviously, they had been totally indifferent to the fate of a large batch of red-tape gobbledygook marked "Finance Forms."

Clutching the precious package to his chest, Colonel Ind hurried back to his car and leaped inside; he and his aide drove back to Brisbane, guided in the darkness and downpour only by the vehicle's cat's-eyes.[3] At AIB headquarters, it required several men fifteen hours just to count the pesos, which totaled the equivalent of a million U.S. dollars.

Two nights later, the American submarine *Tambor* was boring through the sea toward Pagadian Bay on the south coast of Mindanao. On board was the Fifty Party. In a last-minute change of leadership, the AIB had decided that Chick Parsons would replace Charlie Smith, who would be the number two man. Smith himself had suggested the switch on the basis that his pal had far more knowledge of Mindanao, its terrain and its people. Along with the two Americans and three Moros, the *Tambor* carried seven tons of cargo for the guerrillas.

Lying off Pagadian Bay's shore under a veil of darkness, the submarine crew lowered a rubber dinghy, and Parsons and two Moros climbed in and began paddling. All were tense, eyes straining to split the night. Now they were almost to the beach. Suddenly, the quiet was shattered. Red and yellow tracer bullets, fired from the shadows, hissed past the intruders' heads and ricocheted off the water. The Moros froze. Parsons shouted at them to keep paddling.

They began rowing again—frantically. Shortly thereafter, the shooting stopped. After the dinghy crunched onto the silent and ominous beach, Parsons crawled forward several yards, paused, listened, heard nothing, and stood up. A moment later, a rifle was poked in his face from out of a thicket. Now it was his turn to freeze.

Parsons could make out the dim silhouette of a man holding the weapon. Glancing down, he could detect bare feet. A wave of relief flooded his being: Japanese soldiers always wore shoes—this man had to be a native guerrilla.

The American called out, "I come from General MacArthur!"

After a long moment of silence, the guerrilla came out of the vegetation and sized up the intruder and the dinghy, which was barely discernible on the beach. Without a word, the native spun on his heel and ran shouting back into the jungle. Parsons was ready to try to return to the submarine when a large number of cheering, laughing, shouting Philippine guerrillas charged out of the jungle to greet MacArthur's emissary. The navy commander gave a deep sigh of relief.

As it developed, the intruders had landed directly at an outpost of Wendell Fertig's force. Quite clearly, these largely undisciplined natives subscribed to the doctrine of shooting first and asking questions later. Now strong hands lifted Parsons onto shoulders, and he was carried amid loud cheering into the jungle, much like a Notre Dame halfback who had scored the winning touchdown in the final seconds of a football game against its old foe Michigan.

Within the next few hours, scores of native guerrillas unloaded the seven tons of weapons, ammunition, and supplies from the submarine, and by daybreak all of the containers had been carried into the thick jungle for future distribution. Chick Parsons, Charlie Smith, and a contingent of armed guerrillas now pushed inland to Wendell Fertig's headquarters on the side of a towering mountain.

Once there, Parsons presented Fertig with his lieutenant colonel's leaves and official commission and then explained in detail his mission to Mindanao. One of his most important tasks was to reconnoiter numerous potential landing beaches on the southern portion of the island, for it was Mindanao where Douglas MacArthur planned to invade. However, there was a major obstacle: How would Parsons be able to travel to these far-flung locales?

Fertig was silent in thought. Then he told Parsons to come with him, and they made a trek through the jungle to a small cove along the shoreline where Fertig's prized possession was carefully hidden—a diesel-powered sixty-foot launch. Parsons was astonished that the guerrilla chief would have such a large, modern, powered boat at his disposal.

"Where'd you get it?" Parsons asked.

"Borrowed it from the Japanese."

"Well, where's its Japanese crew?"

"They died—suddenly."

Parsons knew how badly Fertig needed and wanted to keep the craft, but he turned it over to the newcomer. The lieutenant colonel suggested that Parsons travel by night and hole up along the shoreline in daytime and that he head up the west coast for Medina, on the far tip of the island. There, a Fertig lieutenant, Ernest McLish, had his headquarters.

"He's one of my best commanders," Fertig said. "I'll radio him that you're coming."[4]

Soon, Chick and a few native guerrillas were sailing up the dark coastline. On each side of the launch was painted the Rising Sun emblem of the Empire of Japan, a fact that gave the navy commander a strange feeling although he realized that, hopefully, the identification would keep Japanese gunners on shore from blasting away if the craft were discerned in the pale rays of the tropical moon.

Two nights later, Parsons reached the headquarters of Ernest McLish, a former Manila businessman whom Parsons had known for several years prior to the war. The two greeted one another effusively, after which McLish arranged to refuel the launch and to arm it with an ancient .50-caliber machine gun, which might or might not shoot. That night, Parsons and his craft resumed his trek to reconnoiter the shores of Mindanao.

At a predesignated point on northern Mindanao, Parsons sneaked ashore and contacted a small band of guerrillas. They had alarming news: Japanese patrol boats on Surigao Strait were looking for the Allied spy at that very moment. Undaunted, Q-10 waited until nightfall, then set a northward course for Leyte across the thirty-mile-wide strait. All hands were tense. Japanese craft could be discerned dashing around the waters. One enemy patrol boat headed directly toward Parsons' vessel, but when within shouting distance, it suddenly veered and kept on going, apparently mistaking the commandeered boat for one of their own.

Q-10's mission on Leyte was to organize a guerrilla force, but he discovered, much to his consternation, that in addition to the official war going on against Japan, there were at least six private wars raging between competitive groups of guerrillas under junior American officers. Unification was badly needed, so Parsons began searching for Colonel Ruperto K. Kangleon, former commander of the Philippine army for Leyte and Samar, a nearby island. It was Chick's intention to convince the highly respected Kangleon that he was the one man to take charge and unify the squabbling guerrilla cliques.

Finally finding the Filipino colonel's hideout, Parsons, an eloquent man, had to roll out all his persuasive powers. Kangleon was past middle age, was war-weary and not in good health, and was despondent over the Japanese takeover of his beloved country.

"But Colonel Kangleon, it's your *duty!*" the American declared.

Finally, the Old Soldier agreed. Parsons assuaged the wounded egos of the other guerrilla leaders on Leyte by taking it upon himself to promote them and make them aides to Colonel Kangleon.[5]

In the weeks ahead, Chick Parsons continued to roam the central Philippine islands, escaping the clutches of the Kempei Tai and certain death time and again. Among the guerrillas, he came to be known as the Cat with Nine Lives. When his clandestine travels took him back to Leyte, he discovered that Ruperto Kangleon's combined guerrilla force was functioning like a well-oiled machine.

While Q-10 was stalking the Philippines on April 15, 1943, Admiral Bull Halsey boarded a plane at his headquarters on New Caledonia and flew to Brisbane for three days of talks with General MacArthur. Halsey, who held tactical command under MacArthur's strategic supervision, wanted the Supreme Commander's approval for an invasion of New Georgia in the Solomons by U.S. Marines. MacArthur instantly agreed: In fact, he already had drawn up plans for just such an operation as a springboard to the most western Solomon island, Bougainville.

A few days later, U.S. Marine Lieutenant Milton N. Vedder's plane was riddled in a dogfight off the southern coast of New Georgia while engaged in a bombing and strafing mission for the looming invasion of that island. After bailing out, Vedder paddled seven miles to shore in a rubber raft. There he was promptly confronted by a band of hostile native warriors, most of whom were body-painted with grotesque designs. Knowing that most natives on New Georgia were friendly to the Japanese, the pilot realized he was doomed unless he somehow could win over the natives. Lighting a cigarette, Vedder sat on a log and began blowing a chain of smoke rings. His "hosts" watched in fascination and soon were no longer hostile.

Within forty-eight hours, Donald Kennedy, the Ferdinand operative at nearby Segi Point, learned about Lieutenant Vedder's presence and radioed Townsville. Seventy-two hours later, a Catalina flying boat splashed down offshore and Vedder was picked up. Winging back to his base, the Marine pilot blessed his skill for blowing smoke rings, a talent that may have saved his life.

Meanwhile, in Indooroopilly, Australia, Colonel Sidney Mashbir, head of the AIB's translator and interpreter section, and his staff were rapidly refining techniques for "breaking" Japanese prisoners—which were amazingly few in number. At Guadalcanal, for example, an estimated 20,000 Japanese were killed or died of starvation, while only about 550 were captured, usually those who were dazed by concussions or wounded.

Mashbir, who had spent many years in Dai Nippon before the war and knew the people and their customs, directed that each POW be handled as a separate psychological experiment. Only a knowledge of Japanese psychology could successfully draw out information.

One of the first Japanese taken prisoner on New Guinea was brought to Mashbir's headquarters in an old, rundown estate at Indooroopilly, eight miles outside Brisbane. The sullen POW refused to utter a word. When he finally spoke, all he would say was, "You can kill me or torture me, but I won't talk."

Unusual for a Japanese, he was wearing a beard. So he was brought into a room where a camera was set up and a barber chair prepared. Standing by was a barber with razor, brush, and lather cup.

Mashbir said to the POW: "You see that barber chair? Well, we are going to shave you and then photograph you. Your picture will be published in countries all over the world as one of the first Japanese prisoners."

After a few moments of thought, the Japanese muttered, "*Hakitai*" (I must vomit)—and he promptly did. From that point on, in law enforcement terms, the captive sang like a canary. He had no intention of losing enormous face by having his photo displayed around the globe and identified as one of the first to refuse to die for his emperor.[6]

In another psychological ploy about a week before Christmas 1942, six Japanese naval men taken prisoner off Guadalcanal after their boat was sunk had refused to speak and were hustled off to Indooroopilly. Mashbir and his staff made a casual attempt to talk with the newcomers, but without success. The POWs were left alone for a week. Then, on New Year's morning, each captive was given a few cookies and some soft drinks, appropriately tied as a New Year's gift. Expecting to be tortured and eventually killed, the display of kindness caused all six Japanese to break down and cry.

Expressing amazement that their blood enemy was so chivalrous as to recognize their greatest holy day, they talked freely thereafter, telling everything they knew about units, plans, and command problems. Sid Mashbir's intimate grasp of Japanese psychology had paid off handsomely.

One of the captives had been a draftsman at a major shipyard since boyhood, and in his eagerness to show his gratitude, he sketched from memory detailed drawings, including cross-sections of many types of ships, two of which the American high command had not yet known existed, a carrier and an airplane-carrying submarine.

A few of the other POWs revealed some of the most significant naval information obtained up to that time and that was then totally unknown, among which were details of torpedoes of a size and range that already had sunk several U.S. ships.[7]

During the early months of 1943, Colonel Mashbir and his staff developed other psychological techniques to be used against the Japanese to dramatize that the Americans were civilized people who respected the religious beliefs of even their enemies. The idea was to soften the treatment of tens of thousands of GIs being held in POW camps, hoping in this way to rouse a spark of chivalry.

In war zones, the Japanese cremated their dead, and the ashes were shipped home in individual boxes marked to the Yasukuni Jinja, which is the shrine in Dai Nippon sacred to the souls and spirits of soldiers who died on the field of battle. On New Guinea, a large number of these boxes, already prepared for shipment to Japan, were captured. After consultation with the Australian officer in charge of psychological warfare at that time, Mashbir decided that these boxes of ashes would be dropped by parachute on a nearby Japanese force to show the Americans' humanity and compassion for dead enemy soldiers.

A short time later, Sid Mashbir and his artful dodgers concocted a psychological scheme designed to crack the morale of Japanese troops. So far in the war, a large number of postal savings books had been taken from the Japanese corpses and shipped to Indooroopilly. These represented the savings of soldiers who had made deposits at Japanese army field post offices.

These captured postal savings books were packed into bundles along with messages printed on the letterhead of "General Headquarters, Supreme Commander." The notes were addressed to the Imperial Japanese government, although aimed at the fighting men. The messages said that even though the soldiers were dead, their money should be paid to their next of kin and that the government should not confiscate their savings. Then these bundles were parachuted onto Japanese garrisons in New Guinea and elsewhere—with undetermined results.

Early in the war, American psychological warfare efforts proved to be amateurish and generally ineffective. As a result of instructions from Washington, thousands of packages of cigarettes, each with a surrender-now message inserted, were dropped by airplanes on Japanese positions. This was a total waste of time: Japanese officers simply told their men that the cigarettes were impregnated with cholera and syphilis, a diabolical Yankee scheme to fell thousands of soldiers. The result was that the cigarette packages were left untouched.

Propaganda leaflets prepared by agencies in Washington and sent to the AIB were very elaborate and beautifully crafted—and absolutely useless. Whoever had prepared them had just enough knowledge of the Japanese classics to enable him to mix his Japanese aphorisms as thoroughly as though he had used an eggbeater. Colonel Mashbir sent back a comment: "It is [our] opinion that this leaflet would make just as much sense to the Japanese as would a leaflet dropped on American troops which read: 'Here are some beautiful Vermont maple leaves. Therefore you must surrender because a rolling stone is worth two in the bush.' "[8]

The constructive criticism apparently was well received in Washington, however, and gradually the quality of the leaflets put out there improved markedly as to psychological impact, format, and context.

While Sid Mashbir and his men at Indooroopilly were developing psychological techniques to undermine Japanese morale and coerce information from POWs, a momentous undercover operation was unfolding elsewhere in the South Pacific. The target: Japan's most revered military hero.

"Fan the Peacock's Tail!" 10

E arly on the morning of April 14, 1943, American technicians were monitoring coded Japanese radio messages from a concrete bunker in Dutch Harbor, a bleak, gray town in the Aleutians, a chain of volcanic islands that extends like a long finger more than nine hundred miles westward from the tip of the Alaska Peninsula. High above the fogbound cliffs in Dutch Harbor climbed seven three-hundred-foot radio masts. Nearly a year after the Japanese high command became suspicious that its naval code had been broken after an American-Australian naval force intercepted and turned back a Japanese armada bent on capturing Port Moresby, the same cipher system was still in use.

Now, at 6:30 A.M. in Dutch Harbor, a bored monitoring soldier tensed: He was picking up a cipher signal from Truk, a Japanese-held island in the Pacific, that bore the code sign of Admiral Isoroku Yamamoto, commander in chief of the Combined Imperial Fleet and architect of the sneak attack on Pearl Harbor. Not knowing what he was scribbling, the GI finished taking down the entire lengthy message.

Following standing orders when Japanese naval radio traffic was intercepted, the message was rushed to Washington without the Dutch Harbor outpost having the foggiest notion that it had handled one of the most electrifying intercepts of the war in the Pacific. At Naval Intelligence, code-breakers studied the groups of intercepted figures and compared them with their secret key charts. By 11:00 A.M, they had decoded and translated the intercept. Dai Nippon's most revered admiral and folk hero, fifty-nine-year-old Isoroku Yamamoto, soon would be flying from the Japanese bastion of Rabaul to Kahili airfield on Bougainville, in the northwestern Solomons, on an inspection trip.

Admiral Yamamoto was the most Westernized of Japanese military leaders. In the early 1920s, Yamamoto, one of the Imperial Navy's most promising young officers, was sent to Harvard University, where he learned to speak English fluently, became a poker addict, and amused his American friends with his impromptu acrobatics, such as standing on his head on a chair for nearly a half hour. During those years at the Cambridge, Massachusetts, seat of higher learning, Yamamoto came to admire the United States and made many American friends.

After his Harvard graduation, the navy commander was assigned to Washington as naval attaché and studied U.S. defenses and ship-building programs. Back in Tokyo in 1934, Yamamoto, by now a vice admiral, got into a heated squabble with old-line Japanese battleship admirals and rammed through an accelerated construction program for aircraft carriers.[1]

Yamamoto was soon widely recognized in Dai Nippon as the country's most brilliant and visionary naval officer. Those under his command received vigorous and sometimes unorthodox training. An inveterate gambler, he required his aides to learn poker as mind training for the arts of bluff and surprise. And he sometimes put tacks on the seats of their chairs as a pointed reminder of the need for a naval officer to be vigilant at all times.

Now, within hours of the radio interception by the electronic snoopers in Dutch Harbor, many high-ranking officials in Washington and top commanders in the Pacific were exhilarated by the looming opportunity to gun down Admiral Yamamoto. But should the United States conduct what the Japanese called a *fukushu saku* (revenge military operation)? There was another prodigious factor to be considered: Was it worth the possible loss of the enormous advantage of having broken the Japanese naval code to kill one admiral?

At Port Moresby, Douglas MacArthur felt it was worth the risk. In Hawaii, Admiral Chester Nimitz was cautious, but he finally concluded that the enormous psychological reward of a successful attack on Yamamoto would offset the chance that the Japanese would change their naval code. At his headquarters on New Caledonia, Vice Admiral William F. "Bull" Halsey, the salty U.S. naval commander in the South Pacific, made no bones about how he felt. Yamamoto was third on the peppery Halsey's "personal shit-list," trailing only Emperor Hirohito and General Hideki Tojo. Halsey was delighted over a vision of Yamamoto being shot down in flames. He had called the Japanese admiral the Peacock because of Yamamoto's penchant for never appearing in public without being in full dress uniform, complete with a chestful of decorations, white gloves, and a ceremonial saber.[2]

After musing over the opportunity for twenty-four hours, top military and government officials in Washington reached no decision, so the matter was bucked up the chain of command to the President of the United States. Franklin Roosevelt never hesitated: He gave the green light to what would be dubbed Operation Vengeance.

Word was flashed to the southwest Pacific, where the crack U.S. 339th Fighter Squadron, based at Henderson Field on Guadalcanal, was selected for the mission. Two auxiliary tanks would be attached to each plane in order to provide sufficient fuel for the twin-boomed P-38s to make the circuitous eight-hundred-mile flight to eastern Bougainville and back.[3]

Led by Major John W. Mitchell, all eighteen P-38s would go on what the Japanese called a *damashi uchi* (sneak attack). These sleek fighter planes, recently arrived in the southwest Pacific, were ideal for the task. Although the Japanese Zero was more maneuverable, the P-38 more than neutralized this disadvantage by superior speed, diving ability, and altitude tolerance.

Henderson Field erupted in a beehive of activity. Planners had to come up with a meticulous timetable. They even deduced that Yamamoto's flight would be fifteen minutes early because meteorologists said that the usual southeast wind would not be blowing on the morning of April 18. It was estimated that if the P-38s flew at optimum speed, they would have only five to ten minutes over the target in which to tangle with the Zero escorts and shoot down Yamamoto's twin-engined Mitsubishi bomber.

Shortly before the P-38 flight was to lift off, Magic intercepted another message reaffirming details of the punctual Yamamoto's flight. After reading the decoded intercept, Bull Halsey radioed the air commander on Guadalcanal: "It appears the Peacock will be on time. Fan his tail."[4]

Meanwhile, at Rabaul, Yamamoto's aides tried until the final minutes to talk him out of taking the one-day trip. The Imperial Air Force no longer dominated the skies of the southwest Pacific, they pointed out. The admiral brushed off the suggestion, declaring that his garrisons in the forward bases could use a morale booster.

When Yamamoto learned that the Rabaul air commander had laid on twenty Zeros as escorts, the admiral erupted in fury. Six Zeros were plenty, he barked, adding that the remaining Zeros could be put to better use escorting bomber raids or attacking enemy positions.

Precisely at 8:00 A.M. (Guadalcanal time) on April 18, the admiral's bomber (known as a Betty) raced down the runway at Rabaul and lifted off. Coming along behind was a second Betty with Yamamoto's chief of staff, Vice Admiral Matome Ugaki, on board. Taking two planes was a security measure: In case one craft went down, the surviving admiral would provide a continuity of command. Unspoken was the fact that if the flight were intercepted by chance, the American pilots would not know in which Betty the navy's commander in chief was a passenger.

As soon as the two bombers were airborne, the six Zeros climbed into the sky and hovered around the Bettys like mother hens protecting their broods. Flying at forty-five hundred feet, the tiny sky armada set a southeasterly course for the 315-mile flight to Bougainville.

Earlier that morning at Henderson Field, Major John Mitchell and his solemn pilots were going over the flight plan once again. If ever a mission needed teamwork, split-second timing, and pinpoint navigation, this was it. The P-38s would wave-hop almost to Bougainville to avoid detection by Japanese radar, then Mitchell and thirteen of his pilots would climb to twenty thousand feet in order to pounce on the escorting Zeros from above. At the same time, the four other Lightnings, led by Lieutenant Thomas G. Lanphier, Jr., would go after Yamamoto's bomber and shoot it down.

Chosen to be triggermen along with Lanphier were Lieutenants Rex Barber, James McLanahan, and Joseph Moore. All four pilots had performed skillfully eleven days before when they tangled with a large flight of Zeros and blasted a total of seven of them out of the sky. At the same time, the Marines, flying Wildcat and Corsair fighters, had lost seven airplanes to the Zeros.

If a P-38 were to develop mechanical trouble or be disabled in a dog-fight, the other planes were to continue with the mission, abandoning their comrade to what probably would be a watery grave. Likewise, if a pilot ran out of fuel on the way home, he would have to be left to his own devices.

Every pilot, planner, and air commander knew that Operation Vengeance was a longshot, that it well could result in a monumental disaster for the 339th Fighter Squadron. Magic had not been able to pick up the number of Zero fighters that would be Yamamoto's escort, but veteran airmen predicted that they would number from twenty to twenty-five. And there was the distinct possibility that all one hundred Japanese fighter planes known to be based on Bougainville might jump the P-38s.

A few minutes before the 7:10 A.M. (Guadalcanal time) takeoff, John Mitchell and his men received an enormous boost in morale. A Magic intercept disclosed that there would be only six Zeros escorting Yamamoto's bomber.

Precisely on time, Major Mitchell's eighteen Lightnings began racing down the runway, one after the other. James McLanahan's plane blew a tire on takeoff, and he had to be left behind. There was no time to dig up a replacement plane and pilot. Circling overhead until all were airborne, the P-38s set a course for eastern Bougainville. Less than a half hour later, Joseph Moore's plane developed mechanical trouble, and he had to turn back. Mitchell immediately signaled two of his other pilots, Lieutenants Besby Holmes and Ray Hine, to join Tom Lanphier and Rex Barber as triggermen.

Now there were sixteen P-38s to go after Admiral Yamamoto.

Almost at once danger reared its ugly head. Skimming along just above the waves, the pilots were nearly blinded by the mist that caressed the water. Buffeted by the wind, the P-38s flew at heights of ten to fifty feet, their propellers leaving long wakes like those of motorboats on a lake. A sudden downdraft nearly plunged one pilot into the sea, but he righted the plane just before impact. It was of little comfort to Major Mitchell and his men to catch close-up glimpses of large sharks playing about in the blue Pacific.

As the clock ticked on, the pilots were growing tense and restless from the strain of keeping their planes so close to the water and knowing that they could plunge into the sea and sink to the bottom—provided they didn't become shark food first. The haze steadily dissipated, and Mitchell signaled the Lightnings to begin climbing to their designated attack plateaus. Minutes later, off in the distance, Bougainville was sighted. In a marvel of pinpoint navigation, the P-38 flight was approaching the coast southeast of Empress Augusta Bay—right on target.

But where was Yamamoto's flight? The P-38 pilots would have only a few minutes to spare over the target before the fuel situation became critical.

Moments later, Lieutenant Douglas Canning spotted the prey: the six Zeros and not one, but *two* bombers, each exactly like the other. This was a jolting development: No mention had been made in the Magic intercepts of two bombers. Which one held Admiral Yamamoto?

Over the intercom, Major Mitchell promptly gave revised orders. Tom Lanphier and his three other triggermen would tangle with *both* bombers, while Mitchell and the remaining P-38s would take out after the Zeros. Almost at once, this new scheme went awry. Auxiliary fuel tanks were to be jettisoned to provide increased maneuverability and to lessen the danger of fire should one of the tanks be hit by bullets, but Besby Holmes and Ray Hine, both Lanphier's pilots, were unable to shake loose their spare tanks and had to drop out of formation.

Probably due to the fact that none of the Japanese sky convoy expected to encounter American warplanes so far from their bases, the P-38s had not been sighted yet. Then, a Zero pilot caught a glimpse of the silvery flash of a jettisoned fuel tank and spread the alarm.

According to a prearranged plan in the event of attack, Yamamoto's bomber turned sharply and dove downward, skimming just above the treetops on eastern Bougainville. Ugaki's Betty turned the other way, out to sea.

Dropping their belly tanks to lighten their planes for combat, the six Zeros nosed over in a group and three of them raced toward Lanphier and his wingman, Rex Barber. Lanphier's .50-caliber machine guns chattered angrily, ripping the wing away from the first Zero, and it began spinning crazily toward the sea.

Then, Lanphier kicked his P-38 over on its back, and he began looking down for the lead Betty. In seconds, he spotted it, skimming above the jungle heading hell-bent for the Kahili airfield. Lanphier pounced on the bomber and put a long steady burst into the right engine and then the right wing. Moments later, the Betty crashed into the thick jungle and exploded, killing all on board instantly—including Admiral Isoroku Yamamoto.[5]

Meanwhile, Rex Barber chased after Ugaki's bomber and loosened a fusillade of bullets into it. Pieces flew off the bomber, and it began to smoke and headed downward in a long glide. Barber never saw it crash— he was too busy trying to shake the three Zeros on his tail.

Down below, swarms of Zeros based at Kahili airfield were frantically preparing to lift off and join in the aerial free-for-all to save Admiral Yamamoto. No one on the ground had anticipated the sky ambush, so it required several minutes to scramble for the fighter planes.

High in the sky, Besby Holmes and Ray Hine succeeded in dropping their faulty auxiliary fuel tanks, and now they joined the fray. Holmes raced after the three Zeros that were chasing Rex Barber and blasted two of them out of the air with his machine guns and .20-millimeter cannon. Then, Holmes squeezed off a fusillade of bullets into Ugaki's bomber, which was already smoking and in a downward glide after Barber had riddled it. Seconds later, the Betty appeared to disintegrate on contact with the sea.

Actually, the veteran Betty pilot, knowing that he could not outrun Rex Barber's P-38 in the earlier encounter, had deliberately crash-landed his plane. Both wings were ripped off in the crunching impact, but Admiral Ugaki and two others managed to scramble out of the fuselage before it sank and were rescued by motor launches.

Now the Zeros on Kahili airfield were soaring into the sky and dashing about like angry hornets. In one dogfight, Ray Hine was shot down. Moments later, the calm voice of Major John Mitchell came over the radio. "Head for home, boys!"

The entire aerial melee had lasted only five minutes.

A few P-38s had lost touch with the formation and straggled back. After Major Mitchell and several others landed on Guadalcanal, Tom Lanphier came in alone.

Scrambling from his P-38, he ran across the field yelling, "I got Yamamoto! I got Yamamoto!"

A few minutes later, Rex Barber was on the ground, shouting that he had shot down Yamamoto. Then along came Besby Holmes, who swore that he sent the famous Japanese admiral to his doom.

In the debriefing hut, the confusion was compounded. Combat intelligence officers finally gave credit to Lanphier, Holmes, and Barber for one Betty each. That would make three bombers shot down, when there had been only two of them in the Yamamoto flight. Outside of the three P-38 pilots involved, no one in the Allied camp really cared who had shot down what; it seemed clear that the architect of the sneak attack on Pearl Harbor was dead.[6]

Joy was unrestrained at Henderson Field. The Operation Vengeance pilots were presented with a case of coveted whiskey, none of which went to waste. Then came a message from irrepressible Bull Halsey: "Congratulations to the hunters—sounds as though one of the ducks in [your] bag was a peacock."[7]

In New Guinea, Douglas MacArthur solemnly told aides that he could "almost hear the rising crescendo of sound from thousands of glistening white skeletons at the bottom of Pearl Harbor."[8]

Although American commanders in the Pacific were eager to tell the world of the demise of Isoroku Yamamoto, security officers bottled up the blockbuster story. They didn't want the Japanese to suspect that their naval code had been broken.

Within a few hours, a bevy of media correspondents and cameramen on Guadalcanal knew the whole story. Newsreel photographers shot hundreds of feet of film of America's latest heroes. Print reporters had notebooks chock full from interviews. All the film was confiscated, and the reporters were threatened with a dire fate should they as much as hint what had happened over Bougainville.

A day later, another flight of P-38s was sent to Kahili airfield to drop a few bombs and strafe in order to give the impression that the Americans had begun routine fighter sweeps in that region the day before.

At Henderson Field, the seventeen surviving pilots on the mission were grounded and sent back to the United States. Each stop along the way, they were threatened with severe consequences should they breathe a word of the Yamamoto escapade. Reaching California, the pilots were congratulated by high brass, decorated, promoted, and muzzled. Other Americans everywhere who were involved in or knew about Operation Vengeance were sworn to secrecy.

Unbeknownst to the U.S. commanders in the Pacific, Admiral Yamamoto's remains had been cremated on Bougainville, and his ashes were placed in an urn and flown to Rabaul. There, the container was put aboard the huge battleship *Musashi* and placed in the "commander-in-chief's quarters" for the trip back to Tokyo. Alongside the urn were the admiral's decorations, white gloves, and ceremonial saber that had been salvaged from his wrecked bomber.[9]

As time passed, MacArthur, Nimitz, Halsey, and other American leaders in the Pacific waited anxiously for some word from Japan concerning Yamamoto's fate. Had he truly been killed? Or was Imperial General Headquarters engaging in some sort of psychological warfare ploy? Finally, on May 24, five weeks after the aerial melee over eastern Bougainville, Radio Tokyo, the mouthpiece of the high command, reported, "Admiral Isoroku Yamamoto, while directing strategy on the front line in April, engaged in combat with the enemy and met gallant death in a warplane."[10]

Elation erupted in Allied ranks from Port Moresby all the way to the White House in Washington. A day later, however, those involved in Operation Vengeance were given a jolt. An Australian newspaper published a story about the Yamamoto ambush and identified Lieutenant Thomas G. Lanphier, Jr., as the triggerman. A grossly unprincipled reporter had broken the story even though he must have known that by doing so he would endanger Allied security. American intelligence knew that Japanese monitors regularly picked up the contents in Australian newspapers by intercepting radio broadcasts from South America. Unaccountably, the monitors apparently failed to intercept this blockbuster story, so the Imperial Navy went right on using its "unbreakable" code.

On September 12, nearly five months after the Yamamoto ambush, Tom Lanphier's brother, Marine Lieutenant Charles Lanphier, led a flight of Corsair fighter planes on a strafing and bombing raid at Kahili airfield. Charles' plane was disabled in a dogfight and he parachuted onto Bougainville, where he was captured. Incredibly, he had landed only a short distance from the spot where Yamamoto's bomber had crashed.

Charles Lanphier was taken to a POW camp at Rabaul. That situation brought new worries to American commanders. If the Japanese learned that they had in their clutches the brother of the pilot who had gunned down their revered admiral, Charles would, no doubt, be subjected to agonizing torture and beheaded. The Japanese, however, apparently never realized the brother connection, for Charles continued to receive only the normal mistreatment and abuse.[11]

While the Yamamoto scenario had been unfolding, elsewhere in the southwest Pacific an equally spectacular secret mission was in the works, this one designed to cause the Japanese to lose great face.

11

Boom and Bang in Singapore Harbor

Captain Ivan Lyon, smartly clad in the brass-buttoned uniform and rakish tam of Britain's Gordon Highlanders, was grim and businesslike as he briefed controllers of the AIB in Brisbane on a scheme he had conceived to inflict great damage on Japanese ships and to cause the enemy enormous embarrassment and chagrin. Lyon's proposal was so audacious that even the AIB officials, long conversant with "impossible missions" that succeeded, were astonished. Together with a handful of men, Lyon would penetrate two thousand miles through Japanese-controlled waters, sneak into tightly guarded Singapore harbor, and blow up enemy ships. It was now May 1943.

Captain Lyon, who had been one of the handful of British fighting men to escape from Singapore when it was captured by the Japanese in February 1942, had a burning passion to strike a telling blow at the enemy, because Lyon had been compelled to leave behind his wife and young daughter. Since those dark days, reports had trickled in to Brisbane about the prodigious bloodbath the conquerors had inflicted on the civilian population.

Thousands of civilians in Singapore's multinational population had been rounded up. The main targets for Japanese wrath were former employees of the British colonial government and Chinese residents. The fate of many was sealed when traitorous informants, hooded to conceal their identities, picked out those allegedly having actively participated in Singapore's defense. Hundreds of other civilians were murdered because they had tattoo marks. In Japan, these markings were a sign that the wearer had a criminal record. Among many in Singapore, the tattoos were merely popular adornments, but the Japanese decided they also meant membership in a secret anti-Japanese society.

The mass executions were supervised by the Kempei Tai. The doomed were shot on the spot, or beheaded, or bayoneted, or trussed up, taken into Singapore harbor in boats, and thrown overboard. Other civilians were trucked en masse to area beaches, lined up in rows, and machine-gunned.[1]

As the weeks passed and news of the civilian slaughter in Singapore reached Australia, Captain Lyon learned that his wife and daughter were among those who had been murdered by the conquerors. Keeping his grief locked up, Lyon swore vengeance.

Now, after hearing Lyon's bold proposal for a boom-and-bang raid on Singapore harbor, the AIB chiefs sent him to Lieutenant Colonel G. S. Mott, who was head of the Services Reconnaissance Department (SRD), a component of the AIB. Despite its benign title, the SRD's function was to blow up anything that was of value to the Japanese.

Moody on occasion, sharp-witted, and tough, Colonel Mott burned with intense resentment against the Japanese because he was among the outmanned British contingent that had been routed out of Burma and later out of Java. So the SRD boss's excitement heightened as Captain Lyon detailed his Singapore scheme.

Lyon would recruit a small party of tough, resourceful men for the expedition through enemy waters. Centerpiece of the operation would be a decrepit, seventy-foot fishing boat, the *Krait*, which would serve as a modern-day Trojan horse. Hopefully, Japanese warships and patrol boats encountered along the way would regard the *Krait* as one of their own, as she had once been owned by a Japanese firm. On board would be a Rising Sun flag to hoist when a hostile craft approached.

Concealed on the *Krait* would be three canoes, which the raiders would paddle the remaining few miles into Singapore harbor under cover of darkness. There, Lyon and his men would sneak up to Japanese ships and attach limpets at the water's edge. Looking like rectangular chunks of rusty iron, the limpets measured eleven by eight by three inches and each weighed fourteen pounds, ten of which were plastic explosives. The ensuing blast could blow a hole five feet square in the plates of a ship. A fuse and time pencil could be set for detonation any time up to six hours. This would permit the raiders to cover a considerable distance in their getaway before booms and bangs erupted in Singapore harbor.

Colonel Mott was delighted with Lyon's bold proposal. There was no doubt in his mind that with stouthearted men and proper training— and a generous helping of good luck—the raid could be pulled off. Mott, however, wise to the nuances and subtleties of the high command, was convinced that MacArthur's headquarters would turn thumbs down on the scheme.

So with a twinkle in his eye, Mott declared, "Well, Ivan, we're simply going to have to provide the brass hats with a convincing demonstration. We'll have to actually slip into one of our own tightly guarded harbors and bug every ship in it with limpets—without the explosives, of course."[2]

Typically, Captain Lyon was eager. "I can do it!" he replied enthusiastically.

"No, Captain, not you," Mott responded. "You'll have to be saved for the real show. There'll be hell to pay at GHQ [general headquarters] when they discover we pulled it off." Pausing briefly, Mott added, "Carey, of course! Who else?"[3]

A few days later, Captain F. W. Carey of the Australian army reported to a secret, closely guarded training camp along the coast some fifty miles above Townsville. In the week ahead, night and day, strenuous exercises were held in the sea just off the training camp. Canoes. Men in swimming trunks. Much dashing about. Wearing a private's uniform as a security measure, Captain Lyon took it all in from a vantage point on shore.

A target was selected for the boom-and-bang demonstration—Townsville harbor. Once a small, sleepy port, Townsville had burgeoned into a combination Allied naval base and unloading point for thousands of tons of supplies and weapons coming from the United States and elsewhere. Merchant ships and transports of all sizes and tonnage were tied up or waiting for their chance to berth. American and Australian warships were nesting side by side while their crews, except for those on watch, were living it up in boisterous Townsville.

On the appointed night, canoes began moving leisurely between the ships. Later, lookouts would recall hearing sharp, metallic clicks (small magnetic devices that caused the limpets to adhere to steel ships). Apparently, no one on watch considered this to be of any consequence.

Just before dawn, shouts rang out from one ship—a limpet attached to its hull had been spotted. Moments later, the shriek of a siren split the air over Townsville harbor. Searchlights crisscrossed the water. An anti-demolitions party was hurriedly dispatched to examine the limpet, which conceivably could blow the men to smithereens at any moment. Military police commanders on shore began telephoning feverishly, demanding a blackout be enforced—clearly, Townsville harbor was under attack by Japanese commandos or frogmen.[4]

Bedlam continued until after dawn broke. It was as though every major ship in the harbor had been mined by secret devices and the whole place could blow up at any second.

Meanwhile, Captain Carey and his stealthy raiders had rendezvoused at a designated spot. Carey changed into his regular Australian army uniform and walked into Townsville, which was still in an uproar. Checking into a hotel, the exhausted captain went to sleep.

In some unknown manner, military authorities in the Townsville region learned about the SRD stunt. They were advised to locate and arrest one C. W. Carey, said to be a captain in the Australian army, who was the ringleader of the nocturnal highjinks. Carey was found sleeping peacefully in his hotel room.

Calm and collected as always, Carey answered all questions hurled at him by the angry authorities. He advised them to contact the AIB, which would confirm that he had been sent on a harmless training mission. Official suspicion grew more intense; none of the military officials in Townsville had heard of the AIB.

Now Carey's predicament intensified. He gave his interrogators a secret number to call, but when the AIB was contacted, officers there said they had no knowledge of a Captain Carey nor did they know anything about a secret training mission in Townsville harbor. For whatever his reasons, Colonel Mott had not advised anyone at AIB headquarters of the demonstration scheme.

Strangely, Mott could not be located. When he finally surfaced, he was curiously vague as to who had authorized the caper in Townsville harbor. Secretly, he was elated over the success of the mock raid. Carey was taken off the hot seat and transferred to New Guinea by the AIB. There followed a heavy turnover of officials charged with the security of Townsville harbor.

Perhaps impressed by the success of the "Destruction of Townsville Harbor," the AIB's leadership approved the Singapore mission. It was code-named Jaywick. Located at the southern tip of the Malay Peninsula, Singapore had a population of 1 million persons and was the base for the powerful Japanese Southern Fleet.

As soon as the AIB gave him the green light, Ivan Lyon selected his raiders from the Flinders Naval Depot, an Australian installation, and four months of rigorous training began in a clandestine camp near Sydney. Many candidates were weeded out, and when it was time to depart, the Jaywick party would consist of Captain Lyon, three other officers, and ten naval ratings (enlisted men).

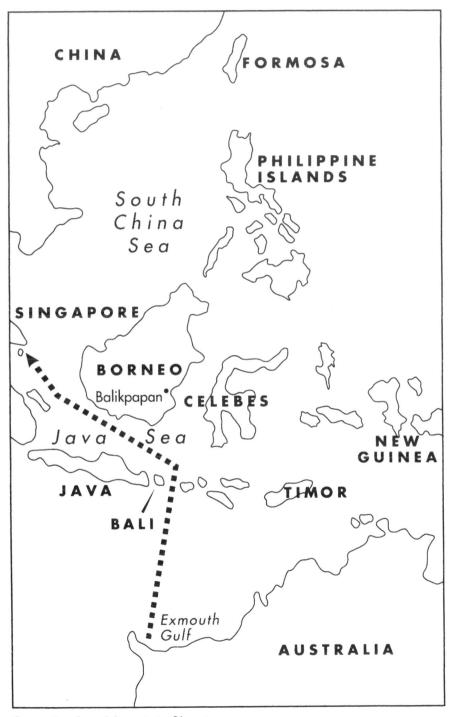

Operation Jaywick route to Singapore

On September 2, 1943, the creaking old *Krait* chugged out of Exmouth Gulf, north of Perth on Australia's western coast. The third day out, Lyon called his men together and told them the target.

Singapore! More than one thousand miles inside the new Japanese Empire. Elated, the raiders let loose with a mighty cheer.

A few days later, all of the party began darkening their skin with a special dye that had been brought along for the purpose. It was a sticky, foul-smelling mixture. Because of the heavy alcohol fumes in the concoction, the men had to leave white rings around their eyes. Sweat and sea spray steadily eroded the dye, and it had to be reapplied again and again. Each man donned a native sarong, triggering much ribald humor. All of this might confuse the Japanese and the natives from a distance, but close up, the white circles around the eyes, which gave the raiders a raccoon look, would give them away.

If the *Krait* were approached by a Japanese warship or patrol boat, the three darkest "natives" were to rush to the stern and point excitedly at the Japanese flag they had hoisted. The captured Japanese flag they had brought with them was new and clean. So they scuffed it around on deck with their dirty bare feet, pitched buckets of seawater on it, and wadded it into a ball time and again until it looked sufficiently weather-beaten.

Ivan Lyon and his second in command, Lieutenant Paddy McDowell, had hoped for foul weather to mask the intruding boat from hostile eyes. However, for eight days the blue sky was clear and the sun was beaming brightly. Although there had been occasional heavy tides, the trip so far had been largely uneventful, as though the Jaywickers had been on a peacetime cruise. Still, there was tension aboard. The *Krait* was now in range of land-based Japanese airplanes.

Just before dawn on September 14, Lieutenant H. E. Carse, the navigator, shook Ivan Lyon awake. With a slight tone of concern in his voice, he said, "Skipper, there're junks and sampans all over the sea—and we're right in the midst of them!"

"Any Jap patrol boats?"

"Can't see."

With dawn breaking, Lyon ordered the fishing net to be dragged over the stern.

"We've got to look like one of them," he declared.[5]

After continuing for a short distance, they heard a voice hailing the raiders from a nearby boat. Ignoring the call, the *Krait* kept going and soon left the collection of boats behind. All hands issued sighs of relief.

For two more days, the God of Raiders smiled benignly on the tiny group of men in the creaking old boat. Suddenly, a crewman called out, "Look!" Off in the distance, not far above the waves, a Japanese airplane could be seen. It was heading hell-bent toward the *Krait*. Most of the men were ordered to take cover, and Lyon and three others quickly donned native straw hats and began tending to their fish nets. As the roar of the airplane engine grew louder, hearts began to pump furiously, stomachs knotted, and palms perspired. Had this aircraft with the Rising Sun emblems glistening in the sun spotted the *Krait* earlier and was now closing in for the kill?

With a mighty roar, the Japanese aircraft was almost overhead. Lyon and the other "Malay fishermen" on deck looked up and waved at the pilot, a natural thing to do. Then he was gone and soon out of sight. The raiders gave silent thanks for the Japanese flag flapping in the breeze at the stern of the *Krait*.

Seventeen days after leaving Australia, navigator Carse scribbled in his log: "I don't know how the day is going to end—We are within about thirty miles of Singapore and getting closer by means of a staggered course, praying for dark. No lovers ever longed for darkness as we do."[6]

It was about half past seven o'clock that night when Lyon called out, "There she is!" All eyes peered forward, looking at the reflections of the lights of Singapore twinkling only twenty miles away. The raiders were excited, slapping one another on the back. Suddenly, the joy vanished. From a nearby island came the bright finger of a Japanese searchlight, probing the sea all around the *Krait*. Now the God of Raiders again showed his hand: A heavy rain squall erupted, obscuring the searchlight beam.

The storm passed, and two hours later, the *Krait* was hovering silently in Otters Bay, on the largely uninhabited island of Panjang. Now the precious canoes were placed in the dark water and loaded with the necessities needed to accomplish the mission: weapons, ammunition, charts, binoculars, protective clothing, food, water for a month, and the lethal limpets.

Ivan Lyon and five of his men climbed into the three fragile canoes. *Krait*, with the remaining Jaywick operatives on board, prepared to pull out for Borneo. A rendezvous with the Singapore boom-and-bang men would be on Pompong Island, forty miles southeast of Panjang, after dark on October 1, eleven days away. If the harbor raiders failed to appear at that time, they were considered to be expendable, and the *Krait* would return to Exmouth Gulf in Australia.

As the old Japanese fishing vessel chugged off and was swallowed by the night, the six raiders, two to each canoe, felt extremely lonely and isolated, deposited a thousand miles inside Japanese territory and all lifelines to their own comrades and resources severed. If Lyon and his men got into big trouble, they were on their own.

With its combat load and two operatives—a seaman in front and an officer behind—each canoe weighed about eight hundred pounds. Riding low in the water, sluggish, and hard to paddle, the canoes had to hold all that weight or the mission would be jeopardized.

Within fifteen minutes of splitting with the *Krait*, Lyon and the other canoeists heard a frightening sound: the mutter of a powerboat engine. All hands froze, and the canoes drifted aimlessly in the blackness. Then the dim silhouette of a Japanese patrol boat could be faintly discerned, including the snouts of machine guns. Helpless, the Jaywick men held their breaths as the enemy craft continued toward them. Then, for whatever its reason, the eighty-foot Japanese boat slightly altered its course and slid on past the canoes and was gobbled up by the darkness. Lyon and the others went limp, but moments later the paddling resumed.

Just after midnight, seventy-two hours after this close call, the Jaywickers reached their final "hide-up"—Pulau Dongas, a tiny island only eight miles south of Singapore. Nearly exhausted, the raiders flung themselves on the ground and slept.

At mid-morning, Ivan Lyon and Lieutenant Donald N. Davidson scrambled up the highest point on the uninhabited (except for a colony of ill-tempered crocodiles) island. The men were elated by the view. Working in shifts, they kept a constant watch. In periods of good visibility, the snoopers could see the ships in Singapore harbor, and they charted their locations.

At night, Lyon and his men were delighted that it appeared no special defensive precautions were being taken in the port city—not even a blackout. The headlights of cars tooling along Beach Road could be clearly seen. No harbor or navigation lights were burning and all ships were stationary. Evidently, the Japanese felt there was not an armed Allied soldier within two thousand miles of the stronghold.

On the third day after holing up on Pulau Dongas, Captain Lyon called a council of war. Every ship they had seen in the harbor was carefully plotted, and targeted vessels were assigned to each two-man canoe team. Lieutenant Don Davidson and W. G. Falls were to attack the group of ships lying snugly in Singapore Roads, leading into the harbor. Lieutenant Robert Page, son of the prewar deputy governor of Australian New Guinea, and his companion, A. W. Jones, would take on ships berthed at wharves, and Captain Lyon and A. W. Huston would deal with a group of vessels anchored in the harbor.

After dark, the Jaywick men said solemn goodbyes, checked the fastenings on their skintight black garb and hoods, climbed into the narrow circular openings of the canoes, and with a final salute with paddles cast off for Singapore harbor.

Two hours later, Davidson and Falls, drenched with perspiration and arm-weary, were paddling across the inner harbor of Singapore. It was eerily quiet. It hardly seemed possible to the men that they could be passing unobserved into the heart of the Japanese bastion. Had the Jaywick party been detected earlier? Were they entering an ambush? Suddenly, Falls spotted a vessel with navigation lights moving directly toward them. As it drew closer, the two men could see that it was a large Japanese tug. They ceased paddling and held their breaths. It seemed impossible that the raiders would not be sighted or crushed by the oncoming vessel. Then the tug veered off just before reaching the canoe and disappeared into the night. Davidson and Falls were badly shaken, but they rapidly recovered their composures.

Again Davidson and Falls forged ahead and reached a wharf where, from their observation post on Pulau Dongas the night before, Ivan Lyon and Davidson had sighted two large freighters tied up. Davidson and Falls saw that their quarries had departed. They silently paddled back out into the harbor and soon found themselves amid several large Japanese ships of some six thousand tons each. There were limpets enough for three of the vessels. Davidson held up his right fist, a predesignated signal, and the two men paddled quietly to the first ship and began drifting along its hull. On deck, only some twenty feet above the raiders, crew members could be heard chattering and laughing.

Amidships, Davidson steadied the canoe while Falls set the fuse on a limpet and snapped the magnets against the hull well below the waterline. As they worked, Davidson and Falls could hear the chimes in the clock on Singapore's Victoria Hall counting out the quarter hours. The procedure was repeated routinely on the second ship, but the third vessel had arc lights burning brightly on deck, illuminating the dark waters around it. Undaunted, the canoeists paddled alongside and placed the limpet.

By 1:00 A.M., the job had been completed. Elated and cocky, Davidson and Falls headed out of the harbor to their preselected hideout on Batam Island. The mines were timed to blow at 5:00 A.M.

A few miles to the west of them, the other two canoes had remained together until almost in the harbor, where they split. Lieutenant Bob Page and

A. W. Jones made a beeline for the Pulau Bukum docks, while Ivan Lyon and A. W. Huston headed for an anchorage where several ships were at rest.

An hour later, Page and Jones ran into the first real obstacles. They found that the docks were brightly lighted and that sentries were on duty at the ships' gangways. However, at great personal peril, the two men paddled the entire length of the wharves to pick out the most likely target. Finally, they settled on a large freighter. Slipping up to it, Jones attached the limpets. Above them, Japanese sailors were talking with one another while unloading cargo onto a barge on the far side of the ship. As the canoe drifted away, Page and Jones were gripped by a sudden surge of fear. Standing on the dock, armed with a rifle, a Japanese sentry appeared to be peering directly toward the two raiders, who were presumably visible in the glow of the arc lights on the ship. Moments later, the enemy soldier casually turned around and walked away.

In the meantime, Ivan Lyon and A. W. Huston paddled directly into the midst of a large number of ships lying at anchor. All were blacked out, and a spit of land blocked any chance of the two men determining a target from the glow of Singapore's lights. Then Lyon spotted a dim red light; he knew that the ruby glow signified that it was on a tanker. Stealing toward the beckoning light, the two men edged up to the tanker's stern, where Huston placed the leechlike limpets.

Lyon and Huston then slipped along the tanker toward the engine room and prepared two more limpets for placement. Suddenly, a slight noise was heard from above. The two Aussies instinctively looked up and froze. Protruding from a porthole only ten feet above them, a face was watching the two raiders.

There was a long moment of silence. For whatever may have been his reason, the Face continued to stare at Lyon and Huston but did not utter a word. Not knowing what other action to take, Huston continued fastening the limpets, then the two men began backing away in the canoe. Glancing over his shoulder, Lyon saw the Face withdraw and apparently light a lamp in his quarters.

High-tailing it away, Lyon and Huston expected all hell to break loose in the harbor at any moment, but the Face apparently gave no warning and presumably went to bed.

Their mischief accomplished in Singapore harbor, the men in the three canoes rendezvoused at Pulau Dongas, eight miles away, between 4:45 and 5:01 A.M. Talking on top of one another, the raiders excitedly related their adventures deep inside the Japanese bastion. En masse, the six Jaywick men clawed their way up the high elevation they had used earlier as an observation post. Moments later . . . *boom!* Then, *boom, boom!* In rapid order, five more explosions. Ivan Lyon and his men leaped up and down in exhilaration.

As the sun rose and cleared off the morning haze, Lyon, through his binoculars, surveyed the harbor. One ship was half submerged. Fierce fires were blazing from the tanker on which the Face had been staring down at Lyon and Huston only a few hours earlier. Thick clouds of black smoke billowed across Singapore.

Meanwhile, bedlam erupted along the Singapore waterfront. Sirens screamed. Japanese patrol ships darted out of the harbor and began to fan out in search of the culprits. Just past 6:00 A.M., a flight of warplanes lifted off from an airfield near the port and began scouring the sea approaches to Singapore. One of the planes skimmed directly over the patch of land on which the Jaywick men were hiding and waiting for nightfall.

Throughout the day, Captain Lyon and the others could see Zero and Zeke planes and light aircraft crisscrossing the wide harbor. Launches sped back and forth like so many waterbugs scurrying about.

After paddling relentlessly for the next two nights, the Jaywickers reached Fisherman's Bay on Pompong, where they were to link up with the returning *Krait*. Now came a renewed surge of concern: With what Lyon and his five men were convinced was much of the Japanese navy and air force searching for them, the *Krait* was nowhere to be seen. Had the old tub been sunk? Had the Japanese captured her crew, tortured them, and forced them to disclose the rendezvous point? If so, Ivan Lyon and his companions were doomed.

All day and into the night, an uneasy watch was kept. As the minutes and then the hours ticked past, hopes sank. Three nights later, the Jaywickers heard a boat engine offshore, and they picked up their weapons to do battle. As the vessel drew closer, Donald Davidson called out, "Hold it. It's our old tub!" Delayed by stormy weather and violent seas, the *Krait* had arrived.

On October 18, *Krait* sailed into Exmouth Gulf, forty-eight days and four thousand miles after it had departed.

Meanwhile, Japanese commanders at Singapore, who had lost enormous face, never learned the true identity of the culprits nor that they had come all the way from Australia. In due course, a report was sent to Tokyo, which read in part: "Singapore shipping espionage had been carried out by Malayan criminals. It was commanded by Europeans hiding in the neighborhood of Jahore. As a result of this clever plan, seven ships were sunk by explosives."[7]

An All-Out 12
Propaganda Blitz

I n the spring of 1943, Douglas MacArthur planned to intensify his clandestine war against the Japanese in the Philippines in order to lay a sturdy foundation for his eventual Great Return. The Supreme Commander wanted a special secret agency, working in conjunction with Charles Willoughby's AIB, devoted exclusively to coordinating the scores of scattered bands of guerrillas, supplying them with field radios on a systematic basis, and collecting intelligence.[1]

The Supreme Commander asked the Pentagon to send him Colonel Courtney Whitney, Sr., an old friend from Manila days, who had spent fifteen years in the Philippines as a corporation lawyer before war broke out in the Pacific. He knew the islands and the Filipinos intimately.

Whitney happened to be in Washington at the time MacArthur's request arrived at the War Department, preparing to leave for China to be intelligence officer for Major General Clare Chennault's new 14th Air Force. Now, with the change of plans, Whitney, who had been a fighter pilot in World War I, was eager to get to the southwest Pacific to play a key role in undermining the Japanese.

Before departing Washington, Whitney scoured army sources there in search of portable radios that would be crucial if a widespread communications net involving MacArthur's headquarters and spies and guerrillas were to be expanded. He managed to locate a few transmitters: Each of them weighed one ton, far too heavy for guerrillas to lug through thick jungles, especially if pursuing Japanese were snapping at their heels. So Whitney's search reached across the Atlantic to London, where, with the help of British intelligence friends, he located transmitters that could be carried on a man's back. Possibly exceeding his authority, the colonel ordered dozens of them; he would worry later about procedures for paying for the electronic devices.

After arriving on the west coast, Whitney inspected two regiments of Filipino soldiers training there. After countless one-on-one interviews, MacArthur's new cloak-and-dagger officer selected the best men for future assignments of sneaking through Japanese positions and establishing radio espionage posts throughout the Philippine Islands.

Upon his arrival in Brisbane on May 24, 1943, Colonel Whitney was greeted warmly by the Supreme Commander. Without wasting time, the general filled in the details of the task Whitney had been brought to the Pacific to perform. MacArthur stressed that it would be left to Whitney's imagination and ingenuity to achieve the objectives.

When Whitney rose to leave, he looked MacArthur directly in the eye and said, "General, I will deliver your periodic reports from my own operatives in the city of Manila within three months!"

With a twinkle in his eye, the Supreme Commander replied, "And what will be the penalty if you fail?"[2]

A day later, Whitney moved into an office near MacArthur's Brisbane headquarters. He would be in charge of a new Philippine Regional Section (PRS), an offshoot of the AIB. But Whitney was told he would report not to the AIB, but to General Dick Sutherland, who had been MacArthur's chief of staff since before the war. At the same time, Whitney would keep the AIB advised of his major operations to avoid duplication of effort or, conceivably, a violent clash in the field between unknowing PRS and AIB operatives.

Perhaps for the first time, Court Whitney fully comprehended the new world of clandestine machinations into which he had plunged. His work was so secret that even most of the other officers in MacArthur's headquarters were unaware that the PRS existed. Those who did know that Whitney had ensconced himself in a Brisbane office presumed that he was involved in some sort of paper-shuffling function. Consequently, the colonel had to be on guard at all times lest a slip of the tongue would give away his true function.

So while the vast majority of MacArthur's staff officers never would have an inkling of what was going on, the Supreme Commander himself followed the PRS operation with keen interest and personally approved or revised every major move that Whitney made. Reports from PRS radio operators in the Philippines would be the first things he would read and evaluate when he arrived at his office each morning.

Whitney and his staff worked out countless separate codes to maintain the secrecy of his covert communications. The large number of Filipinos he had selected while they were in training on the west coast were speeded to Australia at MacArthur's urgent request. When all of them had arrived, they were sent to a secret camp forty miles south of Brisbane, where they were put through a rigorous course in radio operations, codes, intelligence, sabotage, and related subjects.

In the early months after Whitney's arrival (and prior to that time), supplies and individuals were sneaked into the Philippines on submarines that had other missions in the southwest Pacific and could stop off briefly in the islands to discharge undercover agents in rubber rafts. However, no doubt at MacArthur's intervention with Washington brass, a few submarines were assigned to the PRS exclusively for cloak-and-dagger operations. Two of these were huge cargo-carrying submarines, which could hold a hundred tons of arms, ammunition, and other supplies as well as provide room for fifteen passengers.

A few months after Court Whitney began operations, MacArthur and a few aides became deeply concerned that the Japanese propaganda that had been saturating the islands for the past twenty-one months was steadily eroding the morale of Filipino civilians and the guerrillas. The conquerors controlled all sources of internal propaganda—radio, newspapers, magazines, and billboards.

In their radio messages to the PRS, guerrilla leaders repeatedly begged for some dramatic action to counter the barrage of false Japanese propaganda. Consequently, in September 1943, Colonel Whitney and his artful dodgers at the PRS launched a massive retaliatory campaign designed to give new hope to Filipino civilians and the guerrillas.

Various items known to be scarce in the Philippines, such as cigarettes, matches, chewing gum, candy bars, sewing kits, and pencils, were sent to the islands in submarines by the millions for widespread distribution. Each package bore on one side the crossed American and Philippine flags and on the other the quotation "I shall return!" printed over a facsimile of General MacArthur's signature. Never mind that few Filipinos spoke English—each man, woman, and child knew the phrase "I shall return!"

Special stamps for a Guerrilla Postal Service were struck, and when they were shipped into the islands by the hundreds of thousands, the partisans began using them in outlying areas. Many reached the Manila post office, where workers, affecting not to notice them, routinely processed the letters with the bogus stamps. Some of these letters even were delivered to addresses occupied by Japanese government officials.

Around Manila and elsewhere in the islands, "I shall return!" was crudely painted on walls as well as on the sides of buildings. On occasion, dawn breaking over Manila would find a large billboard with "I shall return!" leaping out at passersby. These defiant words were even found on stickers pasted on the backs of Japanese military buses and trains, at the entrances to theaters, at railroad stations, and even outside brothels.

In Australia, hundreds of thousands of copies of a pictorial magazine entitled *Free Philippines* were printed each month and shipped into the islands in the huge cargo-carrying submarines. Splashed across the cover in large, bold letters were the words "I shall return!" Loaded with pertinent photographs, the magazines reviewed the progress of the war on a factual basis. Maps, with angry-looking arrows pointing directly toward the Philippines, helped explain the true war picture—and MacArthur's goal—to the hard-pressed natives and guerrillas.

Newspapers and periodicals from the United States flooded the Philippines. Reaction to them far exceeded PRS hopes. Lieutenant Colonel Wendell Fertig, the American who led thousands of guerrillas on the big island of Mindanao, radioed Brisbane. "Advise that article about Ibn Saud, King of Saudi Arabia, in *Life* on 31 May, be reprinted for distribution among Mohammedans of the Celebes, Borneo, and all Moro provinces in Mindanao and Salu. Expressions of friendship by the King for the USA are extremely important. Many Mindanao Moros have made pilgrimage to Mecca. That single issue of *Life* has destroyed much pro-Jap support in this region."[3]

Another report from the Philippines dramatized the impact of the American counterpropaganda barrage. "Smuggled *Life* mag selling for twenty-five pesos [$12.50] each in Manila."

On October 6, 1943, MacArthur received a message from Washington: "The President [Roosevelt] and President Quezon are much concerned over the progress of Japanese propaganda in the Philippines. The substance of the message of the President to Congress [today] should be impressed upon the minds of the Filipinos by every practical means. . . . Text of the President's message is being sent you."[4]

While MacArthur remained outwardly serene on receipt of this order from the White House braintrust, his staff felt no such compunctions. What in the blazes, they howled in picturesque language, did the nabobs in Washington think the PRS and the guerrillas who put their lives on the line to distribute the tons of American literature had been doing for months? The Supreme Commander, however, replied that he would see that Roosevelt's speech got the widest possible distribution in the Philippines.

Perhaps inserting a needle into the Washington hierarchy, who apparently were fearful that the Filipinos would leap suddenly over to the side of the Japanese, MacArthur closed by declaring, "Have no fear. The Philippine people will remain loyal at heart, and the day we set foot on the islands, they will rally as a unit to our call."

Roosevelt's speechwriters had fashioned his talk to Congress in lofty, philosophical phrases, dwelling on reassuring promises for the future. They totally neglected the present. What the Filipinos wanted most, MacArthur and Whitney knew, was to have the Japanese yoke lifted from around their collective necks. They wanted relief from the perils that were a part of their daily lives. Because Roosevelt's message failed to mention any of these crucial things, MacArthur moved to fill the gap.

On the Supreme Commander's official stationery, and over the facsimile of his signature, tons of printed leaflets were prepared for delivery by submarine. Below the President's message, MacArthur inserted these pertinent words (in part). "I am fully conscious of the heavy burden that is resting on you during this trying time in Philippine history, and along with the President's proposals for your future postwar welfare and security, I . . . convey to you my personal assurances that our military operations, designed to effect your complete liberation, are proceeding successfully. . . . I shall return to Philippine soil to lead our combined forces in a destructive blow aimed at your permanent release from the threat of subjugation by the Japanese Empire."[5]

The Roosevelt/MacArthur document proved to be a blockbuster, numerous guerrilla leaders and AIB operatives radioed Brisbane.

In response to the PRS propaganda blitz, the Japanese launched a major operation to track down "subversives" in the Philippines. Through bribes and rewards, the occupiers managed to track down several guerrilla bands and their leaders. When few Filipinos succumbed to the offered rewards, the frustrated Japanese responded with barbarism. Entire barrios, suspected of harboring guerrillas, were razed and many of their civilians murdered.

With extensive backgrounds in infiltrating the sleazy waterfronts of Shanghai and Singapore, Kempei Tai agents were especially active in the dingy bars, whorehouses, saloons, and restaurants in the disreputable suburbs of Manila. Hoping to feather their own nests, the hardened ex-convicts, drug addicts, and other Filipinos who inhabited those haunts readily agreed to become stool pigeons for the conquerors.

One of the better known habitués of these Manila dens of iniquity was Franco Vera Reyes, who had been doing a long stretch for forgery and larceny in Old Bilibid prison when the Japanese captured Manila. He promptly cut a deal with the Kempei Tai: He would become a stoolie in return for being sprung out of Bilibid.

Now Reyes was in his element. He did not have to work. His Japanese controllers kept plenty of money in his pockets. Best of all, he could hang out in the shady nightclubs and flash large rolls of currency in front of admiring prostitutes and assorted crooks. In return for this bonanza from heaven, all he had to do was to rat on his patriotic countrymen to the Kempei Tai. Treachery came easy for Franco Reyes.

Soon Reyes began spreading his slimy wings beyond the underworld haunts. Portraying himself as an AIB agent, he made contact with José Ozamis, a senator before the war who was now active in the Free Philippines committee, a clandestine group of substantial Manila citizens involved in gathering intelligence and working with patriotic underground groups. The Japanese stoolie had an oily tongue, and he soon convinced Ozamis, a sophisticated man, that he, Reyes, was indeed an AIB operative.

Senator Ozamis confided in a fellow Filipino, Colonel Orestes Manzano, about his new AIB contact. Manzano had been an engineer officer with a Philippine division and became a prisoner when Corregidor fell. Along with other Filipino officers and men, he had been seriously ill at the Camp O'Donnell POW camp, and the Japanese sent him home to die. Manzano, however, chose to recover and got in touch with a trusted assistant, Lieutenant Osmundo Mondonedo, for the purpose of organizing an underground sabotage and intelligence network. Manzano operated from Manila, while Mondonedo was based at Los Banos, in southern Luzon.[6]

On learning about the reputed AIB agent named Franco Reyes from his friend Senator Ozamis, Colonel Manzano became highly suspicious. So he sought out Reyes and invited him to lunch at Tom's Dixie Kitchen, long a popular dining establishment. Tom was an American, but the Japanese, for whatever their reasons, permitted him to operate the restaurant.

Before leaving for his engagement at Tom's Dixie Kitchen, Manzano arranged to have two veteran members of the prewar Manila police force to be seated separately in the establishment. Both men knew on sight most of Manila's criminal element. Reyes would be, in essence, the subject of an informal police lineup.

At lunch, Reyes was typically friendly and loquacious. He spoke of the great work AIB operatives were doing in Manila and elsewhere in the islands. Manzano, however, was aware that the ex-convict was trying to draw him out, to slyly entice the colonel into making damaging revelations about the underground. Manzano refused to snap at the bait.

Later that day, Manzano met secretly with the two former policemen. He could tell by their demeanor that they had alarming news. Franco Reyes, they told him, was not only a habitual criminal and notorious liar, but, far worse, he was a Japanese stool pigeon who should be avoided.

Colonel Manzano rushed to warn José Ozamis, who refused to believe that the gracious, personable Reyes could be a traitor, one whose perfidy had doomed a large number of Filipino patriots.

In earlier conversations, Senator Ozamis had confided to Reyes enough information to implicate himself in anti-Japanese activities, but the Kempei Tai apparently decided not to arrest the former senator. Rather, they would tail him in the hope that he would unwittingly disclose the identity of others in the Free Philippines organization.

Unaware that he was a marked man, Ozamis traveled to Mindanao, where he contacted guerrilla bands whose leaders were in touch with the AIB in Australia. When he returned, Ozamis brought with him several letters from the Filipino guerrillas for personal delivery to their specified loved ones in Manila.

Ozamis showed the guerrilla letters to a few leaders of the Free Philippines group, all of whom advised him not to deliver them because the Kempei Tai might have the addresses under surveillance. Perhaps out of the softness of his heart and having seen the miserable and lonely conditions the guerrillas were enduring in the jungles of Mindanao, Ozamis chose to disregard the urgent advice of his comrades.

In some manner, Franco Reyes learned about the letters—perhaps from his "friend" Ozamis himself. Now the Kempei Tai struck—swiftly and hard. Along with Ozamis, nine Filipinos and several women were arrested and hurled into the dungeons at Fort Santiago prison. Most of them were beheaded as spies.

Filipino patriots launched an intense manhunt for the traitorous Franco Reyes, who apparently had gone into hiding. Perhaps the quest had been successful, because the turncoat was never seen around Manila again. Or had he changed his name, fled to some remote island in the Philippines, and spent the rest of his days counting his blood money?[7]

While the oily Franco Reyes was weaving his traitorous web in Manila, 150 miles to the north another Filipino, twenty-six-year-old Mario Bansen, became a staunch collaborator with the Japanese in the town of Bontoc. A former lieutenant in a Philippine regiment on Bataan, Bansen had been captured and put in a POW hellhole known as Camp O'Donnell. After imprisonment for several months, Bansen agreed to take a "reindoctrination course," conducted by the Japanese, where he heard daily about how a greedy United States had exploited the Philippines for decades.

When the Camp O'Donnell authorities were convinced that Bansen had been sold on Japan's theme of "Asia for the Asians," he was released on the condition that he join the Philippine Constabulary, a Japanese-sponsored police organization whose function was to root out guerrilla bands and other Filipino "subversives."

Bansen was assigned to the headquarters of the constabulary in Bontoc in a key position, chief clerk. In that role, he was entrusted with all correspondence and secret messages that arrived daily from Japanese army agencies in Manila and elsewhere on Luzon. He quickly earned the praise of his Japanese bosses, who regarded him as one of the most hard-working and dedicated members of the constabulary. However, he led a lonely life, for he was scorned and snubbed by his own countrymen. They had no way of knowing that Bansen was one of the AIB's most productive spies, who was saving the lives of large numbers of guerrillas who were marauding in the mountains of northern Luzon.

Within a few weeks of arriving at his post in Bontoc, Mario Bansen learned that the prime target of the constabulary there was Lieutenant Colonel Russell Volckmann, an American who had escaped when Bataan fell and had organized a guerrilla force of ten thousand Filipinos. Bansen hoped to make secret contact with Volckmann. Through reading Japanese dispatches, he learned that the American's suspected headquarters was on a jungle-covered mountain.

One day, a native courier, who refused to give his name or where he lived, found his way to Volckmann's hideout and brought a message signed by Mario Bansen, formerly of General MacArthur's forces. In his note, Bansen explained that joining the constabulary was the only way he could have escaped eventual death in the Camp O'Donnell hellhole and at the same time be in a position where he could help his country.[8]

Russ Volckmann smelled the proverbial rat. While he and a Lieutenant Mario Bansen had served in the same regiment on Bataan, the guerrilla chief had no way of knowing whether the message actually came from Bansen or a Japanese plant using his name. Then there was always the chance that the genuine Lieutenant Bansen had sold out to the Japanese, in which case the note might be a ploy to capture Volckmann, who had a heavy price on his head—dead or alive.

By the same courier, Volckmann sent back a message telling Bansen to prove his loyalty by sending the guerrilla leader secret information culled from his position as the constabulary's chief clerk.

Mario Bansen proved to be an intelligence gold mine. Unnoticed by his trusting Japanese bosses, he always placed an extra sheet of paper in his typewriter for all secret reports, so within hours, Russ Volckmann and his intelligence officer would be poring over the identical documents that were meant only for the eyes of Japanese commanders. This high-grade information was promptly radioed to Courtney Whitney's PRS in Brisbane.[9]

As time passed, the Japanese officers in Bontoc led heavily-armed constabulary bands on raids of Colonel Volckmann's ever-shifting hideouts. Always, the prey and his guerrilla staff had just vacated. Some-one in the know was tipping off the American "bandit," the Japanese became convinced. None suspected the enlightened, industrious chief clerk, Mario Bansen.

13 Rendezvous with MacArthur's Master Spy

I n mid-July 1943, a slight, middle-aged Filipino arrived one night at Brisbane airport after a long flight from the United States. Carried on the passenger manifest as Hector Rodriguiz, the man was met by two Americans in civilian business suits. They escorted him to an unmarked, black Buick sedan and drove to the Brisbane headquarters of General MacArthur. There he conferred for nearly an hour with the Supreme Commander.

Hector Rodriguiz was the cover name for Dr. Emigidio Cruz, a prominent Manila doctor, and the plainclothes men who had met him at the airport were military officers belonging to the AIB. Quiet and unassuming, Cruz briefed MacArthur on his reason for being in Brisbane. As the personal physician to Philippine Commonwealth President Manuel Quezon, he had been sent from Quezon's residence in exile in Washington to penetrate Manila on a perilous espionage mission.

President Quezon had grown extremely worried about news that his onetime top Philippine government officials, who were also his social friends, were collaborating with the Japanese, a fact long known by the AIB. Quezon's scheme was to infiltrate a trusted aide—Dr. Cruz—into Manila to contact the one man he felt could give an accurate assessment of the political situation there. That contact was Manuel y Acuña Roxas, a wealthy, influential friend of the Philippine president.

Puffing on a cigar, MacArthur listened thoughtfully to Cruz's recitation and then remarked that he considered the chance of a man totally untrained in espionage work of sneaking into Manila as about ten percent; his chance of making his way back out, zero.[1]

MacArthur himself had been disturbed since his days on Corregidor by a flow of reports about Manuel Quezon's high-ranking officials collaborating with the Japanese. Like Quezon, who was far more emotionally involved, the Supreme Commander would have liked to know the true political picture in Manila.

Collaborators were a mixed breed. Their motives varied. Some were frightened by the conquerors, others preferred Oriental rulers to Occidental ones, and many were outright opportunists seeking personal gain. Then there were genuine patriots who thought they could best serve their country by cooperating with the Japanese.

Collaborators had begun to surface in January 1942, even as the Battling Bastards of Bataan were starving and fighting for their lives after the fall of Manila. At that time, General Masaharu Homma, commander of the invading army, had appointed a commission of Philippine politicians headed by Jorge Vargas, who had been Quezon's confidential secretary, to help run the country. The first act of the Vargas commission was to cable President Franklin Roosevelt, demanding an immediate American surrender throughout the Philippines.[2]

Then, in mid-1943, the Vargas commission was abolished and replaced by the Independent Philippine Republic headed by José Laurel, a former associate justice of the Commonwealth's supreme court and a close friend of Quezon. Laurel was the only Filipino to hold an honorary degree from Tokyo University. MacArthur was outraged over the fact that the puppet government's mainstays were the Philippines' prewar elite—his former friends and Quezon's colleagues.[3]

All the while, Manual Roxas remained in Manila, watching closely the political gymnastics taking place in the puppet government. Roxas, fifty-two years of age, had been born to wealth and long had been a ranking member of the Philippine economic and government establishment. Owner of three newspapers, including the influential *Manila Daily News*, he had been a regent at the University of the Philippines, and was a reserve brigadier general in the U.S. Army. As a senator in the Philippine legislature, Roxas had favored early independence for the islands.

Before President Quezon was spirited out of besieged Corregidor on a submarine in March 1942, he asked his pal Roxas to go with him into exile. Although the introverted Sergio Osmeña (his nickname was Sphinx) was the vice president of the Commonwealth, Quezon wanted Roxas to be the next president. Roxas, however, refused the invitation to leave the country.

There was good reason for Roxas's decision: Unbeknownst to Quezon and Osmeña, MacArthur had asked the brigadier general to remain in the Philippines in order to provide MacArthur with firsthand intelligence on the political scene in the islands. G-2 Charles Willoughby, one of the few Americans who was aware of Roxas's espionage role, told a confidant, "Roxas has been our man [in Manila] all the time."[4]

When General Wainwright had surrendered the Philippines in May 1942, Manual Roxas was captured on Mindanao. A week later, an order authorized in the name of General Masaharu Homma arrived at the headquarters of Major General Toroa Ikuta, the commander on Mindanao, at Davao. Homma ordered Ikuta to execute Roxas "secretly and immediately."

Ikuta turned over the job to his chief of staff, Colonel Nobuhiko Jimbo, who, with his shaven head, horn-rimmed glasses, and mustache, resembled the big boss, Hideki Tojo. Jimbo was a devout Catholic, as was Roxas, and his task disturbed the Japanese officer as he drove the Filipino and another high-ranking captive to the site of the execution. During the hour-long trip, Roxas acted nobly on the verge of death, and Jimbo found himself with a great deal in common with the man he was about to execute. So Jimbo decided to try to save Roxas, although doing so could mean his own life as forfeiture.

Finding an excuse to postpone the killings, Colonel Jimbo left Roxas and the other captive, an island governor, under guard in a small village while he raced back to Davao to try to persuade General Ikuta to ignore the execution order. Jimbo's pleas fell on sympathetic ears: Ikuta had assigned the task to Jimbo because he, himself, could not bear to carry it out.

Ikuta and Jimbo decided that they would keep Manual Roxas hidden, on the theory that the execution order would be forgotten by those who had issued it in Manila. They were wrong. Word seeped out (probably through a disloyalist on Ikuta's staff) and an officer arrived from Manila to tell Colonel Jimbo that he was to be court-martialed for disobeying orders. However, he was not put under arrest.

Knowing that his life and certainly his career were at stake, Jimbo flew to Manila to plead his case. General Homma was out of his office, so Jimbo spoke with Major General Takaji Wachi, his chief of staff. Wachi was stunned. No such order had been authorized by Homma. Jimbo showed him the original execution document, which was stamped by Major General Yoshihide Hayashi, military administrator in Homma's Fourteenth Army.

Unauthorized to countermand orders stamped with Homma's name, the chief of staff issued a temporary suspension of Manual Roxas's execution. While Jimbo waited, the angry Wachi charged into Hayashi's next-door office, where the general was conferring with four staff officers. A violent dispute erupted. Jimbo could hear loud voices.

"Did you issue this order to execute General Roxas?" Wachi thundered.

Hayashi denied it, for such an order would be in violation of Homma's strict orders to grant clemency to high Philippine officials, he declared.

Still red-faced with fury, Wachi yelled for Colonel Jimbo. When Jimbo pulled out the execution order, Hayashi's feigned innocence evaporated, and he admitted that he and the four staff officers in the room had stamped the document.

Then Hayashi wheeled on Jimbo and shouted, "You have done a terrible thing to us!"[5]

"Us," it developed, was a small but influential group of Homma's own subordinates, who had been secretly sending out orders over Homma's name for the execution of top Philippine authorities.

That night, General Wachi paid a call on Colonel Jimbo at the Manila Hotel, which once had been home for Douglas MacArthur and his family. Homma was pleased with the initiative displayed by Jimbo, the colonel was told, and orders already had gone out countermanding the Roxas execution. Had any of the Japanese known that Roxas had remained in the Philippines to be MacArthur's prime espionage agent, matters may have turned out differently.[6]

Now, a year later, master spy Roxas was playing a dangerous, high-stakes poker game. Early on, he had ingratiated himself so deeply with the conquerors that he, Roxas, was their first choice to head the puppet government, not Vargas. Pleading that he had suffered a coronary (which was untrue), he declined the offer with profuse apologies. Then, in the months ahead, Manila newspapers showed pictures of Roxas signing documents in Malacañan Palace, the seat of government before and after the occupation. Loyal Filipinos, especially the guerrillas, were furious. Unaware of his clandestine role for MacArthur, they branded their prominent countryman an arch-traitor.

Against this backdrop of Manila intrigue, Dr. Emigidio Cruz, who had not been advised by MacArthur of Roxas's espionage role, climbed into the submarine USS *Thresher* at Perth, Australia, for the first leg of his journey to Manila. His initial stop would be for a rendezvous with guerrilla leader Jesus Villamor (W-10 at the AIB), on the Philippines island of Negros. Crammed into the submarine were a few other Filipinos in peasant garb (other spies to be slipped into the islands) and some seven tons of arms and ammunition consigned to guerrillas.

On the morning of July 9, 1943, the *Thresher* prepared to surface at the designated landing spot in southwestern Negros. Through the periscope, the skipper detected an alarming sight: A Japanese cruiser was patrolling the shore. If it seemed strange that this particular stretch of beach would be the subject of a warship's attention, Cruz gave no indication of it.

Shifting to a nearby locale, the *Thresher* remained submerged all day and then surfaced after darkness fell. Dr. Cruz, clad in a wide-brimmed straw hat, shorts, and a thin shirt—typical native dress on Negros—paddled ashore in a rubber dinghy and contacted a band of guerrillas. In the remarkable span of only forty-five minutes, all seven tons of weapons and ammunition was removed from the submarine and taken ashore by the guerrillas.

An hour later, Cruz met with Jesus Villamor (cover name Ramon Hernandez), who was directing the AIB's Planet operation from his hideout on Negros. Rightly concerned with the security of Planet, Villamor was appalled when he discovered that the amateur espionage agent (Cruz) had in his possession a fountain pen of a popular American brand that had not been distributed in the Philippines since before the war. Also in Cruz's pocket was a cigarette lighter that had been purchased recently in the United States. If the physician was caught by the Kempei Tai—a likely possibility, Villamor thought—these accoutrements would nail down the physician's coffin.

Now, on the heels of a Japanese cruiser's presence along the initial landing beach, there came a series of other curious happenings that might indicate that someone, somewhere, had tipped off the Japanese. Only seventy-two hours after Cruz linked up with Villamor, an enemy raiding party stormed ashore at the doctor's landing spot. After a brief shootout, the guerrillas were scattered. Then the Japanese rushed to the precise place where the weapons and ammunition carried from the submarine had been hidden, a remarkable feat, indeed, without prior information.

There were other indications of treachery. While a group of Japanese was lugging a large amount of the weapons and ammunition back to their boat lying offshore, other Japanese hurried directly to the carefully camouflaged radio station that Villamor used to communicate with the AIB in Australia. The radio was also hauled away, and the raiders departed.

When Cruz was ready to march to the next stopover, northern Negros, on his odyssey to Manila, Villamor warned him that it would not be safe to continue.

"There are too many, even among the guerrillas, who know your true identity," W-10 declared.

The doctor, however, managed to obtain a native guide and left for the hideout of Alfredo Montelibano, who was the governor of Negros.

After a week of rugged walking through the jungle, Cruz and his guide reached Montelibano's headquarters, which was perched at the top of the Caloan volcano and guarded by guerrillas. Five days later, some two hundred Japanese soldiers scrambled up the mountainside and launched a surprise raid on the camp. Caught off-guard, the guerrillas, along with Cruz and the governor, fled deep into the thick vegetation, where they reorganized. For three days, a fierce firefight raged, and when the Japanese pulled back, they left sixty of their comrades lying dead.

When peace returned, Cruz learned from a guerrilla that a friend, Major Emilio Roberto, was holed up in the hills nearby, and the physician set out for his hideout. By a stroke of amazing good fortune, Cruz discovered that Roberto had a sailboat concealed near the northern Negros port of Cadiz and that the major had a five-man crew that was stranded on the island and eager to get back to their homes on Luzon.

Posing as a trader, Cruz loaded the vessel with dried fish and chickens. Then the boat cast off and set a course through the Visayan Sea for Luzon, 250 miles to the north. It was a tedious and dangerous trip. Along the way, the vessel stopped at several islands to dispose of the goods and replenish them with fresh ones.

As the turtlelike trek continued, a lookout suddenly called out, "Jap patrol boat!"

Tension gripped those aboard the Manila-bound craft. Minutes later, the Japanese vessel pulled alongside, and its skipper, an interpreter, and five armed sailors boarded. While Cruz and his companions looked on, the enemy crewmen began picking through the dried fish and chicken. Moments later, the doctor thought he was a goner: The search was leading directly toward a small tin box that held letters from President Quezon to Manuel Roxas. Just before the probing hands would have touched the container, the Japanese gave up the search.

Now the patrol boat's skipper began to grill Cruz. "We want information on a Major Suylan who brought arms to the bandits on Negros," the Japanese said to Cruz, who felt a surge of panic.[7] Major Suylan was the cover name the physician had been assigned in Australia for his trip to Manila.

Hoping that his voice would not quake, Cruz replied that he knew nothing about a Major Suylan—that he, Cruz, was just a poor peddler of fish and chickens, trying to eke out a living. After forcing the doctor to go through his story time and again, the Japanese skipper shrugged, and he and his men climbed back into the patrol boat and departed.

Two nights later, the little vessel chugged into a small port in southern Luzon. Back on familiar territory, Cruz adopted Emilio C. Corde as a new alias and made his way to Magdalena, a coastal village controlled by the Japanese. Still masquerading as a peddler, he sought out the elderly Japanese who had been appointed mayor. When Cruz flashed a handful of pesos, the mayor responded by providing a local residence certificate, which was required for travel, made out to "Emilio C. Corde, merchant." Now Lady Luck again smiled on Cruz. He contacted a Chinese merchant named Tiong Hing, who had lived in these parts for several decades and was bound for Manila with a load of lumber and flour. An amiable chap, the Chinese man agreed to take Cruz along. They would depart at dawn.

That night, a band of eight armed guerrillas, led by an American, barged into the house where Cruz was holed up and roughly demanded to know what he was doing in town. The newcomers were belligerent and threatening.

"You're a goddamned Jap spy!" their leader shouted.

Cruz's protestations were of no avail. Forcing the doctor to carry a shovel to dig his own grave, the guerrillas marched him through the night toward a large field.

"Now we're going to show you how we deal with Jap spies!" the leader declared.

With his feet getting heavier with each step, Cruz asked the American, "You're not really going to kill a Bataan Boy, are you?"

There were moments of silence. Then the American said, "You mean you're a Bataan Boy? I fought on Bataan, too!"[8]

The execution party concluded. For nearly an hour, the two men exchanged their experiences about escaping from Japanese clutches on the doomed peninsula a year and a half earlier.

On October 23, nearly four months after he had left Perth on his secret mission for President Quezon, Cruz reached Manila. It was arranged that he would meet a friend, the nephew of Doña Aurora Quezon, the Philippine president's wife (who was in the United States with her husband), in Quiapo Church. There, means would be provided to escort him to yet another contact, who would arrange a clandestine meeting with Manuel Roxas.

Inside the stately old church, Cruz knelt in a pew, and minutes later a figure knelt next to him. Glancing out of the corner of one eye, the doctor saw the anxious face of his friend, President Quezon's nephew. The other's hand gripped his arm, and in a slight whisper he called attention to a Filipino standing near a door to one side. Holding his head still, Cruz rotated his eyes and saw that the man was staring intently toward the pair in the pew.

Both Cruz and the younger Quezon sneaked peeks and saw the stranger go out the front door and approach Japanese military police who were apparently on duty there. Without a word, the physician and his companion slipped along the wall toward another side door. The nephew walked off briskly in one direction and Cruz, in his haste, almost bumped into a parked car with a man seated at the wheel.

"Get inside," the driver called out, pushing open a door. Cruz needed no second urging. He scrambled inside and the car sped away. Cruz said a quick prayer to the Virgin Mary: He had stumbled into the very man who had been sent to make contact with him and arrange for the rendezvous with Manuel Roxas. The driver was an old friend and had immediately recognized the physician.

Cruz was taken to a safe house, where word was sent to him that the Kempei Tai was searching for an unidentified aide of President Quezon. Since the wanted individual was said to be wearing a black mustache, Cruz promptly shaved off his facial hair.

Amid much secrecy—no one in Manila could tell who was a collaborator and who was loyal to the Commonwealth—Cruz and Roxas met that night in a house at 893 Lepanto Street. Outside, lurking in the shadows, were two of Roxas's trusted assistants who were lookouts for the approach of danger. Roxas and Cruz talked through most of the night. Roxas gave his friend an exhaustive rundown on which of the Philippine high-ranking politicians were true collaborators and who were playing a perilous double game to secretly serve their country and its people.

Daily conversations were held in which Roxas, the only prominent Philippine figure who had found excuses not to sign an oath of allegiance to the Japanese Empire, provided abundant information on the enemy's troop strengths and installations on Luzon. Roxas also advised Cruz that he had a secret understanding with General Eulogio Franciso, a patriot who was masquerading as a Japanese sympathizer, that if the occupiers were to draft Filipinos into the Japanese army (a likely possibility), loyal Filipino officers would be assigned to key positions so that they could turn the entire conscripted army against the Japanese when Douglas MacArthur invaded the islands.

"You can be sure that ninety-five percent of the Filipino people are loyal to the United States and to President Quezon," Roxas declared.[9]

After Dr. Cruz had been in Manila for a week, he knew it was time to leave and return to Australia. Good luck had played a major role in getting him to Manila. Perhaps he recalled that General MacArthur had told him frankly that he estimated Cruz's chances of getting back were zero. His desire to leave promptly was hastened after Roxas told him that, through contacts in the Manila police department, he had learned that the Japanese knew that President Quezon's physician was in Manila on a secret mission and that they were searching desperately for him.

Before departing, Cruz was given a large container that Roxas wanted the doctor to take back to the United States and give to Quezon. Inside the box was a gold mine of intelligence: copies of a complete set of the Philippine Gazette containing the official reports and the records of all the bureaus and departments in the puppet government, including the speeches given by the top politicians.[10]

With the Philippine Gazette and pages of copious notes he had taken during his week in Manila concealed in a small bamboo trunk beneath cigars, handbags, and wooden shoes, Cruz donned shabby clothes and headed southward. Once again, he became Emilio C. Corde, peddler. There began weeks of island hopping and dodging Japanese bands on the ground and patrol boats on the sea. On the tiny island of Gigantangian, he was preparing for the next leap when the region was struck by a typhoon, which blew a Japanese patrol boat and its crew into the hamlet where he was hiding.

Finally, on February 12, 1944, the physician/spy was picked up by the submarine *Narwhal*, and a few days later he reached Australia. His travels deep into the heart of Japanese-controlled territories had taken more than seven months.

In Brisbane, General MacArthur's staff arranged for Emigidio Cruz to come to headquarters to be decorated. Three o'clock came and went, and the doctor never showed up; he had been so engrossed in writing up countless pages of intelligence collected in Manila that he had forgotten about the affair in his honor.

That night, top AIB officers had a gala dinner in Cruz's honor at Lennon's Hotel. This time, the amateur spy remembered to attend.

Spying on the Conquerors 14

In the summer of 1943, Manila was one of the south Pacific's most bustling ports. On any given day, scores of Japanese ships were being loaded or unloaded at the docks. For nearly two years, a large group of American POWs had been working as stevedores under U.S. Navy Lieutenant Commander George G. Harrison. Calling themselves "G.G.'s 400 Thieves," the POWs had become so familiar to their Japanese guards that virtually no attention was paid to the Americans' activities—besides, the POWs were dedicated workers. But while the guards loitered in the shade, sipping sake and chatting among themselves, the stevedores sabotaged nearly every enemy ship filled with the accoutrements of war and food bound for Japanese soldiers in the southwest Pacific.

Harrison's "thieves" became quite skilled in creating innovative means to sabotage the enemy ships without implicating themselves, which would have meant instant beheading. They loaded vessels in such a way as to cause them to capsize in stormy weather. These ships vanished, the stevedores would learn. The Americans also created a technique for boring small holes in the hull and then concealing the openings. When the ship got out to sea, the POWs knew, the heavy swells would expand the size of the holes. These vessels would also never be heard from again.

An elderly, mild-mannered Filipino harbor official, whose peacetime function for many years had been to coordinate the arrival and departure of ships and to assign them dock space, was retained in his post after the Japanese captured the city once known as the Pearl of the Orient because of its broad, palm-lined thoroughfares and majestic buildings. To keep the heavy Manila Bay shipping operating efficiently, his services were crucial. Besides, what harm could an old man cause the Empire of Japan?

Early on, the harbor official had explained that he could not allocate berths unless the Japanese informed him of the tonnage and the cargo of each ship. So each morning, he was provided with this detailed data. Members of the ships' Japanese crews often would return from a night on the town reeking of sake and reeling. The friendly old Filipino engaged them in casual conversation and often learned the destination of their vessels as well as their sailing dates.

Each day, through a covert arrangement, the harbor official slipped information to a popular Filipino radio broadcaster, who stood in good stead with the occupiers because he closed each program with a brief sentence that seemed to be eulogizing the Japanese. Actually, it was a predesignated code that tipped off AIB electronic monitors about the approximate shipping tonnage that had entered and departed Manila Bay during the previous twenty-four hours, as well as the destination of some of the vessels.

Likewise, Filipino workers in the Manila railroad yards reported regularly to the spy network on trains running in and out of the city, particularly with regard to troop trains. Young Filipina women sauntered around the railroad station, striking up conversations with homesick Japanese soldiers and often prying from them detailed information on the identity of their units and destinations. This intelligence, too, reached the AIB.

Manila was infested with MacArthur's spies, most of them Filipinos. These undercover operatives, who received no pay and would seldom receive public recognition, came from all walks of life. While going about their legitimate daily routines, they collected countless pieces of intelligence about the Japanese occupiers and their military machine. Despite their diverse backgrounds, ranging from the wealthy to the poverty-stricken, the amateur spies had one common denominator: Each lived under the constant threat of arrest and beheading by the Kempei Tai.

A fireball sun was hanging high in the cloudless blue sky as Field Marshal Count Haisichi Terauchi, supreme commander of the Japanese Southern Armies, strolled into the magnificent lobby of the swank Manila Hotel after an eleven-hundred-mile flight from his headquarters in Saigon. Pompous, shrewd, and tough, Terauchi came to evaluate the war situation in the southwest Pacific. It was September 2, 1943.

Forewarned of the field marshal's arrival, the hotel's Filipino manager and staff, decked out in formal attire, were arrayed just inside the front door to provide a warm and gracious welcome to the distinguished guest, whose military juggernaut had conquered their country two and a half years earlier. The Filipino employees were friendly, even deferential, to Terauchi as he made his way to the ornate, seven-room penthouse with its breathtaking view of beautiful, blue Manila Bay.

Hardly had the field marshal ensconced himself in the luxury suite than word of his presence was flashed by a clandestine radio network to the AIB in Brisbane, Australia. Source of this information had been the Manila Hotel's executive staff, desk clerks, bellhops, and elevator operators who long had been risking their lives daily as AIB spies.

A few hours later, MacArthur was shown the message disclosing that Field Marshal Terauchi was a guest in the Imperial Suite of the Manila Hotel. This was the same apartment where the general and his wife, Jean, had lived for several years until being forced to flee when the Japanese invaders approached Manila in late December 1941. Left behind in the penthouse were the family furnishings and mementos, including priceless keepsakes handed down by Douglas's father, General Arthur MacArthur, who had served in the Philippines many years earlier.

Handing back to his aide the message from the Manila underground, Douglas MacArthur remarked dryly, "Well, I'm glad to know who is occupying the suite. [Terauchi] should like the pair of vases given by the [Japanese] emperor to my father in 1905."[1]

For more than a year, the Filipino spies among the employees of the Manila Hotel had subtly extracted information from the high-ranking Japanese military officers and government nabobs from Tokyo who had been parading in and out. A beaming elevator operator would inquire casually about how long the guest planned to remain in Manila and the purpose of his visit. To catch a Japanese dignitary off-guard, a bellboy would slip in offhand comments about how deplorable it was that some unthinking Filipinos resented the presence of the Japanese in the Philippines.

It was common for the Japanese guests to bring with them their wives or mistresses posing as wives. These ladies of refinement required frequent visits to the hotel's high-fashion beauty salon, where the Filipina stylists engaged the customers in amiable conversation. These relaxed encounters often produced important intelligence for the Manila spy network.

Elsewhere in Manila, a young Filipino architect, slight of stature and with a boyish face, rented a studio in one of the city's finest office buildings—which also happened to have the Kempei Tai as a tenant. Cheerful and amiable at all times, the architect rapidly made friends with the Japanese sentries at the building's front door. Bowing and beaming, the Filipino invariably stopped to chat when leaving, and the guards ceased the normal checks and searches given to others. Clearly, the architect was no threat to Japanese security. Had he been a spy, he most certainly would not have moved into a studio adjacent to the Kempei Tai offices.

Soon, the Filipino began hearing from his friends, the Japanese door sentries, about underground ammunition and fuel dumps being built secretly at Nichols Field, a large airport outside of Manila. American POWs captured on Bataan and Corregidor early in the war were being used as slave labor on the massive construction project, an action that was in violation of the Geneva convention.[2]

A few days later, a Filipino who appeared to be a teenager applied for a job as a waterboy on the construction job at Nichols Field and was accepted. Clad in short, ragged pants and a floppy straw hat, he looked much like the other fourteen- and fifteen-year-olds who circulated around the project with fresh water for the American POWs who were laboring in the scorching sun for twelve-hour days. Water was not being provided to the emaciated POWs out of generosity of the Japanese guards, many of whom were brutal; rather, an occasional drink would enable the Americans to labor a little longer.

None of the Japanese guards seemed to notice that the new boy always managed to serve the POWs toiling in the off-limits underground ammunition dump or that he remained after the other waterboys left and the guards had marched the POWs away. They were not around to see the boy sketching rough drawings of the new project, including its proximity to other buildings at Nichols Field.

Toward the end of each day, he went to the home of a friend, donned his business suit, and returned to his office in the building occupied by the Kempei Tai—for the waterboy and the architect with the baby face were one and the same. Over a period of time, he created large, detailed, precisely scaled drawings of the secret underground ammunition dump on long sheets that had to be rolled up.

Now that his drawing task was completed, the architect was faced with a major obstacle: How would he smuggle out the long rolls of paper when the front door was guarded day and night? He decided boldness would be the best course: He would stop and chat briefly with his friends, the two Kempei Tai sentries, and then continue as though it had been just another day at the office.

If caught, he was fully aware that he would be hurled into the slimy dungeons of Fort Santiago prison and tortured hideously to force him to disclose the names of other Filipino spies before being beheaded. A thousand fears raced through his nimble brain. What if there happened to be new sentries who did not know him? Most assuredly they would search him and discover the espionage materials he was carrying. Or what if the usual sentries decided, for whatever their reasons, to check his documents this time? These were chances he would have to take.

Holding the rolls of drawings of the huge underground installation being built at Nichols Field, the young man left his office and approached the front door. He was perspiring profusely, his stomach was tied in knots, and his legs felt like jelly. Moments later, he offered up brief thanks to the Virgin Mary: The old sentries were on duty. Grinning and bowing, the architect forced himself to joke and chat with them for several minutes. The drawings rolled up in his hand seemed to weigh a ton. Finally taking his leave, he went directly to his Manila contact, who took the priceless drawings to a predesignated rendezvous with a U.S. submarine.

Within ten days, officers at the AIB were carefully poring over the espionage bonanza. Later, when American warplanes would thunder over Manila, the Japanese commander would be perplexed over how the bombardiers had managed to pinpoint and destroy the top secret, camouflaged underground ammunition dump at Nichols Field.[3]

A favorite Manila hangout for Japanese officers and high civilian officials was Club Tsubaki. Located near the harbor, the nightspot was owned by thirty-five-year-old Claire Fuentes, a vivacious brunette of Italian birth and Philippine citizenship. Manilans long had regarded her as a despicable traitor, for she had let it be known that Club Tsubaki catered only to the Japanese bigwigs and that even wealthy Filipinos were not welcome.

Club Tsubaki was packed each night with beer-swilling Japanese who lounged in low-slung settees and portable armchairs. Clad in tight-fitting evening gowns with plunging necklines, Fuentes circulated among the patrons, laughing, teasing, and flirting. On any given night, the shameful hussy would spend most of her time at the table of the highest-ranking or most important Japanese. She did little to resist their drunken pawings.

Before the war, the raven-haired, flashy-eyed Fuentes made a living by singing popular ballads in ritzy establishments like the Manila Hotel and the Alcazar Club. Drawing on her entertainment background, she now put on a rousing floor show each night, complete with a five-piece band and featuring her five attractive, skimpily clad dancing girls.

The Japanese officers, most of whom were well oiled by showtime, watched goggle-eyed during the women's on-stage gyrations. The patrons became even more attentive when the female performers mingled with them after the show. The dancers' nimbleness was of great help in eluding the grabs at various parts of their anatomies.

Actually, Claire Fuentes was a master spy for the Americans. She was not an Italian, but a native of the United States who had come to the Philippines just before the war began in the Pacific. She used her popular nightclub to collect information from the Japanese, intelligence that was then sneaked out of Manila and into the hands of American-led guerrillas in the nearby Zambales Mountains.

All of the female stage performers and the male employees were ardent Philippine patriots, and they were valuable cogs in Fuentes's espionage operation in the dead center of Japanese power in the islands.

Fuentes's code name was High Pockets, which was derived from the fact that she carried secret intelligence information and personal valuables in her brassiere. She had gotten into the perilous espionage business when she learned that her American husband of a few months, Sergeant John V. Phillips, had been captured on Bataan, suffered through the Death March, and died a short time later of malnutrition and brutalities at the Cabanatuan POW camp sixty miles north of Manila.[4]

One day, High Pockets received an urgent request from Major John Boone (code-named Compadre), who led a large number of guerrillas in the Zambales and to whom Fuentes had sent hundreds of intelligence messages that were relayed by Boone's radio to AIB headquarters. Boone's terse note said, "Urgent. Find out what is in Jap ship in Manila harbor. Ship painted white with huge red crosses."

High Pockets was acquainted with that particular vessel, for it had been in port for at least three days and its skipper, a stocky, stone-faced man, had visited Club Tsubaki each night. She sent for two teenage Filipinos, who had jobs on the pier unloading ships and served as her eyes and ears there. She asked them to slip aboard the red-cross ship that night and break into one of the crates in the hold to discern the vessel's cargo.

Both youths were terrified. If caught, a distinct possibility, they would be tortured to reveal their accomplices and then killed. Despite her own misgivings—she would be one whose true identity would be disclosed if the boys were caught and tortured—High Pockets tried to reassure them that the ship's skipper and his officers would be in Club Tsubaki until well after midnight, taking in a special floor show and party she conveniently had arranged for them. All that the two youths had to do was dodge a lone sentry on the vessel. Reluctantly, they agreed to the mission.

As soon as the ship's captain and his entourage entered Club Tsubaki that night, he told High Pockets that he would have to leave early, that his vessel had to sail at midnight. Fuentes's heart skipped a beat: The two Filipino boys would be trapped on the ship at that time.

Laboring to overcome her fears, High Pockets ordered the floor show to begin at 10:00 P.M., rather than at a customary starting time of midnight. While the ship's captain was peering at the young Filipina dancers as they went through their sensuous routines, Fuentes took a seat next to him and managed to slip a Mickey Finn (knockout powder) into his glass of beer. A few minutes later, the man turned a ghastly greenish white and slumped in his chair. Two waiters were called to half-carry the groggy skipper to a booth, where he stretched out and fell asleep.

High Pockets sent word to the junior officers at other tables that their boss was "quite tired" and that he wanted to remain with her to rest. That pronouncement was greeted by laughter and bawdy remarks.

While the Japanese skipper lay sprawled and snoring in the booth, the floor show continued until the performers, who were privy to the scenario, were nearly exhausted. Just past 11:30 P.M., the junior officers began to depart. One of them whispered to High Pockets to send the skipper back as soon as possible, punctuating the request with a wink and a broad grin.

When the Japanese officers had cleared the club, a horse-drawn wagon was brought to the back door, and the captain's inert form was placed in it. High Pockets was fearful that he might die, and she didn't want his body to be found in her club. Furtively, the snoozing skipper was dumped along the dark docks near his red-cross ship. Presumably, when awakened, he would surmise that he had tried to make it back to his vessel but, for some reason, had keeled over.

Shortly after daybreak, the two excited Filipino dockhands arrived at the club. They had gotten aboard with no difficulty and had inspected the contents of several crates. One held out a handful of bullets, the type of "red-cross" cargo being carried.

High Pockets scratched out a note to Major Boone and dispatched a teenage girl to take the message, and the bullets, to the guerrilla leader. Within a few hours, AIB headquarters had the information. Presumably, the large white ship with the oversized red crosses was sailing southward to resupply Japanese forces. American submarines, no doubt, would be lurking along the way to properly dispose of the disguised mercy ship.[5]

15 Raid on a Hidden Japanese Base

With the approach of fall 1943, General Hideki Tojo, the supreme warlord, and his aides in Tokyo were taking a grim new look at the strategic situation in the southwest Pacific. Slowly, almost imperceptibly, the Japanese tidal wave had begun to ebb. A series of defeats at Guadalcanal, on the Bismarck Sea, and on New Guinea convinced Tojo that his forces were overextended. So he developed a directive called the New Operational Policy.

Under this plan, Japanese soldiers and airmen would continue to savagely contest every foot of captured territory and hold present positions until the spring of 1944. By that time, Japanese airplane strength would be tripled and significant Imperial Fleet losses replaced. Then, *banzai!* On to Australia!

For his part, Douglas MacArthur had no intention of cooperating with Tojo on his New Operational Policy. In a series of lightning-like leapfrogs up the spine of northern New Guinea, Colonel George M. Jones's U.S. 503rd Parachute Infantry Regiment bailed out over Nadzab island and rapidly seized an airfield there, and amphibious forces captured Salamaua on September 12 and Lae four days later.[1]

Large numbers of Japanese troops were left behind to wither on the vine between these American enclaves. In a desperate effort to feed and supply their marooned garrisons, the Japanese began dispatching sixty-foot motorized barges across Vitiaz Strait from New Britain almost nightly. Within a week, AIB jungle spies on New Britain reported that a main base for launching these barge runs to New Guinea was located a few miles up the Pulie River. Because the site was inland, shrouded by thick foliage, and on a narrow, barely navigable stream, the Japanese apparently felt that it was quite secure.

In New Guinea, a PT-boat raid was laid on to destroy the Pulie River barge base. With three powerful Packard engines, each boat had a crew of twelve and was armed with four .50-caliber machine guns. These speedy, mighty midgets—with the impudence and wallop of Jack the Giant Killer—had become Douglas MacArthur's secret weapon. For their part, the Japanese had come to both hate and fear them. They never knew when, where, or from what direction the craft they called Devil Boats and Green Dragons would strike deep behind their forward positions.

The PT boaters were a new breed of American fighting men, a mixture of seagoing cavalry, commando-type raiders, and Indian scouts out of the Old West. Each skipper had volunteered for PT-boat duty, fully aware that in the savagery of the Pacific, there would be no grandstands, no cheering, no glamour. The only "fan" reaction would be in the form of hisses from Tokyo.

A lone PT boat would go on the secret mission to Pulie River. Skippered by Lieutenant Oliver J. "Ollie" Schneiders, the craft left New Guinea at dusk and set a course across Vitiaz Strait. The starless night was dark and hot. Two hours after casting off, Schneiders' boat, its engines muffled, slipped up to the mouth of the Pulie. It was deathly quiet. All on board were tense since they expected the entrance to such an important base to be guarded by machine guns. A minuscule trace of light from the PT boat's radarscope was the lone challenge to the blackness.

Inching ahead at five knots, the boat edged into the river and headed upstream. Thick with brush and trees, the banks were only a few yards to each side—ideal locations for an ambush. Anxiety increased as exotic birds in the jungle cawed and screamed.

One sailor stood on the bow and repeatedly lowered a weighted line to measure the depth of the water. If the boat were to run aground, right in the enemy's bailiwick, it could be curtains for the raiders. Perhaps forty-five minutes after entering the Pulie, Lieutenant Schneiders detected the dim outlines of a group of huts and a small wharf jutting out into the river. There it was—the secret Japanese barge terminal!

Schneiders held a hasty, whispered discussion with the Nisei who had been brought along as an interpreter. Then, the Nisei faced the dark huts, cupped his hands, and called out in flawless Japanese, "Where can we tie our barge?"

Silence. A stifling pall of apprehension gripped the PT-boat men. They hardly dared to breathe. Some felt their thumping hearts would be heard and give away the intruders' presence. Moments later, a Japanese voice boomed from out of the blackness, and lights flashed on along the wharf. In plain view of the Americans were the structures at the base: huts, warehouses, and sheds, all nestled among majestic palm trees.

Then . . . "Fire!" It was Ollie Schneiders's voice. Every gun on the floating arsenal began pouring streams of tracers into the structures, igniting several small fires that rapidly spread. The racket was ear-splitting. Suddenly rousted from sleep, scores of Japanese could be seen dashing hither and yon. Some charged directly into the American machine-gun fire and were cut down. Others fled for the protection of the jungle. Soon the entire base was a raging inferno. A mighty roar shook the region as an ammunition dump exploded, sending fiery orange balls into the black sky.

The machine guns ceased firing. An eerie silence returned, punctuated by the angry crackle of the flames that were consuming the base. From the PT boat could be seen the crumpled forms of many dead Japanese.

"Okay, let's haul ass!" Ollie Schneiders called out. There was no time for elation over having wiped out an enemy barge terminal. No doubt the rattle of the shooting could have been heard for miles. And there was only one escape route—back down the Pulie.

Laboriously, the PT boat turned around, its movements constrained by the narrowness of the stream. Then the craft began to head back—and ground to a halt. It had become stuck on the bottom of the shallow river—right in the glare of the raging fires. After the engine huffed and puffed for what seemed to the navy men to be ages, the boat tore free. Those on board resumed breathing.

To the astonishment of the Americans, the PT boat slipped back downriver without a shot being fired at it. Before dawn, Ollie Schneiders and his bluejackets tied up at the rickety wharf at their base on Morobe atoll. Another telling blow had been struck in General MacArthur's undercover war.[2]

In the meantime, at Nouméa in New Caledonia, an island about the size of New Jersey lying 750 miles east of Australia, Admiral Bull Halsey had a visitor from Washington. Nouméa was headquarters for the admiral's South Pacific Area, a hybrid command in which Halsey was under the strategic control of General MacArthur yet had to depend on Admiral Nimitz in Hawaii for his troops, ships, and supplies.

Halsey's visitor, a lieutenant commander, had been sent by Wild Bill Donovan, the OSS chief in Washington. A wild-eyed professor, he billed himself as an authority on Tibet and therefore, by implication, indispensable to the South Pacific campaign. Halsey was unable to grasp any connection between his theater of operations and Tibet, a far-off land whose snow-covered mountains and windswept plateaus are the highest in the world.

Donovan's man was so wrapped up in his cloak-and-dagger role that he whispered even in Halsey's office. The admiral had received the professor as a courtesy to Bill Donovan, but, at the same time, he was hard put to learn why the visitor was there.

Halsey, dragging furiously on a cigarette and growing steadily more impatient, finally got the idea that the man was promoting a one-man collapsible rubber submarine. When Halsey asked him to describe it, he took furtive glances over his shoulder, then whispered, "Sir, I'd rather not. It's highly confidential."

Halsey, a four-star admiral, assured the visitor that his discretion could be trusted, and finally the professor admitted, "The fact is, admiral, we haven't got one yet, but I'll tell Washington to develop it."

The Bull was furious. Rising to his feet, he shouted, "Get the hell out of here!"[3]

OSS boss Bill Donovan, it appeared, had not given up trying to get his agency's toe inside the southwest Pacific door.

Douglas MacArthur's "hit-'em-where-they-ain't" campaign along New Guinea's long northern coast was picking up momentum. Finschhafen, at the tip of the Huon Peninsula, fell on October 2, and the Australian diggers seized Wau and were struggling along jungle trails toward Madang, a New Guinea port one hundred sixty miles northwest of Lae. Flights of up to a hundred of George Kenney's bombers were blasting the Japanese Eighteenth Army headquarters at Wewak, two hundred miles west of Lae, destroying large numbers of Japanese fighters and bombers there on the ground.

Meanwhile, Admiral Bull Halsey, who was under MacArthur's strategic control, had conquered or bypassed Japanese strongholds west of Guadalcanal in the central Solomons. Now he was focused on Bougainville, the large, westernmost island in the chain. In the twenty-one months that the Japanese had occupied it, they had transformed Bougainville into a formidable fortress. Five airfields had been built and a sixth one was under construction.

While a likely invasion point on Bougainville was the subject of intense study at Halsey's New Caledonia headquarters, word was received from Jack Reed and Paul Mason, the two highly active Ferdinand jungle spies on the island, that, while most of the natives were friendly to the Allies, the Japanese had managed to win over a few villages. Once Bougainville was invaded, the villages sympathetic to the Japanese could be a serious threat to the Allied rear areas.

As soon as a village sympathetic to the Japanese was identified by the Ferdinand jungle spies, the Allies would bomb it and then drop pidgin English leaflets on the nearby villages, warning them not to invite bombs on themselves. One message dropped on Bougainville said:

SITROG PELA TOK BILOG NAMBAYWAN KIAP BILOG OMASTA.
(A serious warning from the big white chief.)

OL IUPELA MAN BILOG BUKAPASIS NO BILOG BUIN NA KIETA.
(To all natives of Buka Passage, Buin, and Kieta.)

DISPELA TOK MIGIVIM IU I STRAITPELA TOK.
(This is straight talk.)

PLES KANAK OLIKOLIM SORUM I AMBAG TUNAS LOG KIAP
(The village of Sorum has been disloyal)

HIRAM TOK BILOG JAPAN NAU ALPIM JAPAN.
(and has taken orders from the Japs and helped the Japs.)

ORIAT TROWEI BOMB OLSEM DAINAMAIT LOG IN NAU.
(We have now bombed them.)

I NO LONGTAIM NO MIPELA OLGETA IKAM WANTAIM OLD SOLJA BILOG
AMERIKA
(Before long we will come with all the American)

NA RAUSIM OLD JAPAN NA KILIM OLGETA NAU MEKIN
(soldiers to dislodge the Japanese and kill them all and punish)

SAVE OLMAN I ALPIM JAPAN.
(all natives who helped them.)

IUPELA I LUKAUT.
(You have been warned.)

Before the American invasion of Bougainville, an elaborate deception was staged at Shortland, an island just off the southern tip of Bougainville. AIB operatives slipped ashore at several points along the coasts of Shortland and deliberately left evidence that they had been there. Almost daily, photo-reconnaissance planes made leisurely, low-level flights across these same beaches, and then Kenney's bombers dropped their cargos around the supposed landing beaches. Japanese commanders on Bougainville swallowed the bait and began moving troops, artillery, and heavy equipment the short distance over water to Shortland.

L-Day for the invasion of Bougainville was November 1, 1943. At 6:31 A.M, the deception was given a new boost when a task force of four light cruisers and eight destroyers stood offshore and pumped hundreds of shells into Shortland. Then, the first assault boats filled with U.S. Marines hit the beach—not at Shortland, but sixty miles to the north at Empress Augustus Bay.

There were only some three hundred Japanese soldiers in the region to contest the invasion. Half of them were killed, and the remainder fled deep into the jungle. By L-Day plus 10, the Marines had driven far enough inland for work to begin on airfields, from where Kenney's bombers would soon be plastering the Rabaul stronghold.

Now that MacArthur was nearly halfway along New Guinea's northern coast, he set his sights on New Britain, the large Japanese-held island forty miles across Vitiaz Strait from Finschhafen. At the northeastern tip of New Britain was the Japanese stronghold of Rabaul, with its fleet anchorage, five military airfields, and sixty thousand dug-in troops.

During the first week of December 1943, two AIB operatives, one Australian and the other American, along with nine natives who had undergone extensive espionage training, climbed onto a PT boat at Morobe off eastern New Guinea. Skippered by Lieutenant Edward I. Farley, the boat (nicknamed *Jack O'Diamonds*) was on a top secret mission that Lieutenant Commander Barry Atkins, the squadron commander, declared "might provide some excitement."

Atkins, who would go along on the jaunt as tactical commander, explained that the AIB operatives and the nine natives would be put ashore under cover of night to reconnoiter enemy positions and determine his strength around Cape Gloucester on the southwestern tip of New Britain. That was all that Atkins knew about the urgent mission—or was willing to tell. If captured and tortured, Ed Farley and his men could not reveal to the Japanese what they didn't know. Only much later would Farley and his crew learn the true purpose of the mission: General MacArthur's forces would conduct an amphibious landing at Cape Gloucester on the day after Christmas. The Supreme Commander's primary objective was to seize an airfield from where George Kenney's bombers could rain explosives on Rabaul from dawn until dusk.[4]

Not only would Ed Farley's boat be heading directly into heavy Japanese concentrations, but the course through Siassi Straits was a treacherous one. It was also the shortest route and offered the best chance of sneaking through to Cape Gloucester undetected. The success of the venture would rest to a great extent on Lieutenant Eric N. Howitt, Royal Australian Navy, who would guide the *Jack O'Diamonds* through the Straits. Howitt was an AIB operative. In peacetime, the fifty-two-year-old officer had operated a copra plantation, and he had sailed the coastal waters of new Britain and New Guinea for fifteen years.

Jack O'Diamonds shoved off at twilight. As anticipated, the trek through the Straits was slow and torturous. Lieutenant Farley was at the wheel and carefully responding to a continuing flow of instructions from the imperturbable Eric Howitt. It took more than an hour to negotiate the six-mile-long Straits.

Just past 11:00 P.M., the boat's radar man reported objects off the port bow on his screen. Engines were shut off. A short time later, less than fifty yards away, four Japanese barges loaded with troops were stealing through the darkness in a line in the opposite direction. Farley's gunners eagerly fingered triggers: This juicy target could be wiped out with one Sunday punch from *Jack O'Diamonds'* .50-caliber machine guns.

Commander Barry Atkins was sorely tempted to give the order to blast the barges. However, the secret mission had priority, so *Jack O'Diamonds*, with engines muffled, crawled onward while the barges slipped past in the opposite direction.

When the designated beach near Cape Gloucester was reached, the boat's engines again were shut off and *Jack O'Diamonds* lay to a hundred yards off the beach. It was unearthly silent. Crewmen whispered that they could smell the Japanese cooking aromas. The black night was ideal for sneaking ashore—and for stumbling into an ambush.

Faces blackened with grease and gear securely taped to prevent telltale rattles, the American and Australian AIB agents gingerly slithered into a pair of rubber rafts and were followed by the nine natives. These were tense moments. The slightest noise might betray their presence. Then, as the last man scrambled into a raft, someone inadvertently knocked an oar overboard. It made only a small splash, but to the intruders and to the PT-boat crew it sounded like a cannon going off. They were convinced that Tojo in Tokyo had been awakened by the noise.

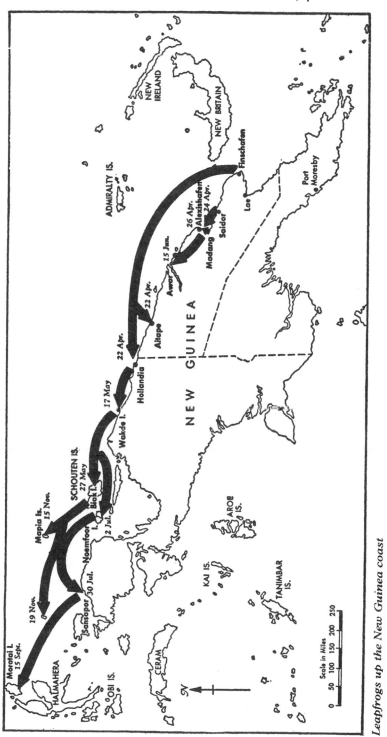

Leapfrogs up the New Guinea coast

The rafts, however, were paddled as silently as possible, and the landing party stole onto the beach, hid the rafts in the underbrush, and disappeared into the jungle. It had been arranged for brief radio contact so the PT-boat skippers would know that the AIB agents had gotten ashore and were trudging inland. Now, only a stone's throw from the beach, Lieutenant George Walbridge, on *Jack O'Diamonds*, was listening closely to a walkie-talkie. Then, a booming voice with an Australian accent thundered over the walkie-talkie, "Okay, Yanks, we're all set!"[5]

Walbridge winced. If the paddle-splash had not rousted Tojo out of bed, this roaring verbal report no doubt would do so.

"Good luck!" Walbridge whispered. Then, the PT boat headed back to Morobe.

Two weeks later, Lieutenant Ed Farley and the *Jack O'Diamonds* returned to the same beach to retrieve the reconnoitering team. Few, if any, on the boat expected to see the AIB agents and their natives again. But, exhausted, bearded, filthy, yet chipper, the landing party kept the rendezvous. Climbing onto the PT boat just offshore, the Australian boomed out, "Boy, what a bloody two weeks!"

"Let's get the hell out of here," Skipper Farley whispered.[6]

Forty-eight hours later, the American and Australian operatives were at General MacArthur's headquarters, pouring out an avalanche of details on Japanese troop strengths, positions, and fortifications along and behind Cape Gloucester.

On December 26, as planned, the U.S. 1st Marine Division stormed ashore at Cape Gloucester. After four weeks of stiff fighting, they seized the airfield there. Many Marines who survived had no way of knowing that they owed their lives to the American and Australian AIB operatives and their nine native helpers.[7]

Lt. Col. Guillermo Nakar, Filipino guerrilla leader, was captured and executed. (National Archives)

Lt. Col. Wendell Fertig, guerrilla chief of Mindanao, as daring as he was eccentric. (U.S. Army)

After rescuing General MacArthur from Corregidor and "kidnapping" President Quezon, Lt. John D. Bulkeley (second from left) and other PT boaters continued the fight as jungle spies on Mindanao. (Courtesy of Alice Bulkeley)

Japanese propaganda poster in the Philippines depicts President Roosevelt as a greedy monster seeking to gobble up the Pacific. (National Archives)

Ferdinand coastwatcher and his assistant operate a hidden radio control station in the Solomons. (Australian War Memorial)

USS *Nautilus* was one of MacArthur's submarines running arms and supplies to jungle spies and guerrillas. (U.S. Navy)

U.S. Army Sgt. Richard M. Sakakida spent much of the war as a spy in Japanese headquarters. (U.S. Army)

U.S. Navy Cmdr. Joseph J. Rochefort broke the Japanese naval code, permitting ambush of Adm. Isoroku Yamamoto. (U.S. Navy)

Two weeks before his plane was ambushed over Bougainville, Admiral Yamamoto exhorts pilots at Rabaul to hit hard at the American fleet. (National Archives)

Lt. Thomas G. Lanphier, Jr. (kneeling at right), was credited with shooting down Admiral Yamamoto's bomber. Lt. Rex Barber (standing, third from left) brought down the second bomber with Adm. Matome Ugaki aboard. (U.S. Navy)

An American Nisei (far right) scans a captured document at a conference of the Allied Translator and Interpreter Section. ATIS chief Col. Sidney F. Mashbir is fourth from the right. (U.S. Army)

P-38 Lightnings over New Guinea. This type of plane was used in the 1943 ambush of Admiral Yamamoto. (U.S. Air Force)

Ferdinand jungle spies observing Japanese movements from concealment.
(Australian War Memorial)

Limpet mines of the type used by the Operation Jaywick raiders in Singapore harbor.
(Australian War Museum)

Mister X (Charles A. Lindbergh) returns to the New Guinea airstrip after a combat flight while on a secret mission for MacArthur. Maj. Thomas B. McGuire is at left. (U.S. Air Force)

American Nisei scanning Japanese documents at the Allied Translator and Interpreter Section. The photo was taken from the back so these American soldiers of Japanese ancestry could not be identified if captured during frequent tours of frontline duty. (U.S. Navy)

Ferdinand jungle spy Donald Kennedy used this plantation house at Segi Point, New Georgia, as his headquarters. (National Archives)

Donald Kennedy's men at Segi Point bring to a Catalina Flying boat U.S. Marine Lt. Milton Vedder, shot down off New Georgia in April 1943. (National Archives)

Guerrillas gather around their leader, U.S. Army Capt. Donald LeCouvre, who is mounted on the unit's sole transportation. (U.S. Army)

U.S. Lt. Col. Russell Volckmann (right), guerrilla leader on northern Luzon, and a Filipino aide. (U.S. Army)

Guerrillas paddle out to meet MacArthur's invasion force off southern Luzon. (U.S. Army)

> Let us join hands!
>
> Don't lose your lovely native lands
>
> Trust not the sly Americans.
>
> Come, join hands and help us build
>
> A true home of our God sent East.

Japanese propaganda leaflet of the kind distributed in conquered territories in the southwest Pacific. (National Archives)

Adm. Mineichi Koga, head of the Combined Fleet. Conjecture was that he was the Japanese admiral held captive by guerrillas on Cebu in the Philippines. (U.S. Navy)

General MacArthur going ashore at Leyte with Philippine President Sergio Osmeña (left). U.S.-led guerrillas rescued Osmeña's family from the Japanese secret police. (MacArthur Memorial)

American PT boaters haul Japanese sailors from the ocean. These prisoners often provided valuable intelligence for the Allied Intelligence Bureau. (Courtesy of Alyce Mary Guthrie)

Many secret missions far behind Japanese positions were carried out by crews of swift PT boats. (Courtesy of Alyce Mary Guthrie)

GIs on Leyte advance through a waist-deep swamp, which was typical of the terrain over which MacArthur's troops fought. (U.S. Army)

Col. Sidney Mashbir (right), whose Nisei unit played a key role in MacArthur's undercover war, receives Gen. Takashiro Kawabe as the Japanese surrender-arrangement delegation arrives in Manila. (U.S. Army)

Maj. Gen. Charles A. Willoughby (tall man at left), chief of the Allied Intelligence Bureau, shows General Kawabe his chair at the surrender-arrangement conference in Manila. (U.S. Army)

An Intelligence 16
Bonanza in a Briefcase

By New Year's Day 1944, General Douglas MacArthur was re-appraising his strategy. For nearly a year and a half, the leapfrog campaign up the coast of New Guinea had advanced his forces 240 miles—still 2,000 miles short of Mindanao, in the Philippines, where he intended to invade. At the current pace, it might take ten years to reach Tokyo. To speed the offensive, the Supreme Commander decided to make longer leaps.

MacArthur's eye was on the Vogelkop Peninsula at the western tip of New Guinea. Beyond that point lay the Moluccas, an ideal spring-board for a mighty jump all the way to Mindanao. However, between his forward forces and Mindanao were a great number of Japanese on various islands. Although the AIB jungle spies had performed (and would continue to perform) invaluable services that had saved countless lives, most of them were civilians.

So MacArthur wanted to create a relatively small, elite band of specially trained soldiers whose task it would be to sneak behind Japanese positions and return with specific reports on enemy weapons, fortifications, and troop identities. He wanted a force whose men could live in the jungle for long periods on scant food and water, who could move swiftly, silently, and invisibly, stalking and killing Japanese and snatching prisoners for interrogation.

Christened the Alamo Scouts, this unique outfit would perform in the tradition of Davy Crockett and his frontiersmen who had put up an epic fight against overwhelming hordes of Mexicans at the Alamo in Texas in 1836. These modern-day Crocketts were to be MacArthur's newest secret weapon in his undercover war.

Selected to command the Alamo Scouts was Colonel Frederick W. Bradshaw, who had been a lawyer in Jackson, Mississippi. Bradshaw selected as his executive officer (second in command) Major Gibson Niles, a New Yorker who had been a varsity athlete at West Point. A call for volunteers was put out to men already in the southwest Pacific. Wanted were tough soldiers of high individual initiative, of competitive spirit, and temperamentally drawn by a game of high stakes.

Fergusson Island, five miles off eastern New Guinea, became the training center for the Alamo Scouts. Many of the volunteers were eliminated during the grueling six-week training course—they could not measure up to the high physical and mental standards. Those who did survive developed the esprit de corps desired—the Alamo Scouts were the elite, and they knew it.[1]

Colonel Bradshaw and his eager men wasted no time in going into action on a dangerous secret mission—they planned to kidnap General Hatazo Adachi, commander of the Japanese Eighteenth Army in New Guinea. Stealing ashore under the blanket of night, a team of five Alamo Scouts hid near Adachi's headquarters and watched his movements for a week. Always the Americans were in danger of discovery and certain death.

After the team returned to the Alamo Scouts' camp, they told debriefing officers a wealth of details about General Adachi's habits, including the jungle trail he followed on daily horseback rides. He always had a bevy of heavily armed bodyguards with him. And the Eighteenth Army headquarters was guarded by a large number of troops armed with machine guns and rifles.

Despite the prohibitive odds against snatching the Japanese commander in New Guinea, the Alamo Scouts, to a man, were eager to make the effort. But the bold venture was rejected by Lieutenant General Walter Krueger, commander of the U.S. Sixth Army. He agreed that the kidnapping would be a spectacular propaganda bonanza, but, in his view, the scheme was not worth the life of a single Alamo Scout. Krueger doubted if any of the raiders would get back alive.[2]

Disappointed, but undaunted, the Alamo Scouts would soon be assigned another secret mission deep behind Japanese lines as bold as the one to snatch General Adachi.

In mid-January 1944, Douglas MacArthur was ready to make another giant leap on the road to Tokyo. His twin targets were Los Negros and Manus Islands in the Admiralties, 225 miles northwest of the Japanese bastion of Rabaul. In the Admiralties, MacArthur would acquire priceless airfields and an anchorage large enough to accommodate his entire amphibious strike force.

MacArthur's staff was stunned. The invasion would be an especially enormous risk. The AIB had reported that Los Negros was "lousy with Japs." His officers stressed that if the invasion force ran into a hornet's nest, the nearest Allied troop replacement base was at Finschhafen, three hundred miles to the south, too far to rush reinforcements to the beachhead. MacArthur replied that he would bring in troops by air. What if the airfield was not in Allied hands? It would be, the Supreme Commander declared.

MacArthur knew the Admiralties operation would be a close call. So he hedged his bets by designating it a "reconnaissance in force," meaning that if disaster was looming, the invading troops would be evacuated. The Supreme Commander would join the assault convoy in case such a decision had to be made on the spot.

On February 28, MacArthur was on the cruiser *Phoenix* in Milne Bay at the eastern tip of New Guinea. General Walter Krueger came aboard and brought the latest estimates from the AIB. These reports indicated that there were four thousand Japanese prepared to meet the invasion of Los Negros, which would be hit first—a far larger number than was at first anticipated.

MacArthur looked up at the grim faces of his staff officers, the ones who earlier had warned him of the perils involved. Pulling on a cigar, the Supreme Commander said evenly, "We shall continue as planned, gentlemen."[3]

Walter Krueger, an energetic sixty-four-year-old officer who had worked his way up through the ranks from private to three-star general, was noted for his personal courage. Yet he was aghast when MacArthur advised him that he intended to land with the troops.

"It will be a calamity if anything happens to you," Krueger declared.

MacArthur thanked the Sixth Army commander for his concern, then replied softly, "I have to go!"[4]

Just before dawn the next day, the invasion convoy dropped anchor in Hyane Harbor off Los Negros, where the ships were welcomed by a terrific barrage from shore batteries. One salvo sailed over the *Phoenix*, the second fell short, and men on deck scrambled for anything behind which to take cover, knowing that the third volley might well be dead on target. MacArthur remained standing on the bridge, peering toward shore while chatting with his staff officers, who were struggling to appear nonchalant. Lady Luck was with the Supreme Commander. Before a third salvo could be fired, the shore battery was wiped out by a rain of shells from an American cruiser.

Two hours later, GIs of the U.S. 1st Cavalry Division were ashore on Los Negros and locked in a savage fight with typically tenacious Japanese. Offshore, General MacArthur and his staff officers climbed into a small boat and landed with ensuing assault waves. Conspicuous in a yellowish trench coat, gold-encrusted cap, and corncob pipe, the Supreme Commander began casually strolling inland. One of those accompanying him was the general's personal physician, Major Roger O. Egeberg, who had joined the staff less than a month earlier. Now he vividly recalled that other aides had warned him that accompanying the general in range of Japanese riflemen was something to be avoided at all costs. The physician was terrified, and thoughts of his wife and children back home flashed through his mind.[5]

Major Egeberg, under fire for the first time, was not alone. All of the staff officers with MacArthur were uneasy—uneasy about the Supreme Commander's safety and, more importantly, about their own safety.

Walking along a path through the jungle, MacArthur was called to by a young lieutenant who appeared startled to see a four-star general in the front lines.

"Pardon me, sir," the officer said, "but we killed some Japs up ahead moments ago!"

"Good work, lieutenant," MacArthur replied. "That's just the thing to do with them!"[6]

The hottest spot on Los Negros was the airfield, which the Japanese were determined to hang onto at all costs. Earlier, General George Kenney, the air corps boss, had told MacArthur that the airfield could become "the most important piece of real estate in the southwest Pacific." Now he wished he had eaten his words, for MacArthur was heading directly toward the airstrip.

A vicious battle was going on over who would be the landlord of that small stretch of ground. Rifle and machine-gun bullets were whizzing past in both directions. MacArthur, trailed by his nervous staff officers, wandered up and down the strip, pausing on occasion to scrape the coral surface to see if it was hard enough to hold his own warplanes.[7]

Splattered with mud and soaked to the skin from the heavy rains, MacArthur returned to the *Phoenix* after two hours on shore—much to the relief of the officers who accompanied him. That night, convinced that an evacuation would not be necessary, he sailed back to Finschhafen.

Seven days later, at his suite in Lennon's Hotel in Brisbane, the Supreme Commander got the news he had been anticipating—Los Negros and Manus were secure.

MacArthur, despite the dire warnings of nearly his entire staff and the admirals involved in the Admiralties operation, had pulled off a coup de main. Rabaul, the once mighty stronghold from whence General Tojo planned to launch an invasion of Australia, had been isolated. Sixty thousand of the emperor's soldiers, who had been digging in for months waiting for MacArthur's frontal assault against the fortress, wanted to die for Hirohito, but that chance never came. Rabaul, too, would wither and die on the vine. The loss of face was incalculable.

In Brisbane, messages of congratulations poured in on MacArthur from around the free world. General George Marshall was effusive in his praise. British Prime Minister Winston Churchill called the Admiralties invasion a stroke of genius. In New Guinea, however, the U.S. admirals involved in the operation were far from complimentary.

Grumbled Rear Admiral William F. Fechteler, "We're lucky we didn't get run off the damned islands!"[8]

Two thousand miles north of the Admiralties on the stormy night of March 31, a small band of Filipino guerrillas had taken cover in straw huts in the barrio of Balud, along the eastern shore of the central island of Cebu. They belonged to Lieutenant Colonel James M. Cushing's guerrilla network and were lightly armed: two rifles, a few curved bolos, and long poles with sharp, pointed knives attached to the end.

A prewar civilian mining engineer in the Philippines, Cushing was half Irish, half Mexican, a former boxer, and a hard-drinking free spirit. He would have been satisfied to have sat out the war in the mountains of Cebu with his Filipina wife and child, enjoying the good life. But the people of the island convinced him early on that he alone could unify the feuding guerrilla groups on Cebu.

Cushing had been commissioned in the U.S. Army after he had organized his guerrillas into an effective intelligence-gathering force. Japanese troops were stationed in Cebu City outside of Manila, the Philippines' most important town, and in other populated locales. So Cushing dispersed his guerrilla bands in small groups around the island so that any sudden attack would cause harm only on a local basis.

Not long after midnight, a guerrilla standing guard on the beach near barrio Balud saw a brilliant flash of light a mile offshore on the dark and turbulent sea. At first, he thought it was a bolt of lightning. Then he came to the conclusion that an airplane had crashed and was burning brightly.

Excitedly, the sentry called to his comrades, and within minutes many of them were gathered on the beach peering intently out to sea through the heavy rain, where the blaze cast grotesque orange patterns on low-flying clouds. All agreed that an airplane had crashed. But was it Japanese or American?

Native fishermen also had seen the brilliant flash, and they leaped into canoes and began paddling toward the blaze. The waves were angry, and it took nearly a half hour to reach the burning plane. Just as he was being pulled aboard a canoe, one of the survivors dropped a briefcase to which he had been clinging. By the light of the flames dancing on the sea, a native caught a glimpse of the slowly sinking briefcase and retrieved it just before it disappeared. Unwittingly, the Filipino had been the key figure in one of the great intelligence bonanzas of the war in the Pacific.

About an hour later, the fishermen's canoes crunched onto the beach near Balud. They brought with them ten nearly naked, injured or burned Japanese, the crash survivors, and turned them over to the nearest guerrilla band led by Captain Marcelino Erediano.

A few of the Japanese who subscribed to the Bushido code that held capture was disgraceful demanded that they be shot and killed—a sort of hara-kiri by proxy. However, the guerrillas knew that live Japanese prisoners were few and far between, so these could be valuable sources of intelligence. One middle-aged Japanese seemed to be the leader of the group. He told Captain Erediano, who had studied at Tokyo Imperial University for a year, that they were unimportant staff officers from Japan on a routine inspection of the area. Erediano, however, noticed that the other injured Japanese paid great deference to this man. Perhaps he was a high-ranking general. That theory was strengthened by the fact that a waterproof container in the briefcase had red "Top Secret" markings and obviously was of considerable importance.

None of the Japanese were able to walk, so the guerrillas loaded them onto improvised stretchers and set out for Jim Cushing's hideout at Tupas, ten miles west of Cebu City. In the meantime, runners had been sent to notify Cushing that the ten prisoners were on their way.

Lugging the injured men up one mountain and down another was an arduous and time-consuming task. Under incessant grilling by Captain Erediano, the middle-aged prisoner with the authoritative manner finally "confessed" that he was Japan's "top naval officer." Erediano was jubilant—he had snared in his net one of the biggest of the Japanese fish.

After a torturous all-night trek, the safari of Filipino guerrillas and ten Japanese military men reached Tupas. There, the wounded and burned prisoners were given medical treatment. As the dazed Japanese lay on their cots, Jim Cushing and a few of his guerrillas circulated among them, giving cigarettes to those wanting them.

In the meantime, Colonel Cushing radioed the blockbuster news to the AIB at Heindorf House in Brisbane. "Believe [Japanese] party came from Palaus. One thought Admiral Koga. Recovered case of important documents. Some look like cipher system."[9]

Elation erupted at Heindorf House. If the identity of the Japanese prisoner was accurate, it would be the most spectacular catch of the war in the Pacific. Admiral Mineichi Koga was commander in chief of the Combined Imperial Fleet, having succeeded Admiral Isoroku Yamamoto, who had been ambushed by American fighter planes in mid-1943. What's more, Koga's last known headquarters was on Palau Island, six hundred miles east of Cebu.

The AIB immediately radioed Cushing to transport the ten Japanese to Negros Island, where they would be picked up by a submarine and taken to Australia for interrogation.[10]

Cushing knew that it would be impossible to transport the prisoners on foot all the way across rugged Cebu and then on over thirty miles of water to Negros without being detected. Guerrilla reports reaching Tupas disclosed that large numbers of Japanese marines already were fanning out over Cebu in an all-out effort to recover the prisoners.

While Cushing was mulling over his next step, a printed ultimatum by Lieutenant Colonel Seito Onishi, the commander on Cebu, was plastered at scores of locales in southern Cebu. Unless the captured Japanese were turned over to Onishi within thirty-six hours, large numbers of villages and towns would be burned to the ground and hundreds of Filipino civilians killed.

To prevent the certain bloodbath, Cushing radioed the AIB at Brisbane that he was going to release the prisoners. However, he added that he would send the briefcase with the secret documents to the submarine rendezvous point on Negros.

Within a few hours, a direct order from General MacArthur came back. "Prisoners are to be held by you at all costs."

"Impossible to comply," Cushing radioed.

MacArthur was furious. He relieved Colonel Cushing of command on Cebu and reduced him to the grade of private.

In the meantime, three guerrillas lugging the briefcase to Negros arrived at their destination after several hairbreadth escapes from Japanese patrols. The container was handed over to the submarine skipper and, within minutes, the secret documents were on their way to Brisbane.

Cushing may have become a private on U.S. Army rolls in Australia, but he continued to command at the scene of the action. Before he could conceive a scheme for handing over the prisoners, Cushing and his men were suddenly awakened in the early morning darkness by a heavy fusillade of bullets whistling through and past the straw huts. The Japanese marines had clearly found the captives.

Cushing rapidly sent a few of his guerrillas to the edge of the barrio to fire into the black jungle, while others loaded the prisoners onto litters and stole out of the village. All of the captives were evacuated before the enemy overran Tupas.

Throughout the night, the safari traveled up and over mountains until reaching a barrio a few miles from Tupas. After guards were put out, Cushing spoke at length with the man who claimed to be Admiral Koga. Consequently, the two men agreed on a prisoner-exchange arrangement. The Japanese wrote a note to Colonel Onishi in which he said that the guerrillas would release the captives unharmed if Onishi would abandon his plan to raze towns and execute Filipino civilians. After he signed the note, Jim Cushing penned his signature to it.

An unarmed Filipino guerrilla, along with a Japanese airman captured earlier, set off with the note in the direction of Cebu City, Colonel Onishi's headquarters.

In the meantime, Cushing could only wait and ponder. For months, he had been racked with tropical diseases—now he was sick at heart. Although MacArthur had ordered the prisoners to be held at all costs, the guerrilla boss was convinced that the Supreme Commander did not grasp the true situation on Cebu. Be that as it may, Cushing felt that he would be court-martialed after the war.[11]

These were anxious minutes at the barrio in the mountains. Had the messengers bearing the compromise proposal even reached Onishi's headquarters? If so, would the Filipino be taken into custody and the all-out search for the captives continue? Two hours passed. Five. Eight.

Then, from his high vantage point, Jim Cushing peered through binoculars and spotted the Japanese airman and his own guerrilla scrambling back up the mountainside. They brought with them the reply from Seito Onishi: He agreed to the prisoner-exchange proposal.

Now began one of the strangest scenarios in the savage no-holds-barred war in the Pacific. The man claiming to be Koga was loaded onto a litter. Cushing warmly shook his hand, for by now they had become friends. Even the guerrilla chief's fierce mastiff, who bristled at the other Japanese captives, allowed the friendly admiral to pat him. It was only a moment, a fleeting interlude, but it was unique in the relentless conflict.[12]

Then, an unarmed guerrilla group led by Lieutenant Pedro Villareal headed down the mountain with the litters. From the valley, thirty Japanese soldiers, also unarmed, began climbing up the elevation.

When the two opposing groups were within about fifty yards of one another, they halted. For perhaps a minute, each group stared silently at the other. Slowly, as if on cue, the Japanese soldiers and the Filipino litter-bearers resumed moving and merged. No one spoke. Then a few of the Japanese soldiers held out cigarettes, which were accepted by the Filipinos, and both foes stood silently side by side and smoked. After a few minutes, the stretchers changed hands. Each group turned and began retracing its steps, the Japanese down the mountain, the Filipinos up it.

For three days, peace descended on the region where the Japanese POWs had been handed over. Then the Japanese colonel in Cebu resumed his efforts to kill or capture Jim Cushing and his guerrillas. But by then, the American and his men were holed up on another mountain far away.

Meanwhile, at Heindorf House in Brisbane, the briefcase was opened and a sealed, waterproof container was removed and gingerly pried open. Inside were the top secret documents. Photo reproductions were made of each page. The copies were rushed to Colonel Sid Mashbir's ATIS at nearby Indooroopilly, where every available Nisei labored day and night to convert each Japanese character into readable English.

While the time-consuming and tedious translation was in progress, AIB officials set into motion a scheme to convince the Japanese hierarchy in Tokyo that the secret documents had been lost in the plane crash. It was known from Magic that Japanese divers were being brought to Cebu to sweep the ocean floor at the plane-crash site, presumably in search of the missing briefcase. So the original documents were carefully resealed in their waterproof container, which showed no evidence of having been tampered with, reinserted in the briefcase, and sent back to Cebu on a submarine. Plans were to drop the briefcase back into the ocean at the crash site; hopefully it would be found by the Japanese divers. If the ruse was successful, Tokyo might draw the conclusion that the documents were intact and had not been seen by American eyes.

In the meantime, on Cebu, Colonel Onishi apparently had received orders to locate the briefcase, in the event that it had been brought ashore by the plane-crash survivors. He sent an ultimatum to Jim Cushing: Unless the briefcase was handed over within twenty-four hours, severe reprisals would be inflicted on both captured guerrillas and the civilian population.

Cushing felt that the enemy colonel was bluffing, using the ultimatum as a ruse to find out if the guerrilla boss had the briefcase. Since Cushing had sent the container to Australia, he ignored the threat. True to his word, the Japanese commander on Cebu unleashed his warplanes, which bombed and strafed barrios for ten days, killing and wounding scores of civilians.

At Indoroopilly, meanwhile, Colonel Mashbir's hard-working Nisei had completed their translations, which came to twenty-two typed pages. The secret documents in the container proved to be an intelligence gold mine: they described Combined Fleet Secret Order Number 73 (also known as Plan Z), dated March 8, 1944.

Plan Z called for using most of Japan's remaining aircraft carriers, battleships, cruisers, destroyers, submarines, and land-based planes to hurl back the powerful U.S. fleet charging westward across the central Pacific. The plan detailed the projected land, sea, and air deployments. In the decisive sea battles that would rage around the Philippines in the coming months, the translation of Plan Z would help American admirals to nearly decimate the Imperial Navy.

As time passed, the AIB delved deeply into the identity of the mystery man claiming to be Japan's top naval officer who had survived the plane crash off Cebu. Through Magic intercepts and other clandestine sources, it was learned that Admiral Mineichi Koga had been in Tokyo in late February to attend a conference at Imperial General Headquarters, where the finishing touches were put on Plan Z. After flying back to his headquarters at Palau in the Palau Islands, Koga apparently began to have doubts about the grandiose operation he had conceived for crushing the U.S. fleet in the central and southwest Pacific.

Admiral Koga's pessimism intensified after American naval pilots, in a dazzling exploit against all odds, mined Palau harbor, in which Koga planned to assemble his strike force. So he decided to abandon Palau as a base from which to direct Plan Z and move his headquarters to a site near Davao on Mindanao, six hundred miles to the west.

Early on the night of March 31, a violent storm struck Palau as two Kawanishi flying boats prepared to lift off from the harbor. Koga would travel in one plane and his chief of staff, Vice Admiral Shigeru Fukudome, in the other. In the event one craft should fall victim to the turbulent weather, the admiral in the surviving flying boat would be able to provide continuity of command for Plan Z. Each admiral carried a copy of the battle plan sealed in a container inside a briefcase.

"Let us go out and die together," Admiral Koga said to his chief of staff just before departure. Isoroku Yamamoto, Koga added, had "died at exactly the right time" and he "envied him that fact."[13]

At nine o'clock that night, the admirals took off in the two four-engined Kawanishis for the three-hour flight to Mindanao. Along the way, both flying boats crashed in the raging storm east of Cebu.

So which admiral had been rescued from the flaming wreckage off Cebu and was later turned over to the Japanese colonel by guerrilla leader Jim Cushing: the commander in chief of the Combined Imperial Fleet, Admiral Koga, or his chief of staff, Shigeru Fukudome? Although Cushing's guerrillas swore they had Japan's top admiral in their clutches, evidence developed by the AIB indicated that the mystery man was more likely Admiral Fukudome.

The AIB learned that the ten injured and burned plane-crash survivors had been taken from Cebu to hospitals in Manila, where, it was theorized, Fukudome recovered. More evidence that the mystery man was Fukudome surfaced when Magic intercepts disclosed that Fukudome had been named commander of Japanese air forces for the looming battle of the Philippines.

Had Admiral Koga been the one to survive the flying-boat crash, Radio Tokyo would have trumpeted his feat as yet another example of the invincibility of the emperor's armed forces. As it was, Mineichi Koga simply vanished as far as the AIB could learn.[14]

17 Hoodwinking the Enemy

Early in March 1944, Douglas MacArthur called Charles Willoughby, his king-sized intelligence chief, and instructed him to report any enemy reference to Hollandia culled from radio intercepts. Hollandia was a Japanese bastion on the northern coast of New Guinea and two hundred miles to the rear of enemy strongholds at Madang, Hansa Bay, and Wewak. Based on this order, Willoughby became the first staff officer to gain an inkling that the Supreme Commander was preparing to launch his boldest operation yet: a four-hundred-mile leap to Hollandia.

Doing the electronic snooping for MacArthur would be a hush-hush organization known by the innocuous name Central Bureau. Under the direction of Colonel Spencer Akin, who had been with MacArthur since before the outbreak of hostilities in the Pacific, the Central Bureau went to work decoding hundreds of intercepts, scanning each one closely for some mention of Hollandia.

Akin had long been associated with this quite sensitive work. He looked like a young edition of Abraham Lincoln and had much of the martyred president's dry grassroots humor.

"If you don't keep your humor in this activity," Akin once said, "it'll drive you even crazier than you already are."[1]

When MacArthur unveiled his audacious proposal to his staff, some of the officers were highly pessimistic, fearing that the crafty Japanese would react swiftly and trap the invading force far from MacArthur's main bases hundreds of miles to the east. A few urged that heavily defended Wewak be seized first before jumping to Hollandia. But the Supreme Commander brushed aside the suggestion. Wewak was precisely where the enemy thought he would hit next, he pointed out.

In strategic deliberations with his staff, MacArthur held a trump card he could not reveal at the time: Spencer Akin's electronic sleuths had already advised him that the Japanese had virtually denuded Hollandia and sent their troops to Wewak.

"Hollandia is ripe for plucking," declared MacArthur, "and I intend to pluck it!"[2]

As usual, the Supreme Commander relied on the AIB to slip jungle spies into the Hollandia region in advance of his invasion. Already on the ground was AIB operative Jean Victor de Bruijn, who had landed in a seaplane in December 1942. With him was a Dutch radio operator named Rudy Gout. At twenty-nine years of age, de Bruijn, a tall, handsome man who held a Ph.D. degree, had served for two years as a Dutch colonial administrator in New Guinea, and he knew the region and its tribesmen as well as any Caucasian. He had been on medical leave in Australia when war broke out and had contacted the AIB and volunteered to spy on the Japanese.

On returning to New Guinea, de Bruijn quickly recruited and trained tribesmen to report movements by the Japanese, whom the locals hated. Soon he had a covert force of thirty-eight men, including eight colonial policemen who had helped de Bruijn in peacetime. Energetic and resourceful, the Dutchman then organized a large number of natives to grow food for the spy ring.

In June 1943, a large force of Japanese troops suddenly raided de Bruijn's camp, and he and his men narrowly escaped into the mountainous interior. Food was nonexistent. They ate frogs, rats, and pythons. But de Bruijn's spies continued to prowl around Japanese installations and bring back news of movements, which Rudy Gout radioed to the AIB in Brisbane.

Jean de Bruijn's lot, like that of isolated spies since the beginning of warfare, was a lonely one. He was sending back detailed information on airfields around Hollandia, of troops being shifted eastward (to Wewak), and of aircraft flying away and not returning. Daily he and his men risked their lives, suffered, and hungered. Rudy Gout had developed a painful case of ulcers. But was anyone at the AIB even reading his radio messages? Indeed they were: His intelligence was scrutinized daily by those planning the Hollandia invasion.[3]

General MacArthur set April 22 as invasion day. As the date drew closer, a five-man team of Alamo Scouts, led by Lieutenant John M. Dove, sneaked ashore from a PT boat and spent the day prowling around

the Hollandia region on an intelligence mission. That night, nearly exhausted from continuous marching, Dove and his men headed back to
the rendezvous point on the shore. Slipping along a slimy path, the
Scouts came upon a small village.

Dove halted his team to assess the situation. Creeping through the
underbrush, he discerned two Japanese sentries guarding the trail and
some twenty-five enemy soldiers sprawled in sleep along both sides of the
path that led directly through the village. There were swamps with neck-
high water on both sides, so the Scouts could not skirt the hamlet.

Known as "Hollywood John" because of his birthplace in the California movies mecca, Dove collected the other Alamo Scouts and whispered his plan. Minutes later, the two sentries were killed silently by sharp
trench knives, then the Americans stole through the dark village within a
few feet of the sleeping Japanese soldiers.[4]

A day later, Lieutenant Dove and the other Scouts were debriefed
by intelligence officers on the situation they found in the Hollandia
region. Except for the emperor's snoozing soldiers in the village, they had
seen few troops. That disclosure confirmed MacArthur's evaluation of
the situation gleaned from his electronic snoopers and the jungle spy,
Jean de Bruijn.

Now MacArthur began a masterful deception campaign, a component of his undercover war, to mislead the Japanese about the true target
of his next invasion—Hollandia, the former capital of Dutch New
Guinea. Through an interlocking series of hoaxes and machinations,
feints, and misdirections, MacArthur intended to convince Japanese intelligence that Wewak, the most logical target, was next on the Supreme
Commander's hit list.

George Kenney's fighters and bombers began pounding Wewak,
and low-level photo-reconnaissance flights over Wewak were intensified.
Simultaneously, PT boats dashed along the coast and shot up targets in
the vicinity of Wewak and Aitape. At night, these speedy craft sneaked
in close on both sides of those two enemy strongholds and sent small
parties onto the shore. There they half hid rubber dinghies that would be
found by the Japanese and imply that Allied scouts had been reconnoitering the locales.

In another ploy, dummy rubber paratroopers (each half human size)
were dropped inland from Wewak, close enough to the coast to be seen
by the Japanese there. MacArthur and the AIB were counting on the fact
that enemy patrols would not go into the menacing jungle and discover
the dummy paratroopers. It was known that the Japanese along the New

Guinea coast long had been reluctant to send small patrols inland because, in the past, such excursions had resulted in deadly ambushes by headhunters and cannibals.[5]

Meanwhile, the AIB sent a party under Captain Blue Harris, a bold and resourceful Australian, to slip ashore near the true target, Hollandia, and radio back crucial intelligence gathered from their personal observations. A stocky, lantern-jawed veteran of numerous jaunts far behind enemy lines, Harris was called "Blue" in a curious twist of Australian humor, since his hair was flaming red. Coarse and truculent on the outside, soft-hearted and caring on the inside, the captain was highly regarded by all who knew him.

A few months earlier, Blue Harris had been holed up on Vitu, a tiny island off New Britain, from where he was radioing reports on Japanese shipping and troop movements. Somehow his presence was detected, and enemy troops landed on Vitu and began searching for him. Harris, who had a stray dog with him for company, radioed Port Moresby to rescue him.

"Urgent: time running out," he signaled.

Soon a coded message instructed Harris to meet a seaplane that would try to land in the little harbor of Vitu. Miraculously perhaps, the small aircraft, equipped with pontoons, evaded Japanese planes and splashed down at night. The AIB operative paddled out quietly in a canoe, but he refused to get on board: The pilot said he could not bring his faithful dog with him. Finally, the pilot, growing more nervous each second, agreed to Harris's demand, so the captain and his pooch crowded into the cabin, and moments later the aircraft soared off for Port Moresby.

Now, Blue Harris and his Hollandia-bound AIB party were shoehorned into the American submarine *Dace*, burrowing through a soft New Guinea night. With him was his second in command, Lieutenant R. B. Webber, and five other Caucasians. An Indonesian sergeant would serve as an interpreter, and four former New Guinea policemen were along to deal with any hostile natives. The party had a radio and would be able to use a relay station that had been installed secretly a hundred miles to the south.

When the *Dace* neared the designated landing site, a small bay near Hollandia, the craft's commander felt that the waters had been mined, so, at his insistence, another locale several miles away was agreed upon. Embarking in rubber rafts from the submarine, Harris and his party began paddling. The night was especially quiet. When the intruders were nearly ashore, a series of heavy waves suddenly struck their flimsy rafts, pitching several men, including Harris, into the angry surf. Although he was pulled under by the weight of his clothing and equipment, the Australian managed to make it to the shore, where he and the others lay gasping.

Then came a frightening sight: A brilliant blaze nearby split the darkness. Obviously, the party had been detected. Moments later, dim figures emerged from the thick vegetation. Harris felt a slight surge of relief. These were natives, he was convinced. Had they been Japanese, shooting would have erupted from the strangers.

Pulling himself to his feet, Captain Harris walked forward and began conversing with the tribesmen. They seemed friendly, but intuition acquired in his years as a bushman warned him to beware of trickery. The Australian told the natives that his party intended to go inland and they agreed to provide a guide. Harris was apprehensive. His radio had been lost in the surf, and he would have no way to summon help should the AIB party get into a tight situation.

At daybreak, Harris and his men moved inland. After they had gone a mile, the native guide suddenly vanished. Harris was convinced dirty work was afoot. He edged up to his number two man, Lieutenant Webber, and directed him to drop back over the route just covered and give an alarm if he saw anything ominous.

Two minutes later, Webber rushed back and called out that a large contingent of Japanese soldiers was behind them and coming up rapidly. As Harris suspected might happen, the AIB men had been betrayed by the "friendly" natives encountered on the beach during the night. Suddenly, heavy bursts of fire erupted from the thick vegetation on all sides: Harris and his men had stumbled into an ambush.

Those in the party flopped to the ground as a hailstorm of bullets hissed past. Two men were hit immediately. Above the din, Harris shouted, "Scatter, men, scatter!" It was the only way that a few of the party could survive. Harris himself made no effort to escape the lethal trap. Remaining on the ground, he blasted away with his tommy gun to provide cover for the others while they dispersed. Harris was hit three times by bullets but remained conscious.

Now the shooting ceased. A few of the AIB men had escaped. At the scene of the ambush, the Japanese grabbed the bleeding Harris and propped him against a tree. All the while they tried to extract information about the AIB party's mission, how the intruders had arrived, and what was MacArthur's next invasion target. Harris refused to say a word. Furious, the Japanese repeatedly thrust bayonets into the Australian until he died in agony. [6]

In early April, Colonel Spencer Akin's radio intercepts gave startling evidence that the Hollandia deception scheme was working beyond expectations. A Japanese intelligence officer's "estimate of the situation" declared:

> The signs of an enemy plan to make a new landing in the New Guinea area are quite clear. . . . A landing in the Wewak sector is a probability in light of recent bombings of Hansa, the naval bombardment of Wewak, reconnaissance flights over Wewak, and leaflet drops [there]. . . . Since there was no reconnaissance carried out by submarines, destroyers, or aircraft, in the [Hollandia] sector, the probability of a landing there is thought to be minor.[7]

Apparently based on this intelligence estimate, the Japanese rushed even more troops from Hollandia to Wewak. As the invasion date grew nearer, another ruse was implemented: An Allied task force of warships sneaked up to Wewak under cover of night and heavily shelled the Japanese stronghold.

In the third week of April, while various deception ploys were still in progress, U.S. Vice Admiral Daniel E. "Uncle Dan" Barbey's Task Force 77 (code-named Reckless) shoved off from various harbors on a circuitous, thousand-mile voyage to Hollandia. It was the mightiest sea armada yet assembled in the southwest Pacific: hundreds of troop transports, battleships, cruisers, destroyers, sub-chasers, and aircraft carriers. On board the cruiser *Nashville* was Douglas MacArthur.

On April 21, the invasion fleet rendezvoused west of the Admiralties. Since it was impossible to "hide" such a massive flotilla, MacArthur used it to perpetuate a final hoax on the Japanese. During the daylight, the convoy sailed northward, away from Hollandia; hopefully, Japanese scout planes would spot it. Then, just after darkness, the flotilla veered sharply southwestward in the direction of Hollandia.

Shortly after dawn on the sweltering day of April 22, elements of the U.S. 24th and 41st Infantry Divisions stormed ashore simultaneously at Tanahmerah and Humboldt Bays, thirty miles apart, on either side of Hollandia. Due in a large measure to MacArthur's deception machinations, total surprise had been achieved. Dumbfounded to awaken and find a massive American fleet discharging thousands of troops on their doorstep, some fifteen thousand Japanese soldiers, mainly service and administrative personnel, fled inland to the temporary haven of the jungle. There they would wander aimlessly for many days before dying of starvation.

Without pausing, MacArthur's troops east and west of Hollandia charged ahead and converged south of the great Japanese supply and staging base. Within a few days, Hollandia, caught in the pincers, was captured. Only 154 Allied casualties were suffered during the entire operation. MacArthur himself had nearly become one of the casualties. Over Admiral Barbey's protests, the Supreme Commander insisted on following the first waves ashore in an unarmed, plodding Higgins boat, a small craft used for beach assaults. While on Tanahmerah Bay, the *Nashville* radioed that Japanese warplanes were zooming in at deck level and strafing small craft, so the coxswain was to head for the nearest warship to get the protection of its guns.

MacArthur overruled the order and told the coxswain to continue to the beach, much to the chagrin of the Supreme Commander's aides, who were nervously scanning the sky. Minutes later, a Zero swooped in directly at the Higgins boat, then pulled up without firing a shot.[8]

Military professionals the world over were awed by Douglas MacArthur's audacious triumph at Hollandia. In Washington, even Admiral Ernest King, the chief of naval operations and longtime arch foe of MacArthur, labeled the operation a "master stroke." Newspapers in the United States, however, gave precious little ink to the Hollandia invasion—there simply had not been enough American blood spilled to warrant blaring headlines.[9]

In Tokyo in the spring of 1944, bizarre events were unfolding in the wake of repeated American victories in the Pacific. Prime Minister Hideki Tojo suddenly booted out the army chief of staff, Field Marshal Gen Sugiyama, and replaced the navy chief of staff, Admiral Osami Nagano, with his own man, Navy Minister Shigetaro Shimada. Now the army and the navy were under the direct control of Tojo, who believed that the chain of reversals in the Pacific had resulted from bickering between the service chiefs.

Tojo's bald-face grasp of almost total power was deeply resented by important figures in Tokyo, including Prince Chichibu, the eldest of the emperor's three brothers, and by the influential *jushin* (former prime ministers). These men were convinced that Tojo, himself, was responsible for the military disasters in the Pacific, and they began plotting to eliminate him.

Weeks passed with nothing done to oust Tojo. Finally, one of the plotters, Rear Admiral Sokichi Takagi, met secretly with a small group of navy junior officers he trusted and persuaded them that Dai Nippon could not survive unless Tojo was assassinated. The young officers agreed enthusiastically to carry out the murder plot.

Surreptitiously, the conspirators studied Tojo's daily routine, and Takagi decided that an automobile "accident" would promise the highest degree of success. A plan was drawn up. Riding in three cars, the assassins would intercept a Tojo motorcade. One vehicle would crash into Tojo's car, causing it to halt. The other two vehicles would pull alongside and riddle the prime minister with automatic weapons. Then the assassins would flee to Formosa in a navy plane, while Admiral Takagi would remain in Tokyo to try to manipulate the appointment of a successor to the murdered Tojo.

Unbeknownst to the assassination plotters in the navy, rebels in the army were also conspiring to ambush Tojo. A major named Tsunoda, who had recently been transferred from a combat zone to Imperial General Headquarters, would pitch a specially made hydrocyanic bomb at Tojo's limousine as it slowed on a curve near Hirohito's palace. However, the army plot was betrayed by Prince Mikasa, the emperor's youngest brother, to whom a friend of the schemers had inadvertently revealed the ambush plan.

Instead of being sympathetic to the plot, Prince Mikasa tipped off security officers in the Imperial Palace and the Kempei Tai arrested Major Tsunoda and other army conspirators. All were sentenced to death but were given stays of execution. No doubt Hideki Tojo did not want it known publicly that his own military officers had turned on him and were plotting to kill him.

18 The Mysterious Mister X

On July 7, 1944, Lee van Atta, a correspondent for International News Service, called on General George Kenney at the air chief's Brisbane headquarters and had a piece of intriguing news. Van Atta had just flown in from Hollandia, New Guinea, and said that Charles A. Lindbergh, once the idol of hundreds of millions of people throughout the world, was on that island for some unknown purpose.

Kenney was puzzled. Lindbergh was a civilian, so he could not be on a military mission. A quick check disclosed that no one in Douglas MacArthur's headquarters had even an inkling as to why he was in this theater of operations, nor could any information be dug up concerning who had authorized and provided his passage from the United States to the southwest Pacific.

Knowing that the Supreme Commander was suspicious of intruders into his bailiwick, Kenney immediately notified MacArthur. Because MacArthur wanted Lindbergh's presence kept secret, staff officers were abuzz with conjecture over the identity of this mysterious figure. They referred to Lindbergh as Mister X.

Just after midnight on July 10, Lindbergh, known to his friends as Slim when he was a pioneer airmail pilot two decades earlier, was awakened in his tent at Strip 3 at Hollandia. A message had just arrived "requesting" him to come to Brisbane. It was signed "MacArthur."

At 7:54 A.M., a B-25 bomber lifted off with Lindbergh as a passenger and flew on a southeasterly course across the towering Owen Stanley Range. Dressed in tropical cotton clothing, Mister X was racked by bitter cold as the two-engine plane had to climb to ten thousand feet to top the heavy cloud mass.

Seventeen years earlier, the lanky Lindbergh had electrified the world when he took off from Roosevelt Field outside New York City in a tiny single-winged plane and landed at Le Bourget Field near Paris the next day. After flying nonstop for thirty-six hundred miles in thirty-three and a half hours, Slim was greeted by a delirious throng numbering tens of thousands.[1]

After years of adulation, the Lone Eagle, as he became known, emerged as a highly controversial figure in the United States when ominous war clouds were gathering over Europe in 1939. As the marquee star of the America First Committee, a large and influential isolationist organization, Lindbergh stumped the nation, speaking before huge crowds and demanding that America remain neutral after fighting broke out across the Atlantic.

Lindbergh's series of blistering speeches and proneutral articles he wrote for newspapers and magazines riled Franklin Roosevelt, and when the Lone Eagle called for the President's impeachment before an overflow audience in Des Moines, Iowa, less than three months before the Japanese sneak attack at Pearl Harbor, Roosevelt responded with a public broadside against Lindbergh. Consequently, the aviation pioneer resigned his colonel's commission in the Army Air Corps Reserve.[2]

A few days after the United States was blasted into the global conflict, Lindbergh called at the War Department in the Munitions Building in Washington and offered his services. Apparently he hoped to regain his colonel's commission and go on active duty. But seventy-five-year-old Secretary of War Henry L. Stimson rejected Lindbergh on instructions from the White House. Lindy's anger at President Roosevelt intensified.

In the months ahead, Lindy made notable contributions to the war effort. He went to work for Henry Ford, the eccentric genius, as a technical consultant at the Willow Run bomber plant in Detroit for a monthly salary of $666. Along with a few mass production experts, he and Ford ironed out the kinks and got Willow Run's lines purring with B-24 bombers in one of the most extraordinary manufacturing feats of the war.

Later, the Lone Eagle went to the Mayo Clinic in Minnesota for a series of experiments in the clinic's pressure chambers to test a human's lungs and blood pressure at high altitude. He was the guinea pig. Then he put the new P-47 Thunderbolt fighter through grueling tests and nearly died when his oxygen failed at 42,000 feet.

All the while, Lindbergh longed, even needed, to be with the young Americans who were flying against the enemy and battling them in the skies. He blamed President Roosevelt for preventing him from doing so, but at age forty-two, he was rather old for a combat fighter pilot by army standards.

Although members of the Roosevelt Administration, taking their cue from the Big Chief in the Oval Office, scrupulously avoided any contact with Lindbergh, old friends in the armed forces, now holding high rank in Washington, often invited him to lunch in public. Through these connections, secret passage to the southwest Pacific was arranged. The White House was kept in the dark, lest Lindy's covert trek be cancelled out of spite.

Now in Brisbane, as General Kenney awaited the arrival of Mister X, the air boss was aghast to learn that the Lone Eagle had been on New Guinea for several weeks and had flown on numerous combat missions with navy pilots, including sweeps over the Japanese bastion of Rabaul. Over MacArthur's name, Kenney fired off a rather abrupt message to the navy, demanding to know what right the navy had to send anyone into army territory without first getting permission.

After a one-day stopover at Townsville on his flight from New Guinea, Lindbergh arrived in Brisbane early in the afternoon of July 12 and went directly to Kenney's headquarters. As soon as the Lone Eagle ambled through the door, the mystery of Mister X was unraveled: Every officer knew he was Charles Augustus Lindbergh, who had one of the world's best known faces.

Kenney and Lindbergh had been acquaintances for many years. But hardly had the two men shaken hands than Kenney began berating the other: Didn't Lindbergh know that it was against international law for a civilian to engage in armed combat? "If the Japs captured you, they'd cut off your head!" Kenney all but shouted.[3]

When the scrappy Kenney calmed down, he said that he would provide Lindy with papers legalized for MacArthur's theater of operations but that he would ask him not to fly combat anymore. Kenney spoke about army regulations and the "reaction back home" if the famed pilot, a civilian, were shot down.

Lindy responded that he would follow those orders if given them, but that he didn't want to go back to New Guinea and sit on the ground while the other pilots were flying combat.

With the ice broken, Kenney's eyes twinkled. "Well, it might be possible to put you on observer's status, but, that would not make it legal for you to do any shooting," the general said. "But of course no one back home is going to know whether you use your guns or not."[4]

Lindbergh remarked that the squadrons with which he had been involved were wasting a large percentage of their gasoline by cruising their engines at too high a rate of speed and too low a manifold pressure. So he was taken to see General Dick Sutherland, MacArthur's chief of staff, who, after much hesitation, agreed to put the civilian on observer status "to study the subject of fighter range."

Next, the civilian celebrity was ushered in to see General Mac-Arthur, who knew Lindbergh years earlier. Lindy repeated his claim on fighter range, telling the Supreme Commander that P-38 Lightnings (the type of planes that had ambushed Admiral Yamamoto the previous year) were capable of a 700-mile range instead of the present 570 and that some experienced pilots could get a 750-mile radius.

MacArthur replied that it would be a "gift from heaven" if that could be done and asked if Lindbergh could go back to New Guinea to instruct the squadrons on fuel economy that would make such a radius possible. Lindy replied he could go back at once.

"An increased fighter radius would be of enormous importance to my future plans," the Supreme Commander declared.

MacArthur then took Lindy to a huge wall map and detailed his general plan of action in the weeks and months ahead and the limitations that were imposed by present fighter-plane combat radii.

"Of course, you are not to engage in combat," the general declared with a twinkle in his eye. "You are only an observer."

"Yes, sir, only an observer."[5]

MacArthur was delighted over the possibility of extending the P-38's range, which would allow leapfrogs to be made over longer distances. Lindbergh's presence in the southwest Pacific was wrapped in a thick cloak of security while he carried out his secret mission.

In a borrowed fighter plane, Lindy took off from Brisbane on July 14 and reported to Colonel Charles McDonald's 475th Fighter Group in New Guinea three days later. Although MacArthur and Kenney had urged him to preserve his "observer" status, they had agreed that he could hardly tell combat pilots how to handle their planes if he remained on the ground.

On July 28, the "observer" was flying with McDonald's wing when he found himself in the center of a wild dogfight with a swarm of Japanese Zeros over Elpaputih Island. One Zero suddenly swung around and headed hell-bent directly toward Lindbergh, who squeezed his trigger and sent a stream of tracers into the oncoming craft. Looking around,

Lindy saw the enemy plane spin crazily downward and splash into the sea. He had shot down his first enemy plane.

A few days later, the civilian observer was again with Colonel McDonald's wing when it was jumped by a large force of Zeros. One enemy plane got on Lindbergh's tail and was pumping tracers at him. Moments later, McDonald raced up with machine guns blazing and chased off the Zero that had closed in for the kill. Word of Lindbergh's brush with death spread like wildfire throughout the American command. An order came for him to leave the combat zone and report to MacArthur at Brisbane before going back to the United States.

Men who had flown with the Lone Eagle during the past few months—Americans, Australians, and New Zealanders—were sorry to see him depart. He had engaged in fifty combat missions and flown for 179 hours. In battle, he had displayed courage and ingenuity and proved that flying skill and instinct by a forty-two-year-old pilot could more than make up for youthful reflexes.

In his secret mission, Lindbergh had taught them a great deal about their own planes and extended the P-38's range dramatically—an achievement that would have a marked impact upon the course of the war in the Pacific.

On July 8, about a week after the Stars and Stripes began flying over Hollandia, Lieutenant Charles A. Black, a PT-boat skipper, was summoned to intelligence headquarters at Mios Woendi, a tiny atoll off western New Guinea, and assigned an especially perilous secret mission. He was to carry a team of army scouts to Japanese-held Roemberpon Island in Geelvink Bay, the largest inlet in New Guinea. Black was to lead the team ashore, reconnoiter the beaches, and obtain as much intelligence as possible.

Charlie Black was ideally suited for the daunting task. An adventuresome free spirit, he spoke Japanese and several native dialects. What he had not been told was that Roemberpon had been targeted by Douglas MacArthur for another leap forward.

It was daylight when Black's PT boat shoved off from Mios Woendi, and by midnight the craft was lying off the dark and ominous shore of Roemberpon. Faces blackened, wearing dark clothing, and armed to the teeth with tommy guns and nasty-looking trench knives, Lieutenant Black and his scout team climbed into a rubber dinghy and paddled toward the shore. The intruders stole onto the beach, slipped into a clump of vegetation, and listened intently. The only sound was a faint rustling of tree leaves and the gentle lapping of the surf.

"It's too damned quiet," one scout whispered. "The goddamned Japs are up to something!"

After dawn broke, the raiders began stealing along the beach, staying close to the vegetation for partial concealment. Suddenly, Japanese shouts split the silence. The Americans froze. Clearly, they had been discovered. Since the shouts were down the beach, Charlie Black led his men inland toward a native camp where Ferdinand jungle spies were holed up.

Black and his scouts spent several hours talking with the Ferdinand operatives, from whom they obtained detailed intelligence on Japanese troop strength on Roemberpon, gun positions and the caliber of the weapons, the tides, and which beach would be the most suitable for amphibious landings.

When it was nearing time to rendezvous with the returning PT boat, a native led the column far in advance. Nearing the beach, the native hurried back and excitedly gave Lieutenant Black alarming news: The Japanese had found the hidden rubber dinghy and were deployed along the shore to ambush the Americans when they returned. However, the guide told Black that his tribesmen had hidden a canoe on a stretch of beach not guarded by the Japanese.

At twilight, the raiders reached the site. Peeking through thick vegetation, Black saw a chilling sight: Four Japanese soldiers, carrying rifles at the ready, were standing at the precise spot where the canoe was concealed.

Time was running out. The PT boat would return soon. The Japanese dragnet was growing tighter. None of the raiders held any illusions as to his fate should they be captured. They had to get off Roemberpon that night or else they were doomed. Charlie Black concluded there was only one course of action that might save them—boldness.

When it was dark and Black's features could not be discerned, he left the brush and began walking nonchalantly toward the four Japanese on the beach. They looked at the dim figure and apparently thought the American was a comrade. Obviously, a hunted quarry would not be strolling calmly along the beach toward them.

When Black was only ten feet from the unwary Japanese, he whipped up the pistol he had been holding behind his back and shot all four of them dead. Danger still lurked. The pistol reports seemed to have alerted every enemy soldier in the region, and the Americans could hear loud shouts and the rustling of underbrush as more Japanese raced to the site.

Offshore, Lieutenant Paul T. Rennell, on the PT boat, detected the fiery muzzle blasts from Black's pistol and deduced that the scouting party was in big trouble. Despite the peril to his boat and its crew, Rennell moved the craft near the beach. As the harsh shouts of the closing Japanese rang in his ears, Black and his men scrambled out of the vegetation and waded to the PT boat as bullets whistled past their heads like a swarm of angry bees.

Pulled out of the water and onto the deck, the raiders were exhausted. As the boat started to race away, Charlie Black quipped to his friend Rennell, "Damn it, Paul, what took you so long!"[6]

For weeks, Pacific strategy sessions in the sprawling Pentagon in Washington had been intense and acrimonious. Officers in the school of thought of Admiral Ernest King, the chief of naval operations, had been lobbying to bypass the Philippines and strike directly at Formosa (later Taiwan), a mountain island rising from the South China Sea a hundred miles off the China mainland and three hundred miles north of the Philippines. An equally vocal group of generals wanted to recapture the Philippines before invading Formosa.

President Roosevelt, a patient man, had finally grown weary of the ongoing Pacific strategy dispute, so he decided to travel to Honolulu and get the views of Douglas MacArthur and Admiral Chester Nimitz face to face.

When MacArthur received an order to meet Mr. Big (as the wording described the President for security reasons) in Hawaii, the Supreme Commander considered the looming showdown a case of "me against them." MacArthur had been convinced for months that the navy intended—once his own forces had reached the western end of New Guinea—to take over the war in the Pacific and administer the coup de grace to Japan.[7]

On July 25, MacArthur's four-engine Flying Fortress, the *Bataan*, lifted off from Brisbane and set a course for Hickham Field, Hawaii, twenty-six hours and four time zones away. The shootout on Pacific strategy began in the spacious, book-lined living room of a private mansion outside Honolulu. Acting as the referee, President Roosevelt turned the floor over to Admiral Nimitz, who urged bypassing the Philippines.

As Nimitz concluded his argument, MacArthur set his pipe in an ashtray, rose, and began to present his case. The general, who long had had a gift for mesmerizing listeners, was at his spellbinding best. Along with what he considered sound military logic, he stressed that it would be "morally wrong, grossly unethical, and shameful" to bypass the Philippines. The entire conference lasted only ninety-two minutes.

The next morning, Roosevelt, seated on the immaculately groomed lawn of the mansion under a palm tree from which all the coconuts had been cut lest one drop on the unprotected presidential noggin, met with a clutch of newspaper reporters and photographers.

"We have had an extremely interesting and useful conference," Roosevelt said. "We are going back to the Philippines, and General MacArthur will [lead us there]."[8]

Hardly had the last volley been fired in the Battle of Honolulu than the Supreme Commander rushed back to his new advanced headquarters at Hollandia. On July 30, American troops splashed ashore at Sansapor, clear out on the western tip of the Vogelkop Peninsula and the final whistle-stop on the grueling, fifteen-hundred-mile trek up the spine of New Guinea. Left behind along the coastline during the "hit-'em-where-they-ain't" campaign were an estimated two hundred thousand of the Japanese emperor's troops. Most were doomed to die of starvation and disease.

Standing on the porch of his Hollandia house on the balmy night of August 3, Douglas MacArthur faced northward, puffed on a cigar, and remarked to his two American commanders, Walter Krueger and Lieutenant General Robert L. Eichelberger, "Gentlemen, I can almost see Manila now!"[9]

Indeed he could. By Pacific distances, the Philippines were just over the horizon from Sansapor.

On August 1, a day after GIs splashed ashore at Sansapor, Emperor Hirohito received a distinguished visitor at the Imperial Palace in Tokyo. General Hideki Tojo, in full uniform complete with medals and ceremonial samurai sword, bowed before the emperor and confessed his failures. Since the glory days of two years earlier when the empire of the Rising Sun had extended its rays over enormous expanses of the Pacific, Tojo had watched as the Imperial armed forces had suffered one defeat after the other. Now the Allies had drawn a noose around his still vast domain. General Tojo, the supreme warlord, the instigator of the Pearl Harbor sneak attack, therefore resigned.

Stepping into the disgraced Tojo's boots was another two-fisted, gung-ho army man, General Kuniaki Koiso. The sixty-four-year-old Koiso had two nicknames. He preferred "The Singing Frog," which he felt was a tribute to his deep, resonant voice, but actually was used derisively behind his back. He particularly liked to sing old Japanese folk tunes when amply fortified with sake. But Koiso was better known as "The Korean Tiger" because of the brutalities he had allowed while governor of Korea.

Hideki Tojo's departure would not result in a slackening of Japan's war efforts; a militaristic clique was still in power. General Koiso told the emperor, "We will fight to ultimate victory!"

"They're Waiting for **19**
Me Up There!"

While Douglas MacArthur was planning his next leapfrog, two of his jungle spies, Captain James L. Evans, an American doctor, and Major Vincent Zampanta, who once had been on the staff of a San Francisco luxury hotel, had taken refuge with one of the world's most primitive tribes, the Manobos, on the island of Mindoro, just below Luzon. After shaking off early fears that they might find themselves on the Manobos' dinner menu, the two men had come to feel at home in their aboriginal surroundings.

Early on the morning of September 9, 1944, Captain Evans was awakened by an excited tribesman wearing a bone through his nostrils. Powerful airplane engines could be heard. Evans dashed outside and squinted into the sun-drenched sky. There were some seventy planes—*American* planes.

"MacArthur's back!" the physician shouted joyously. "MacArthur's back!"

A wild celebration, featuring copious amounts of potent *tuba* juice, erupted in the barrio and lasted far into the night. Not knowing what they were celebrating, the Manobos nevertheless joined with zeal. As the tuba juice flowed, the natives clapped each other's shoulders and yelled excitedly, "Muck-artur back! Muck-artur back!"

Only later would Jim Evans and Vincent Zampanta learn that it was not MacArthur but Admiral Bull Halsey who had launched swarms of carrier-based warplanes against the Philippines. Delighted at the chance to bring the war back to the locale in which the Japanese had inflicted a humiliating defeat on America, Halsey's eager pilots roamed the central islands, bombing and strafing. On that first day alone, twelve hundred sorties were flown, a number that was equalled the next day.

After the final plane had been recovered aboard its carrier at the end of the third day of the air assault, a beaming intelligence officer rushed up to Admiral Halsey. "Here's the box score!" he exclaimed.

Halsey scanned the figures and let out a low whistle. His pilots had shot down 173 Japanese planes, destroyed 305 more on the ground (some of which may have been dummies), sunk 59 Japanese vessels, and inflicted heavy damage on enemy installations. Halsey's losses: eight warplanes and ten men.[1]

A few days later, on September 15, far south of the Philippines, General MacArthur struck at Morotai, an egg-shaped island forty-five miles long and lying between Sansapor at the western tip of New Guinea and Davao Gulf in Mindanao, the southernmost island in the Philippines. The Supreme Commander wanted Morotai as an air and naval base before leaping on to Mindanao. Spearheading the invasion was a task force under the command of the Old Reliable, Admiral Dan "The Amphibious Man" Barbey.

As usual, MacArthur accompanied the assault force. Leaving his flagship, the *Nashville,* he headed for shore in the wake of the first waves. Near the beach, his Higgins boat grounded on a rock—much to the chagrin of the youthful coxswain. Impatient to get onto the beach, the general ordered the ramp lowered and promptly stepped off it—into chest-deep water.

While much younger aides struggled to keep up, MacArthur waded ashore. He was in buoyant spirits. There was token opposition, just as he had expected because of Colonel Sid Akin's electronic intercepts and from Alamo Scouts who had reconnoitered the island. Again, he gazed toward Manila and Bataan and Corregidor.

"They're waiting for me up there!" MacArthur remarked to an aide.[2]

Hardly had the Supreme Commander's shoes dried from wading ashore at Morotai than preparations began for his next jump: to Mindanao on November 15, and the central Philippine island of Leyte on December 20. But the bold Bull Halsey, one of the handful of navy brass with whom MacArthur had rapport, proposed the timetable be scrapped in favor of a more audacious jump.

Since the warplanes of Halsey's Third Fleet had pounded the Japanese in the Philippines for several days and had wiped out large numbers of enemy aircraft, he concluded that the central islands were "a hollow shell, with weak defenses and skimpy facilities." The Bull described Leyte as the "vulnerable belly of the Imperial dragon."

MacArthur was electrified by Halsey's proposal. Mindanao would be bypassed; MacArthur would hit Leyte. A-Day at Leyte was set for October 20.

In preparation for the Great Return to the Philippines, Halsey's mighty Third Fleet ranged the region, striking airfields and shipping in the Ryukus, Formosa, Luzon, Mindanao, and Leyte. Through Magic intercepts, Halsey knew that the Imperial Fleet was divided, most of the surface ships being near Singapore, while the carriers were training new pilots in Japan's Inland Sea. Although the precise location of a few ships of the Japanese fleet was in doubt, Allied intelligence had an accurate roster of the names and characteristics of each vessel.

Also compiled through Magic intercepts, captured documents, and U.S. and British action reports, Allied intelligence had a complete listing of where every Japanese naval vessel larger than an escort destroyer had been sunk. In many instances, the Japanese had tried to conceal the losses, both to confuse the Allies and to keep homefront morale from plummeting.

In mid-September, Halsey's intelligence officers received a Magic intercept stating that a powerful Japanese naval force had departed from Amoy, China, for the Philippines, presumably to do battle with the rampaging Third Fleet and to land reinforcements on Luzon. The information had originated from an AIB spy in Chungking, China, and he said the fleet-sailing intelligence had come from a Chinese informant in Amoy.

If this report were true, it could upset the applecart for MacArthur's Leyte invasion, because Halsey would have to discontinue his softening-up strikes and take on this approaching Imperial naval force. A-Day at Leyte, therefore, might have to be postponed.

Navy Captain Marion C. "Mike" Cheek and Lieutenant Harris Cox, intelligence officers for Halsey aboard the battleship *New Jersey*, were flabbergasted by the report from the AIB source in China. Since the two locations of the Imperial Fleet were known, from where did this new naval force suddenly materialize? However, the unidentified informant at Amoy had done his job thoroughly, even listing the names of the Japanese ships involved.

Cheek and Harris immediately recognized the *Mutzu*, a battleship that the Japanese did not know that Allied intelligence knew had been sunk by an accidental internal explosion. All the other ships on the list were ones that had gone to the bottom during the war but whose loss had been kept secret by the Japanese.

Within an hour, Captain Cheek and Lieutenant Cox informed the concerned Bull Halsey that the massive threat to the invasion of the Philippines was a phantom fleet, that every ship on the list already had gone to a watery grave—only the Japanese didn't know that the Allies knew. Clearly, the Japanese had tried to perpetrate a monumental hoax on MacArthur and Halsey in a desperate effort to disrupt any planned invasion of the Philippines. Without doubt, the phony intelligence had been planted by a double agent (one in the employ of both adversaries), for China was a smorgasbord of secret agents, double agents, and triple agents. [3]

While the cloak-and-dagger dueling over the Japanese phantom fleet had been in progress, the British submarine *Porpoise* slipped out of Perth, Australia, on September 12, and set a course toward Singapore, two thousand miles away. Inasmuch as the Operation Jaywick virtuosos had conducted a highly acclaimed show on the Singapore stage less than a year earlier, an encore performance was now underway. Although secret agents always had believed in the motto "Don't Press Your Luck," a half-dozen of the twenty-two AIB operatives on the *Porpoise* had been stars in the first boom-and-bang mission. The return engagement was code-named Operation Rimau.

Hunched over in the submarine's restricted quarters or sprawled on sling bunks were Lieutenant Commander Ivan Lyon, leader of the Jaywick mission, whose wife and child apparently had been murdered by the Japanese in Singapore; his second in command and longtime close crony, Lieutenant Commander Donald Davidson; Captain Robert Page; and three Australian naval ratings, all veterans of Jaywick.

So bold was Operation Rimau that it had to be approved by London before British Colonel H. A. Campbell, who had succeeded Lieutenant Colonel G. S. Mott as chief of the AIB's sabotage unit, now called the SRD, gave his stamp of approval. Campbell knew his business; he was the officer who had coordinated the earlier fabulously successful raid on Singapore harbor.

Operation Rimau had two unique twists: It would involve baby submarines and piracy on the high seas. Perhaps it was the only time in the war that a submarine's mission was not to sink vessels but to capture one.

That night on the *Porpoise*, Ivan Lyon and his longtime sidekick, Donald Davidson, were poring over the Rimau operational plan once again. It called for seizing an Oriental-looking vessel while en route, after which the *Porpoise* would tow it to the island of Maraps, which would be a forward operating base. Meanwhile, the SRD operatives would conceal two one-man submarines and radio equipment on the captured ship, which would be the centerpiece of the scheme to wreak havoc in Singapore harbor.

A few days after casting off from Perth, the *Porpoise* skipper had a Japanese warship in the crosshairs of his periscope, but, much to his anguish, he had to pass up the chance to launch his torpedoes. Had he done so, the secret mission might have been compromised.

Twenty-four hours later, the submarine encountered the precise quarry the raiders were seeking—a large Oriental junk plowing through the sea. The *Porpoise* surfaced and its crewmen fired a shot from a deck gun across the bow of the junk. Then a boarding party of SRD operatives scrambled onto the *Muskita* and confronted its frightened crew of Malayan natives.

After the Malayans were put in canoes and began paddling toward a tiny island on the horizon, the Rimau men wielded hammers, saws, and other tools to redesign the contours of the *Muskita*. All the while, the *Porpoise* stood guard nearby. When the work was completed, the one-man submarines were removed from the *Porpoise* and concealed between the decks of the junk, which had been reconstructed to hold them.

Now the *Porpoise* began towing the junk, which was manned by SRD men who had colored their skin brown and donned native garb to pass as Malayans at a distance. In a few days, the jumpoff island of Maraps was reached at night, and the next morning, the *Porpoise* departed to resume its customary function of stalking Japanese ships. Another British submarine, the *Tantalus*, would retrieve the Rimau party at Maraps after the raid on Singapore.

Hardly had the *Porpoise* shoved off than the *Muskita*, with its SRD operatives aboard, set sail. The junk would penetrate to within a few miles of Singapore harbor, which, secret reports had indicated, was packed with Japanese ships. At a designated point a few miles from the big port, the baby submarines, with Ivan Lyon in one and Donald Davidson in the other, would be launched. Traveling underwater, the tiny submarines would steal into the harbor and the two occupants would place limpets on six of the bigger ships. Before the time fuses ignited the explosives, the baby submarines would return to Maraps Island.

Within twenty-four hours after the *Muskita* set sail, the junk was confronted by a launch filled with Malayan policemen. An intense gun battle erupted after the native police tried to board the *Muskita*, an act that could have tipped off the mission to the Japanese in Singapore once the baby submarines were detected. All the Malayans were killed in the shootout.

Ivan Lyon had to reach an agonizing decision. Aware that the native policemen could have radioed Singapore before the firefight, he decided to scrub the mission, since total surprise was crucial. So the *Muskita* headed back to the *Tantalus* pickup point on Maraps. Within hours, the plodding junk was overtaken by swifter Japanese vessels, so the *Muskita* was scuttled by opening the sea cocks and the crew reached a tiny island. There, Ivan Lyon and his men engaged in a series of running gun battles with the Japanese pursuers.

A few weeks later in Brisbane, Colonel Campbell received radio reports from undercover agents in Singapore. Citing an account in the Japanese-controlled newspaper there, the coded message said that Colonel Ivan Lyon and nine of his men were beheaded in a public square in Singapore. The ultimate fates of the other twelve Rimau raiders would never be known for certain.[4]

At this stage of the war, every major island in the Philippines, as well as many smaller ones, had organized guerrilla forces, which were armed largely by AIB submarines. Some 182,000 guerrillas constituted a lurking "ghost army" that was eagerly anticipating a signal from General MacArthur to arise en masse and strike a heavy blow against the Japanese.

Over the long months of Japanese occupation of the Philippines, MacArthur had urged guerrilla leaders to confine their resistance mainly to obtaining intelligence and radioing it to the AIB. Any concerted uprising by the guerrillas would result in the vengeful slaughter of civilians, he declared. On the brink of the Great Return, however, the Supreme Commander was nearly ready to unleash his ghost army.

To buttress the morale of his guerrillas—and no doubt to taunt the Japanese—MacArthur broadcast instructions that began, "To my commanders in the Philippines." As a psychological ploy to remind the Japanese that there was a large and potent secret army in their midst, these messages were not sent in code but in plain English.

Along with the large guerrilla force in the Philippines, there also was a clandestine network of 126 radio stations and 27 weather-reporting posts, most of which were hidden in thick jungles. One of the weather sleuths, twenty-one-year-old Private First Class Gordon Jenkins of the U.S. Army, had spent months of incessant running and hiding from an enemy bent on his capture in southern Mindanao. Bearded and with shoulder-length hair, Jenkins lived like a hunted animal in the jungle as he operated an improved meteorological station to provide General MacArthur's headquarters with weather conditions in the southern Philippines.

Lonely, pounded by torrential rains, attacked by wild animals, usually hungry, often frightened, and always in danger of being discovered, Private Jenkins radioed weather information almost daily. Because of security precautions, his bulletins were never acknowledged. Eventually, he became bitter and angry. Was anyone even seeing the weather data for which he was risking his life and living like a jungle animal? Whatever may have been the case, the young soldier would continue to do his duty.

For many months, the Japanese had labored mightily to smash or disrupt the Allied sabotage-and-espionage network that had been built throughout the Philippines. These efforts intensified as American forces edged closer to the archipelago. Heavily armed patrols regularly beat the bushes in the remote regions, searching, bribing, arresting, and torturing in an effort to expose Filipino and American spies.

Against this volatile backdrop, the redoubtable Chick Parsons, the renowned Cat with Nine Lives (Q-10 at the AIB), sneaked ashore on Leyte in September, a month before MacArthur's A-Day. The superspy was checking on the readiness of the guerrillas as well as radioing back to the AIB current intelligence on Japanese troop deployments. He was on the run almost constantly, often only a step ahead of the Kempei Tai and enemy patrols.

Parsons's peacetime friends never would have recognized the American "terrorist" (as he was branded by the Japanese). Wearing what he called "my business suit"—old, dirty, and torn trousers and shirt, along with a tattered, saw-toothed straw hat—he went barefoot and had a four weeks' growth of beard. Parsons never carried a gun, preferring to use his agility—mental and physical—to evade the Kempei Tai.

Parsons had become well known to the Kempei Tai after months of espionage activities on Mindanao, Luzon, and Leyte, and there was a hefty price on his head—50,000 U.S. dollars in gold, a fortune to the natives. Yet the civilians regularly provided him with food and shelter, not only disdaining the huge financial reward for betraying him, but risking death if the American's presence in their modest homes was discovered.

In early October, Parsons was radioed an assignment to snoop out the beaches along Leyte Gulf. Clad in his customary "business suit," the master spy was walking along a dirt road. As was his custom, he sent two guerrillas ahead, while a pair of native farmers remained with him. At a road intersection, the scouts halted but gave no indication of danger. So Parsons and the two farmers continued onward.

Moments later, Parsons felt a sharp streak of fear: Rounding the intersection and marching directly toward him was an eighteen-man, heavily armed Japanese patrol. No doubt they were searching for him. His quick wit told Parsons that his only salvation was to act nonchalant: While he shambled along in one direction, the file of Japanese soldiers trudged past in the other direction. Unaccountably, none of the enemy soldiers even glanced at the Caucasian under the wide-brimmed straw hat, even though they came so close that one or two of them had to lurch to one side to avoid bumping into Parsons and his pair of farmers.

After the patrol had passed him, Parsons resisted an overpowering urge to look back over his shoulder. Finally, he halted and stood beside the road, drenched with perspiration and frozen statuelike for what seemed to be several minutes. Finally, he looked at his two equally shaken companions and muttered, "Whew!"

When his underpinnings were once more firm, Parsons walked on to the small port of Tacloban near Leyte Gulf, the only community on the large island that could lay claim to a degree of modernity. It was at Tacloban, with a population of some twenty-five thousand, that General MacArthur planned to establish his headquarters. But Tacloban, which was thought to be an important Japanese supply and communications center, first would have to be heavily bombed and shelled, even though hundreds, perhaps thousands, of Philippine civilians would be slaughtered.

Slipping into town, an extremely risky job considering that he was a Caucasian, Parsons wandered up one street and down the other, his only "protection" being his nativelike attire. After three hours of snooping, he stole back to his hiding place in the jungle where a radio had been concealed. An urgent message was fired off to the AIB advance headquarters in Hollandia, New Guinea: No Japanese troops or facilities in Tacloban. So the town would be spared destruction and a large number of civilian lives would be saved.

During the next few days, Parsons continued to radio intelligence about the Leyte Gulf region. There was an absence of underwater obstacles at the landing beaches, he pointed out. Parsons also sent information on the mines in waters around Leyte Gulf, about enemy strongpoints on the heights at Carmon and other hills a considerable distance inland, and on the location of Japanese units elsewhere.

Fifteen hundred miles to the south of Leyte Gulf, these were exceedingly busy, even hectic, days at General MacArthur's newly constructed headquarters on the banks of Lake Sentani, a beautiful body of water in the Cyclops Mountains of Hollandia. The impending return to the Philippines, code named King II, would be the largest combined operation in the Pacific war up to that time.[5]

Longstanding plans for invading Mindanao had to be scrapped and new ones created for the Leyte operation—and the timetable had to be speeded up by thirty days. MacArthur knew that not only the lives of his men but also his reputation was at stake. After more than two years of trumpeting "I shall return," what if he should fail? The Supreme Commander was grimly determined to succeed, however.

One day, the air chief, George Kenney, called on MacArthur to remind him that the Leyte plan had a serious flaw: Until landing strips could be scraped out or captured from the Japanese, Americans would be fighting five hundred miles beyond fighter cover. In earlier invasions, MacArthur's troops had landed within range of land-based warplanes.

As was his custom while contemplating crucial matters, MacArthur paced the floor of his office. Suddenly, he halted and turned toward Kenney.

"Damn it, George," he exclaimed. "I'm going back there if I have to paddle a canoe with you flying cover for me in your B-17!"[6]

End of discussion.

While the Supreme Commander was laying plans for the Great Return, his headquarters received a lengthy communication from Washington that was turned over to Colonel Sid Mashbir at the ATIS, which also had been involved in psychological and irregular warfare schemes. A chairborne colonel in the Pentagon had gotten the idea that because of their rice diet, all Japanese were color blind. Just why this should be, no one explained.

The brainstormer in the Pentagon wanted Mashbir and his men to examine Japanese prisoners and determine to which color they were blind. Once that color was identified, the theory held, American tanks, planes, and soldiers could be painted that shade and thereby become invisible to the Japanese.

Colonel Mashbir, whose undermanned staff of Nisei was swamped with work, threw up his hands in disgust. Without concerning himself with the niceties of diplomacy, he fired back a letter to the Pentagon. Even if the theory proved to be true, and it was found that the Japanese could not see pink, and if it was decided to send a herd of a thousand pink elephants into Japanese lines to trample them to death, Mashbir wrote that he doubted if there were enough available GIs to paint the animals pink.

No more was heard about the latest pipe dream from Washington.[7]

Rescuing the Philippines' First Family 20

O n October 6, 1944, Imperial General Headquarters in Tokyo received a signal from the Japanese ambassador in Moscow. A high-level official in the Peoples Commissariat for Foreign Affairs had tipped off the emissary that the U.S. air forces in China had been ordered to launch attacks "in the near future" designed to "isolate the Philippines." A few days earlier, Japanese submarines had reported a heavy concentration of American ships at Hollandia. So the intelligence from a supposed ally of the United States—the Soviet Union—was the clinching piece of evidence concerning where MacArthur would strike next.[1]

At his headquarters in Saigon, Field Marshal Hisaichi Terauchi, supreme commander of the Japanese Southern Armies, felt that the American target would be MacArthur's closest island, Mindanao. But he was covering all bets and strengthened forces at locales throughout the Philippines. There were now some three hundred thousand Japanese troops in the chain of islands, nearly all of whom were eager to die for Emperor Hirohito.

Four days after Tokyo received the clandestine warning from Moscow, a Filipino janitor was mopping the lobby in a building along the Pasig River in downtown Manila. While going through his daily chores, the janitor kept a close eye on the goings and comings at the modern office building across the street that served as headquarters of the Japanese Fourteenth Army, the unit charged with defense of the Philippines. This Filipino belonged to the Manila spy network that reported regularly to the AIB in Brisbane.

Now the janitor noticed a staff car pull up in front of the headquarters building and a Japanese general climb out. He was tall, husky, and walked with long strides. Judging from the fawning being made over him by a reception committee of officers, the janitor concluded that a new and very important military figure had arrived.

Indeed, he was important. Investigation by others in the spy network disclosed that he was Lieutenant General Tomoyuki Yamashita, capable, tough, and Dai Nippon's most celebrated folk hero. Yamashita had been rushed to Manila to take command of the Fourteenth Army.

Flamboyant and dynamic, Yamashita was not lacking in confidence. In a press conference with Tokyo reporters a day after his arrival, Yamashita electrified the homefront by declaring that he was going to teach General MacArthur a lesson and dictate surrender terms in the Philippines.

While General Yamashita was preparing to smash Douglas MacArthur's looming onslaught against the Philippines, a special new Psychological Warfare Bureau was ready to bombard the Japanese homefront with radio broadcasts intended to lower morale and energize the population into demanding that the Japanese ruling clique surrender. Head of the bureau was Brigadier General Bonner F. Fellers, the longtime military secretary to MacArthur.

In preparing the broadcasts, Fellers and his staff meshed with Colonel Sid Mashbir, the Japanese expert, and his men at the ATIS. After lengthy discussions, it was decided that the broadcasts beamed to Dai Nippon would tell the unvarnished truth about the progress of the war in the Pacific and also focus on the traditional superstitions of the people.

Mashbir, who had spent many years in Japan prior to the war, stressed that the Japanese were among the most superstitious people on earth. Before a Japanese would build a house, for example, he would consult a soothsayer to learn the most auspicious date on which to begin construction. Mashbir's mind also harkened back to 1937 when he and his wife had invited Prince Iyesato Tokugawa to be their guest at dinner. Before accepting, the prince considered it necessary to consult his own soothsayer to set up the day and precise hour for this social engagement.

After being approved by General MacArthur, the plan for the psychological warfare broadcasts was sent to Washington. The Office of War Information endorsed the plan in its entirety, but the OSS returned the proposal with a large number of criticisms including, "Our experts [in Washington] state that only a few of the older peasants in rural areas have any belief in superstitions."

That remark angered Bonner Fellers, who fired back a reply. "Our experts state that your experts are obviously mere superficial observers."[2]

Sid Mashbir, who would be the narrator on the broadcasts because of his intimate command of the Japanese language, realized that a gimmick would have to be conceived, one that would not only attract listeners in Dai Nippon, but even *compel* them to tune in. Early in the war, Japanese propagandists had hit on a clever scheme that created an enormous listening audience in Australia. During their broadcasts, they would put on the air recordings of the voices and messages of Australian soldiers who were prisoners of war. So many Aussies had been captured in the Allied debacle at Singapore that there was hardly a family Down Under that was not affected. These people glued themselves to radios in the hope of hearing the voice of a loved one.

Now Mashbir and his colleagues came up with a device that would compel the Japanese homefront—and top government and military leaders—to listen to the Allied broadcasts. During each airing, Mashbir would praise one or more Japanese by name for an "act of loyalty"—usually ones who had committed hara-kiri because the war had been lost. At the same time, he would condemn others by name for failure to comply with the warrior's code of Bushido and take their own lives because of their "failures."

The American propagandists were not concerned about whether those named actually had committed hara-kiri. If they had not, it would be up to the target to explain to the homefront why they had not killed themselves in light of their "failures."

Once the Psychological Warfare Bureau began bombarding the Japanese homefront with broadcasts, the gimmick succeeded in attracting huge audiences: The civilians wanted to learn if any friends, relatives, acquaintances, or prominent figures had taken their own lives or shirked their obligation as Bushido warriors.

Mashbir was scrupulously accurate in depicting the course of the war in the Pacific, which clearly was going badly for the emperor's armed forces. At the same time, the colonel weaved in superstitious tales designed to coerce the civilian population into demanding that the nation surrender before it was destroyed. None of this superstitious dialogue was designed to make sense to English-speaking people; it was intended to create unrest among millions of Japanese by using their ingrained beliefs as a target.

Off Hollandia on October 16, Douglas MacArthur led his staff aboard the cruiser *Nashville*, which soon rendezvoused with an American inva-

sion fleet of 738 ships. Destination: The rugged island of Leyte in the
central Philippines, twelve hundred miles to the north.

These were the most poignant days of MacArthur's nearly sixty-five
years of life. Thirty-one months earlier, overwhelming Japanese forces
had inflicted a monumental disaster on his small, starving, inadequately
armed, ill-equipped, and partially trained army in the Philippines. Now
the general was returning with a huge invasion fleet that stretched for a
hundred miles.

As the great armada sailed northward, the general, wearing his
famed gold-braided cap and puffing on his trademark corncob pipe,
strolled the *Nashville*'s decks alone. No doubt his thoughts harkened back
to the early black days of the war when his troops were fighting for their
lives on Bataan and Corregidor.

At dawn on October 20, a mighty roar echoed across placid Leyte Gulf
as hundreds of warship guns began shelling the beaches. The abrasive
rays of the early morning sun cut through the haze and clouds of smoke
that veiled the barely visible shore. On the bridge of the cruiser *Nashville*,
Douglas MacArthur, his face impassive, casually smoked his pipe and
peered through sunglasses at the orange bursts of shellfire exploding in
the thick underbrush on the hills and glistening sands of the landing
beaches.

As was his habit, MacArthur went ashore on the heels of his assault
waves. There large numbers of Japanese snipers, hidden in trees or
crouched in *tako-tsubo* (foxholes), were steadily picking off GIs. A conspicuous figure in his gold-braided cap and khaki uniform, the Supreme
Commander stood on a low knoll and calmly relit his pipe. Waving out
the match, he strolled inland.

That afternoon on the beach, with the crack of Japanese rifles providing background accompaniment, MacArthur stood before a portable
radio microphone to deliver a two-minute address that would carry
throughout the Philippines. A torrential rain erupted. Offshore, the big
navy guns barked. Outwardly a portrait of serenity, the general fought off
the deep emotions that engulfed him as he began to speak.

"People of the Philippines, *I have returned!* Rally around me!"

Standing at the Supreme Commander's side was sixty-six-year-old
Sergio Osmeña, the president of the Philippine Commonwealth. Along
with former president Manuel Quezon, he had escaped from Corregidor
in a submarine at the same time MacArthur departed the Rock in John
Bulkeley's PT-41. Eventually, the two men reached the United States,

where they set up a Philippines government-in-exile. Quezon, who long had been racked by tuberculosis, died at Saranac, New York, on August 1, 1944, and vice president Osmeña became president.

A short time after Quezon's death, Sergio Osmeña called on Franklin Roosevelt at the American president's retreat at Warm Springs, Georgia. Roosevelt asked Osmeña to land with the first troops to return to the Philippines, and the new Commonwealth leader agreed. Roosevelt felt that Osmeña's presence on his home soil would win over any native groups that might tend to be hostile to the American invaders.[3]

With little more than a toehold on Leyte, Douglas MacArthur turned his attention toward officially redeeming his pledge to return to the Philippines. At noon on A-Day plus 2, a ceremony was held in the Commonwealth Building at Tacloban, the town whose citizens and buildings had been spared because of master jungle spy Chick Parsons' audacious reconnoitering a few weeks earlier. Shy, reticent Sergio Osmeña—the Sphinx to his political foes—was duly sworn in as president of the Philippine Commonwealth, and Tacloban was designated as the tentative capital pending the recapture of Manila.

MacArthur and Osmeña spoke over a broadcast network that carried throughout the Philippines, and troopers of the U.S. 1st Cavalry Division hoisted the American and Philippine flags simultaneously on adjoining poles. Then the Supreme Commander and his brass climbed into jeeps and sped off in a swirl of dust. Left behind was a bewildered President Osmeña, who not only lacked a vehicle but didn't know where he would sleep that night.

All through the thirty-one months since Quezon and Osmeña had been forced to flee for their lives from Corregidor, Mrs. Sergio Osmeña and the couple's four children remained at their home in Manila. Unaccountably, the Japanese had not taken them into custody, as had been the fate of other high Philippine officials' loved ones, but the Kempei Tai kept the Osmeña family under close surveillance.

Even after it became known that Sergio Osmeña was the new president of the Commonwealth, his wife and children were not arrested, although Kempei Tai eyes seldom left them. In an effort to escape this endless intense scrutiny, Mrs. Osmeña and her four offspring, together with her son's wife, who was nine months pregnant, moved to Baugio, high in the green mountains of northern Luzon.

Hardly had the Osmeña family reached Baugio than the president's wife learned from secret sources in Manila that the Kempei Tai was about ready to arrest the entire family. This frightening information came virtually on the heels of General MacArthur's invasion of Leyte. No doubt it was clear to the Japanese high command that Leyte would be a MacArthur springboard to leap northward to Luzon, so the Osmeña family was to be taken into custody and held as hostages.

After arriving in Baugio, Mrs. Osmeña learned that an American lieutenant colonel, Russell Volckmann, was a guerrilla chief in northern Luzon, so she sent a trusted agent to seek him out and plead with him to rescue her and her family and stash them away in a reasonably safe mountain hideout. Volckmann, who had escaped after Bataan fell and built up a force of thousands of guerrillas, hesitated. He was haunted by the specter of the fate of the Osmeñas should he try to spirit away the Philippines' first family and fail. He had no intention of being responsible for their deaths. Aware through radio-newscast intercepts from San Francisco, California, that Sergio Osmeña had gone ashore with General MacArthur on Leyte, the guerrilla chief radioed the Supreme Commander's headquarters there to get President Osmeña's view on the proposed "friendly kidnapping."

Word came back that the Osmeña family would be safer if they remained in Baugio. The reply upset the president's wife, who again dispatched her agent to plead with Volckmann to rescue the family. There was no time to be lost, the intermediary stressed. The Osmeñas could be arrested at any moment. This time, the guerrilla leader agreed to the request. Privately, he felt the odds were against success, for Kempei Tai agents in disguise had been tailing family members each time they left home on routine matters.

Russ Volckmann and his key aides began drawing up an action plan for the "friendly kidnapping" of the first family of the Philippines. Nothing Volckmann had learned at West Point prepared him for the unique operation. Timing was delicate: Should the rescue scheme misfire, the Osmeñas, and no doubt numerous guerrillas, could be captured and executed.

Early on the morning of October 30—ten days after MacArthur's invasion of Leyte—the carefully crafted rescue plan began to unfold. The Osmeña clan, seven in all, climbed into a time-worn station wagon in front of their Baugio home. As instructed, they carried no luggage, so as not to arouse suspicions. Outside town, the vehicle took the road that led southward to Manila, where the family was ostensibly going to visit relatives.

Two miles from the city limits, the Osmeñas were confronted by a daunting obstacle: a checkpoint manned by the Japanese-sponsored Philippine Constabulary. Earlier, Volckmann had arranged for the secretly patriotic Filipinos there to record that the Osmeñas had passed through, bound for Manila. That ruse was intended to throw any tailing Kempei Tai off the track.

A short distance past the checkpoint, the driver of the Osmeña vehicle took a sharp turn on a mountain road. Climbing up the narrow, winding route, the escapees spotted a large number of guerrillas half hidden in the thick foliage. Volckmann's men were heavily armed, and their mission was to riddle any Kempei Tai automobile that might be chasing the Osmeñas.

Five more miles along the road, the Osmeñas linked up with Russ Volckmann and a band of his men. The station wagon was pushed off a cliff, and the escapees and their escorts headed across a mountain on a seldom-used trail. Because of her advanced years, Mrs. Osmeña had to be carried on an improvised litter, as did her quite pregnant daughter-in-law.

Once the Philippines' first family was securely ensconced in an isolated camp, word was spread around Baugio that the guerrillas had kidnapped the Osmeñas. This rumor had been instigated by Volckmann's agents in order to avoid Japanese retaliation against other Osmeña relatives or friends.

A month after arriving in the mountain hideaway, the younger Mrs. Osmeña gave birth to Sergio Osmeña III.[4]

Meanwhile, at Tacloban on Leyte, the Japanese made an all-out effort to kill Douglas MacArthur—no doubt in revenge for the ambushing of the Dai Nippon folk hero, Admiral Isoroku Yamamoto, a year and a half earlier. Shortly after landing, MacArthur had established his headquarters in Price House, a two-story stucco mansion in the heart of Tacloban. It was a commodious structure, so large that the Japanese had used it as an officers club, where, according to Taclobans, "a little bit of everything had taken place."

Due to its size and location, Price House stood out like a beacon on a target night, a prime target for the Imperial Air Force.

Within a few days, it became clear to staff officers at Price House that the Japanese had their share of left-behind spies. An announcer over Radio Tokyo declared, "General MacArthur and his staff have established their headquarters in Price House. . . . Our brave pilots will soon take care of the cowardly MacArthur."

Several nervous staff officers suggested that headquarters be moved to another, less conspicuous building. MacArthur scoffed at the proposal.

Soon Price House was pockmarked inside and outside from repeated strafings by Japanese planes. Cannon shells had left yawning holes in the walls. However, they were unable to hit the bull's-eye, although their strenuous efforts had come close. Twelve Filipinos were killed in a building adjacent to Price House, and two civilian correspondents met their deaths in a structure to the other side.

At one point, General MacArthur was working alone at his desk when a flight of Zeros zoomed in at treetop level and riddled the white mansion with bullets. A worried staff officer dashed into the general's office and called out excitedly, "Did they get you?"

Still seated at his desk, MacArthur removed his pipe and replied evenly, "Not this time." Then he pointed to a fresh bullet hole in the wall about a foot above his head.[5]

On a day in late November, two Filipino farmers working in a field in northern Luzon heard the roar of an engine and looked up at a Japanese aircraft approaching from the south. Suddenly, the engine began to cough and sputter, then went dead. Going down in a crazy-quilt spiral, the plane crashed.

Both farmers were agents of Russ Volckmann's guerrilla force, and they rushed word to him at his mountain hideaway, more than thirty miles to the northwest. Volckmann, in turn, arranged for a party of his guerrillas to inspect the airplane wreckage. The passengers were Japanese army officers, all dead.

A large number of documents were salvaged from briefcases belonging to the victims and from elsewhere in the wreckage. These papers were promptly sent to Volckmann for translation and analysis.

Translating Japanese characters into English required a great deal of skill and knowledge of both languages, but Volckmann long had had the services of an elderly Japanese man known only as Mr. Saito. When war had erupted in the Philippines, Mr. Saito, who had lived on Luzon for the past thirty-five years, was taken into custody at Baugio by American soldiers, but after being interrogated for two days because he was Japanese, they released him.

A month later, when the Japanese occupied Baugio, they, too, arrested Mr. Saito, who was suspected of having been friendly to the Americans, a charge leveled by a native collaborator. After six months, the Japanese released Mr. Saito with a stern warning that they intended to keep a sharp eye on him. So the old man went into the nearby mountains to live. There he was taken into custody for the third time by Filipino guerrillas who suspected him of being a spy for the Japanese in Baugio.

Mr. Saito was held for a few weeks and interrogated gently by Colonel Volckmann, who was unable to decide if the elderly civilian was a spy, a double agent, or no spy at all. While in custody, Mr. Saito translated all Japanese documents that fell into the guerrillas' hands. He also became quite adept at extracting intelligence from Japanese prisoners and was cooperative in everything Volckmann asked him to do. So Mr. Saito was released from prisoner status and put on the payroll of Volckmann's force.

Now Mr. Saito was painstakingly examining the documents taken from the Japanese airplane-crash site. After the papers were translated, Volckmann promptly realized that he had an intelligence gold mine in his hands. Among the documents were copious notes that had been taken at a conference with General Tomoyuki Yamashita, Japanese commander in the Philippines, in Manila. Apparently, the officers in the airplane had been flying back to their post at Aparri, on the northern tip of Luzon, when the crash occurred.[6]

The notes seemed to indicate that General Yamashita, an energetic, shrewd officer, had no intention of defending Manila to the last man and the last bullet (as most American military men believed). Rather, Yamashita expected Douglas MacArthur to come ashore at Lingayen Gulf (where the Japanese invaders had landed in December 1941) and drive southward toward Manila. The Japanese general believed that the American invaders would have far superior armored forces, which could only be slowed down, but not halted, on the great plain of Luzon, the conference notes indicated. Therefore, Yamashita was going to pull back his substantial forces in the Manila region and elsewhere on the island to the rugged mountains of northern Luzon, where topographic conditions would favor the Japanese defenders.

This blockbuster information was radioed to MacArthur's headquarters on Leyte, but no reply or acknowledgment was received. Presumably, this overall view of Yamashita's defense plans was utilized in drawing up strategic tactics for the looming Luzon invasion.

Ten days after MacArthur's Great Return, the fight for Leyte had turned into a brutal, bloody slugging match. American foot soldiers were hacking westward in the direction of the key Japanese supply ports, Ormoc and Palompon, on the west coast of the primitive island. Because of the mountains, thickly jungled terrain crisscrossed by steep gorges, there was no continuous front line.

When the Leyte Gulf forces were halfway across the embattled island, General MacArthur was ready to launch another of his dazzling "hit-'em-where-they-ain't" operations. An infantry division would storm ashore three miles south of Ormoc, then drive north and east to link up with the Leyte Gulf invaders pushing westward. MacArthur hoped to catch the formidable Japanese army in a vise between his forces converging from the east and the west.

Just before dawn on December 7, the U.S. 77th Infantry Division charged onto the beach near Ormoc. Armed with detailed intelligence collected by the Scouts, they pushed rapidly ahead and within a few days captured Ormoc and Palompon, thereby denying General Yamashita the ports into which he had been pouring troops and supplies.

Even while the Japanese on Leyte were resisting like cornered beasts, Douglas MacArthur had his eye on Mindoro, the large, wild, mountainous island that was separated from Luzon on the north by seven-mile-wide Verde Island Passage. Mindoro's northern point, Cape Calavite, lay only ninety miles from Manila. N-Day was set for December 15.

Based on radio intercepts and intelligence collected by Alamo Scouts snoopers, MacArthur was banking on the belief that General Yamashita had left Mindoro lightly defended and was concentrating his forces on Luzon for the final showdown in the Philippines. This intelligence proved to be remarkably accurate. On all of Mindoro, there was only a hodgepodge Japanese force of some one thousand men. MacArthur struck with 11,878 U.S. troops, and by N-Day plus 2, the final springboard to Luzon was secure and work began on constructing four airfields.

Nine days later, on December 26, General MacArthur issued an upbeat communique: "The Leyte campaign can now be regarded as closed except for minor mopping up operations." The term "mopping up" infuriated the GIs who had to wield the mop. There were twenty-six thousand Japanese holed up in the wilds of northwestern Leyte, all of whom could be expected to fight until killed.

One of the Supreme Commander's secret weapons, the Magic intercepts, continued to play a crucial role in his operations. Since the American landings on Leyte, the Imperial General Headquarters had been making desperate efforts to reinforce the Philippines, but Magic had been providing U.S. submarines and George Kenney's Fifth Air

Force with precise intelligence on the routes and positions of many convoys. Despite horrendous ship losses, Tokyo apparently still refused to accept the fact that their naval code had been broken.

In early November, the Japanese 23rd Infantry Division, a first-rate veteran outfit, was loaded onto nine transports in Manchuria for a voyage of eighteen hundred miles to the Philippines. Also in the convoy was the escort carrier *Shinyo* loaded with scores of badly needed warplanes. Four antisubmarine frigates served as protection for the flotilla.

Before sailing, the convoy commander radioed Tokyo the precise time of his departure and his course. At almost the same time that the designated recipients were reading the message in Tokyo, U.S. Navy intelligence officers were poring over a decoded version. Consequently, two wolfpacks of American submarines were rushed to a point on the northern end of the East China Sea, where they lay in wait.

On the night of November 17, the wolfpacks pounced on the unsuspecting convoy and a wild battle ensued. Four troop-loaded transports were sunk, and the *Shinyo* was sent to the bottom, together with all of her warplanes. Two weeks later, the surviving transports carrying the remainder of the 23rd Infantry Division limped into Manila Bay, where they were jumped by George Kenney's alerted pilots.[7]

In Manila, two hundred miles north of MacArthur's bridgehead on southern Mindoro, General Tomoyuki Yamashita was fully aware that the climax of the war in the Pacific was at hand—that the Americans were about to strike at Luzon. On December 31, he was being interviewed by a clutch of civilian reporters from Tokyo at his office on the Pasig River. The scribes had been hastily sent in pursuit of favorable war news for homefront consumption. The bullet-headed Yamashita did not disappoint the eager newsmen.

"The loss of one or two islands does not matter," he declared. "There is an extensive area in the Philippines, and we can fight to our heart's content. I shall write a brilliant chapter in history in the Philippines."

Just after New Year's Day 1945, Lieutenant Colonel Russ Volckmann, the guerrilla chief in northern Luzon who had recently observed his thirty-third birthday, received electrifying orders from the AIB. Beginning immediately, the irregulars were to raise merry hell with the Japanese, especially in the region of Lingayen Gulf. Volckmann and his staff were jubilant: Clearly, the Great Return was imminent.

Also dispatched to Volckmann was a shopping list of targets to be demolished: bridges, culverts, defiles, ammunition and fuel dumps, wireless communications, and airplanes hidden at dispersed locations. In addition, the loyal Philippine people in northern Luzon were to be encouraged to get their long-concealed old rifles, bolos, machetes, shotguns, spears, and swords and commit maximum mayhem on the Japanese. Volckmann immediately dispatched orders to subordinate commanders to go into action.

All part-time guerrillas were mobilized within thirty-six hours. This order brought Volckmann's total force to 19,660 officers and men, 6,000 soldiers larger than the standard U.S. infantry division.[8]

On January 7, 1945, Douglas MacArthur was on the cruiser *Boise* heading northward to Lingayen Gulf. Around him was the most powerful land and sea force ever assembled in the Pacific to that time: 1,000 ships, 3,000 landing craft, and 280,000 men. S-Day on Luzon was January 9.

All during the long trek from Leyte Gulf, the invasion convoy was pounced on by the suicide planes known as kamikazes. Several vessels were sunk or badly damaged, and hundreds of Americans were killed or wounded. MacArthur spent much of the time on the *Boise* bridge, puffing serenely on his pipe and squinting into the sky as the Japanese pilots plunged to their deaths on or near the ships.

At 7:00 A.M. on S-Day, an enormous roar swept across Lingayen Gulf as American warships began pounding the beaches. Minutes after the savage bombardment lifted, assault elements rushed onto the shore. Only a few Japanese stragglers were in the region, and they fired random shots before fleeing into the jungle. But all hell broke loose offshore when the feared kamikazes swarmed all over the anchored fleet. Hundreds of American navy men were killed or wounded.

Five hours after the first dogface (as GIs call themselves) set foot on the Lingayen beaches, General MacArthur stepped out of a Higgins boat into knee-deep water and waded ashore. Scores of Filipinos waving small American flags were parading joyously. On spotting the imposing figure with the gold-encrusted cap, corncob pipe, and oversized sunglasses, the natives let out rousing cheers and ran inland to spread the word of the Second Coming.[9]

By nightfall, the invaders had a beachhead eight miles deep in places, and fifty thousand men and their equipment were on Luzon.

Thirty-six hours later, Charles Willoughby, MacArthur's intelligence chief, was conferring with Lieutenant Colonel Russ Volckmann, who had arrived on horseback and brought with him a thick sheaf of detailed sketches of Japanese defenses along and south of Lingayen Gulf. These scaled drawings had been created in recent weeks as the result of countless—and perilous—hours of snooping by bands of guerrillas.

Volckmann also had good news for Sergio Osmeña, the president of the Philippines. His wife, offspring, and infant grandchild had been safely tucked away in a northern Luzon mountain hideout by Volckmann and his men. The Osmeña family sent word that its members were eagerly anticipating an early reunion with the president.

21 Joey's Password Was Courage

Douglas MacArthur's trousers had hardly dried from his wade through Lingayen Gulf at H-Hour plus 5 than he collared his Sixth Army commander, Walter Krueger.

"Get to Manila!" the Supreme Commander ordered. "Go around the Japs, bounce off the Japs, save your men, but get to Manila!"[1]

Krueger, a courageous yet methodical man, was haunted by the specter of two hundred thousand die-hard Japanese soldiers cutting off his flying columns and chewing them up piece by piece. He proposed spending at least two weeks consolidating his gains before advancing behind massive artillery barrages to the capital, which he presumed would be heavily defended. There was a prolonged dispute, but MacArthur, who had recently been promoted to five-star general, did not pull rank on the four-star Krueger. Rather, MacArthur utilized a subtle approach to spur on his field commander—he moved his headquarters forty miles ahead of Krueger's command post.

For days, Krueger's spearheads snaked southward fitfully down a handful of dirt roads and jungle paths, hemmed in on both sides by thick jungles. The wily Japanese melted away. "Our 'front' is thirty miles wide and thirty miles long!" was the standard GI joke.

Soon, Manila was almost in range of MacArthur's binoculars, but the steady advance ground to a halt near Clark Field, fifty miles northwest of the capital, when the Americans ran into a heavily fortified complex that included thirty caves. A vicious fight erupted as teams of flamethrowers began digging out the tenacious Japanese.

Meanwhile, inside Manila, leaders in the Filipino espionage network had become deeply worried. Earlier they had sent American intelligence a detailed map disclosing that a long section on the main road to the capital was free of mines. But now they discovered that the Japanese had heavily mined this region, so it would be crucial to get to the Americans a revised map showing where these dangerous areas were located. Failure to do so could result in many of MacArthur's soldiers losing their lives in the minefield.

Now a desperate question faced the Manila spy-network leaders: How would they slip this revised map through Japanese lines? Wary of having Filipino guerrillas in their rear areas, the Japanese had roadblocks every mile or so north of Manila toward the battlefront. No non-Japanese vehicles were allowed to pass. Neither were Filipino men. However, a small, shabbily dressed woman might be able to sneak through hostile territory with the crucial revised map.

Volunteering for the perilous task was slight, sickly Josefina Guer-rero, a young Filipina mother who had long been one of the spy network's most daring and successful agents. On many occasions, Joey, as she was known to friends, had smuggled documents through Japanese road-blocks. Although she was halted countless times, the sentries had seen her bloated, scarred face and recoiled in terror. To other Japanese guards, Joey had uttered one word to send them scurrying away—leprosy.[2]

Both of Joey's parents had died when she was a young girl, and her grandmother reared her. Years later, while living in Manila, she married a young physician, Dr. Renato Maria Guerrero, and the couple had a daughter, Cynthia. When the girl was two years of age in the fall of 1941, doctors diagnosed her mother as having leprosy. Since children were thought to be susceptible to the disease, Joey, tearfully, packed off Cyn-thia to live with her grandmother.

Medical specialists told the Guerreros that the disease was now recognized as being minutely contagious among adults, so Joey was no menace to others. They told her that the medical care she needed was in the United States, but the young woman knew that it would be far beyond her financial capacity to go there for a prolonged period.

A few months later in early 1942, before Joey's face became bloated, Japanese soldiers were strutting around the streets of Manila. One day, five of them halted Joey and made known their amorous intentions. Without a word, the five-foot, ninety-eight-pound woman walloped the largest Japanese several times with her rolled-up umbrella, then she fled.

That night, Joey got a telephone call from a woman friend who had by happenstance witnessed her attack on the five Sons of Heaven (as the Japanese soldiers called themselves). In response, Joey went to the friend's house where the other's husband invited Joey to join the guerril-las. She protested that she was feeble and had to rest frequently.

"That's okay," replied the man. "Every little bit helps. We'll find just the right role for you."[3]

Joey signed an oath of loyalty and secrecy, expecting to be an undercover agent for the guerrillas for only a few weeks, perhaps a few months.

Her first job was to keep an eye on the bustling Manila waterfront, which was teeming with Japanese ships, many of them bringing troops and the accoutrements of war for the Rising Sun's relentless surge through the southwest Pacific. While making certain that she was not being tailed, Joey took notes about the size, shape, and apparent cargo of the vessels coming in and out of the harbor. When a day's work was completed, she concealed her notes beneath fruit in a basket she carried.

On one occasion, two armed Japanese soldiers approached the woman spy and, not noticing her now puffed face, began pawing the fruit. Joey's heart was pounding furiously. Palms perspired. Stomach knotted. Then the soldiers selected one fruit each and walked away. The espionage notes that would have doomed Joey to a hideous death remained intact.

There were other close calls in the weeks ahead. Once a Japanese soldier halted her, threatened to plunge his bayonet into her, then allowed her to proceed. As she walked away, he gave her braided black hair a tug. Fortunately for Joey, her hair ribbon was tied too tightly to come off. Inside the narrow piece of cloth an intelligence report was concealed.

Joey, a portrait of confidence and courage, had one close brush with detection after another. Then, in mid-September 1944, American carrier-borne fighter planes began pounding Manila and its environs. Clearly, General MacArthur would be back soon. Now Joey received a terse telephone call from a man who identified himself as Manuel Colayco, who had been a professor at Santo Tomás University in Manila. Could Joey meet him—secretly? She was extremely leery; the Japanese had stool pigeons everywhere. This man could be one of them. Finally, she agreed to meet him at a certain remote locale one night. Unbeknownst to Professor Colayco, Joey's guerrilla friends already had hidden in the vegetation around the designated site. One false move and the man who called himself Colayco would be a goner.

As soon as Joey arrived, the man brought out valid credentials that revealed that he was actually Manuel Colayco, that he indeed had taught at Santo Tomás, and that he was now a captain in the AIB. Then he asked her if she would become an agent for the AIB, even though it might mean sacrificing her life. Joey gave off with a slight chuckle. She had been risking her life daily for more than three nerve-racking years.

Colayco, it soon became obvious, had carefully researched Joey before inviting her to the rendezvous. He knew that she was afflicted with leprosy. But what better cover? If she were to be approached by the Japanese for interrogation, she could rapidly convince them that she had leprosy by revealing the ugly sores on her breasts.

Luzon was electric with tension and anxiety after MacArthur landed at Leyte, only four hundred miles to the south. Meanwhile, Joey constantly penetrated Japanese roadblocks and guard posts north of Manila to carry intelligence reports, photographs of Japanese installations, and detailed maps to guerrilla hideouts. Her returns to Manila were not wasted. Guerrilla printers in the hills produced handbills that said in large type, "Liberation is near!" That scheme was intended to afflict the Japanese with nervous tics and to give heart to the Filipinos. In Manila, Joey and a number of volunteers flitted through the night at great personal peril, for they were out after curfew, to widely distribute the printed message.

By now, Joey's lingering illness was taking an even greater toll. Steadily, she grew weaker. Painful headaches were constant companions. Her feet swelled. The sores on her body got redder. She prayed to God that the Americans would reach Manila before she died.

Then came the electrifying news: MacArthur had landed at Lingayen Gulf, and his spearheads were heading southward in the direction of Manila. Now her AIB controller, Captain Manuel Colayco, asked Joey to go on her most hazardous task of them all: infiltrating Japanese lines to the north and delivering the crucial revised map to the U.S. 37th Infantry Division headquarters at Calumpit, forty miles north of Manila.[4]

Feeble as she was, Joey began walking, convinced that this would be her final secret mission. If health problems did not overtake her, the alert Japanese sentries no doubt would do so. On her back was a bulging knapsack under which was taped to her flesh the map of Japanese defenses north of Manila. This map accurately depicted minefields and strongpoints.

Joey had been on the road only about three hours when a Japanese officer approached as if to search her. Taped between her shoulder blades, the telltale map seemed to burn into her skin.

"Lepor! Lepor!" Joey called out. The enemy officer shrank back and waved the courier on.

After two days and nights of walking, Joey, nearly exhausted and suffering intensely from severe headaches and swollen feet, reached the 37th Infantry Division intelligence section at Calumpit and turned over the map. She was aware that the American officers were gawking at her puffed face and the sores that covered much of her body.

Josefina Guerrero's war was over. A short time later, she became a patient at the Philippine government's leprosarium, a collection of leaking shacks in a thick wilderness. Food was scarce. Bedclothes were soiled. Medical care was virtually nonexistent. Racked with pain, her weight far below its normal ninety-eight pounds, Joey was determined to survive. She had proven countless times that she was a survivor.[5]

While Walter Krueger's dogfaces were digging die-hard Japanese out of the caves around Clark Field, Douglas MacArthur felt victory was imminent. Like a champion boxer, the Supreme Commander was feinting, then landing quick, telling blows, dazzling a worthy opponent (General Yamashita) with his footwork. At his new headquarters in Baguio in northern Luzon, Yamashita was desperately shifting troops about in an effort to parry MacArthur's jabs.

All the while, the American general's sights were on python-infested Bataan. There, in the locale of the United States' most humiliating military disaster, the Japanese might make a "historically repetitive stand," in the words of intelligence chief Charles Willoughby. At dawn on January 29, an American naval armada was lying to off the western coast of Luzon near the small town of San Antonio, twenty-five miles north of Bataan. On board were forty thousand GI soldiers.

Just before the warships were ready to bombard the beaches, a "hold your fire!" order rang out. Several small boats, loaded with grinning Filipino guerrillas, were sailing out to greet the invaders. They had been sent by Lieutenant Colonel Gyles Merrill, an American whose large guerrilla force operated in Bataan and Zambales Provinces, to report that there were no Japanese in the region.

Major General Charles "Chink" Hall, who was to command the assault, called off the bombardment and sent his troops ashore at once. The invaders were welcomed by scores of wildly cheering Filipinos. Only one casualty was sustained in the assault: A GI was gored in the posterior by an ill-tempered carabao.

Hall ordered a regiment to rush inland to seize the San Marcelino airstrip, but upon arrival the Americans found that guerrillas led by Filipino Captain Raymond Magsaysay had secured it three days earlier. Shaking hands with the beaming Magsaysay, the dogfaces had no way of knowing that they were being greeted by a future president of the Republic of the Philippines.

In seven days, Hall's men overran Bataan, slamming the door on any possibility that Yamashita could send in troops for a "historically repetitive stand."

While the Americans were drawing a noose around Manila, General Yamashita, at his new command post at Baguio, declared Manila an "open city," the traditional notice to an enemy that there would be no resistance.

"I do not intend to preside over the destruction of Manila," he told his staff. At the same time, he pulled his troops back from the Manila region toward the rugged mountains around Baguio, where, Yamashita was convinced, he could hold out for months—maybe years.

But hard on the departing Yamashita's heels, fanatical Rear Admiral Sanji Iwabuchi rushed into Manila with his seventeen thousand naval combat troops and ordered them to "defend the city to the last stone, to the last bullet, to the death!" Along with four thousand army troops still in the Manila Bay region, Iwabuchi's men blew up the entire port, transportation facilities, the water supply system, and electric power plants.

Near dusk on February 3, patrols of the U.S. 1st Cavalry Division in the north and the U.S. 11th Airborne Division in the south crossed the Manila city limits. Three days later, a MacArthur communiqué declared, "Our forces are rapidly clearing the enemy from Manila. Our converging columns entered the city and surrounded the Jap defenders. Their complete destruction is imminent."[6]

Newsweek's cover story on February 12 read, "Prize of the Pacific War: Manila Fell to MacArthur Like a Ripened Plum." Congratulations poured in on the Supreme Commander from Franklin Roosevelt, Winston Churchill, Chiang Kai-shek, John Curtin, and other world leaders.

Far from being a fallen plum, Manila became one of the great slaughterhouses of the global war. Of the major cities, only Warsaw suffered more devastating destruction. For four weeks, the GIs battled the tenacious enemy sailors house to house and closet to closet. Barbaric atrocities reminiscent of the bloody era of Ghengis Kahn, the Mongolian warlord, were inflicted by the Japanese on the helpless population. During the vicious struggle, the Japanese murdered an estimated one hundred thousand Manila civilians. Hospitals were set on fire after patients were strapped to beds. Females of all ages were brutally raped before being slain. Babies were torn from the arms of hysterical mothers and skewered with bayonets.[7]

In an isolated area of Manila, GIs discovered an unmarked mass grave covered with fresh dirt. A U.S. graves-registration unit was brought in and unearthed twenty-one corpses—all but one of them, it would be learned, were longtime members of the Manila spy network. They included four German priests, two Filipina nuns, and fourteen other men. The victims' arms had been tied behind them, and each had been shot in the head. There was evidence that some of them had been buried while still alive. Apparently those in the communal grave had been under surveillance by the Kempei Tai and were rounded up even as MacArthur's fighting men were closing in on Manila's outskirts.

The Wild Men 22
of Borneo

E arly on the morning of March 2, 1945, Douglas MacArthur and the Bataan Gang climbed into four PT boats moored outside Manila. It had been thirty-six months since the general, who represented America's prestige in the Far East, had slipped out of Corregidor on the first leg of his spectacular escape to Australia. Now he was going to cross Manila Bay to the Rock, the hallowed fortress where he had said long before that the United States flag had been "ground in the dust" by the conquering Japanese.

It had been only hours since the U.S. 503rd Parachute Infantry Regiment and a battalion of the U.S. 24th Infantry Division had completed a ten-day task of wiping out the entire six-thousand-man force defending Corregidor. Since there were still enemy snipers holed up in the maze of underground caves and tunnels, MacArthur was urged to postpone his nostalgic visit. He refused.[1]

MacArthur was in a jovial mood. He turned to the young skipper, Lieutenant Joseph Roberts, and remarked, "So this is PT 373. I left [Corregidor] on Johnny Bulkeley's PT 41."[2]

At 10:00 A.M, the four boats edged up to the North Dock, the same place from which MacArthur left three years earlier. With an agility belying his sixty-five years, he scrambled onto the rickety wharf and stood with hands on hips, gazing around at the shell-and-bomb-battered fortress. It was a highly emotional moment for the Supreme Commander.

Hopping into a jeep driven by paratroop Corporal Sims H. Smith, MacArthur went first to Malinta Tunnel, his headquarters during the agony at Bataan. He promptly walked into the entrance, where Japanese corpses were strewn about. These were anxious moments for Colonel George M. Jones, the thirty-four-year-old commander of the parachute regiment, who could not be certain that there were no live Japanese still inside.[3]

MacArthur's jeep cavalcade then rolled on around the battered island where the savage fighting had raged a short time earlier, and eventually it reached the parade ground on Topside, the Rock's highest elevation. Alighting from his vehicle, MacArthur walked briskly to where Colonel Jones stood at the head of a battle-weary honor guard in their soiled and torn uniforms. Some wore bandages.

West Pointer Jones saluted and said, "Sir, I present you Fortress Corregidor!"[4]

The day after Douglas MacArthur's emotion-charged triumphant return to Corregidor, Manila fell. Once a magnificent city, the Pearl of the Orient was now a blackened, twisted skeleton. Hardly had the smoke cleared over the capital than MacArthur launched invasions of seven Philippine islands south of Luzon: Cebu, Guimaras, Negros, Palawan, Panay, Tawitawi, and Zamboanga.

Then the Supreme Commander set his sights on Borneo, the big, wild island three hundred miles southwest of Mindanao. There he planned to build airfields to support future jumps into Malaya and Sumatra, west of Borneo. Assigned the task of digging the Japanese out of Borneo were the veteran Australian 7th and 9th Divisions.

The Aussies first chose to infiltrate secret agents onto the island to gather current intelligence and to try to locate Allied prisoners of war and civilian internees. Directing the mission would be Australia's SRD. Major Tom Harrison, who once had spent time in northern Borneo with an Oxford University expedition in anthropology, was selected to lead the special team of seven experts in unconventional warfare.

Original plans called for landing the team (code-named Semut) at night by submarine, but thirty-three-year-old Major Harrison convinced the SRD chiefs that he and his men should be parachuted into the mountainous interior of Sarawak, in northern Borneo, the former bailiwick of Charles Vyner Brooks, the "white raja" who had helped the AIB infiltrate green-turbaned hajji spies into Borneo two years earlier.

Based on intelligence sent to Brisbane from the hajjis, Harrison was reasonably certain that he would be able to recruit the fierce tribesmen in Sarawak to work against the Japanese and to help the secret agents prepare for the amphibious invasion. So on March 25, Harrison and his seven men parachuted from a U.S. B-24 bomber over the unmapped uplands of Sarawak.

By an incredible stroke of luck, Harrison happened to land less than a mile from the village of the Kelabit tribe, a warlike people who hated the Japanese. The Kelabit chief was Lawai Bisarai, who could speak

Malay, the language of the Borneo coast and most of the Dutch East Indies. Chief Bisarai welcomed Harrison, his second in command, Captain Eric Edmeades, and the other six undercover agents.

Blond, sturdily structured Edmeades was an especially resolute warrior. A New Zealander, he had been an instructor in the Australian Parachute School and was said to have made more jumps than anyone else in the country. Edmeades, his mates declared, was not wed to ideas, principles, or philosophies. He took risks just for the hell of it.

Because of the Semut team's miraculous descent from the sky, its assortment of weapons and gold sovereigns—which the Kelabits coveted as tooth replacements rather than money—Tom Harrison was proclaimed as the Raja from Above by the natives. That night, all five hundred members of the local tribe crowded into the village longhouse—the communal building in which all of them lived—for an all-night ceremonial drinking session. The fare was *borak*, a potent local beverage made from fermented rice.

News of the Semut team's arrival from "out of the sky" rapidly passed by word of mouth from tribe to tribe all the way to the northern coast. Barefoot emissaries from many tribes in Sarawak soon arrived, pledged their loyalty to Harrison and his men, and pleaded to be given something to do against the despised Japanese. The Raja from Above quickly put each tribe to work collecting intelligence and wreaking havoc on Japanese outposts and patrols. Within four weeks, Harrison estimated that perhaps as many as fifty thousand tribesmen had become involved in carrying out their missions in northern Borneo.

Meanwhile, Harrison took out across the rugged mountains on a high-priority assignment—reconnoitering Brunei Bay on the northwest coast of the island. That locale was tentatively to be the landing beach of the Australian infantry when the invasion began.

Reports of success radioed back to Australia resulted in two more Semut teams being parachuted into Sarawak. Leading Semut II was Major Tony Carter, a New Zealander who, like Harrison, had a firsthand knowledge of the island. Carter had been an oil company surveyor there before the war and spoke several dialects. In a relatively short period of time, he had organized the tough Kenyah tribe to gain information and wreak havoc on the Japanese.

Major William Sochon was an unlikely figure to head Semut III. Middle-aged and obese, he nevertheless survived the brutal crunch with the ground at the tag end of his parachute jump. He also knew Sarawak well, for he once had been a police officer there. In short order, Sochon was leading a large band of Dayaks, a tribe so untamed and fierce that they gave rise to the term "wild men of Borneo."

As each newcomer parachuted into Sarawak, he was immediately enrolled in the "Tom Harrison Graduate Course," a sort of on-the-job training program. The new Semut man would be assigned some twenty-five tribesmen, most armed with spears and nasty-looking knives, and sent into the mountains to meander around for four weeks and perpetrate mischief against the Japanese should the opportunities arise. When he returned, Major Harrison would reward him with a handshake and dispatch him some distance away to take command of a region perhaps twelve miles by twelve miles square.

All the while, more Semut teams bailed out over northern Borneo, and an intelligence, sabotage, and subversion network was established that stretched for several hundred miles in all directions.

More local recruits steadily drifted into Harrison's camp. A Chinese physician joined up, bringing his wife and thirteen children with him. The family organized and operated a hospital. When medicine and bandages were urgently needed, a team of tribesmen was sent out to raid a Japanese post and bring back the medical supplies. Harrison and his Semut leaders never inquired as to the fate of the enemy soldiers stationed at the post.

In the meantime, Allied airmen who were forced to bail out over the jungle or in water just offshore were gathered in by the major and his warriors. A few bailed-out fliers had survived in the bush for weeks—eating roots, bugs, and mice—prior to being rescued. At one time, there were thirteen American airmen being nurtured back to health at the Chinese doctor's makeshift hospital.

As a security measure, Major Harrison eventually moved his jungle headquarters farther inland to Bawanga territory, where he and other Semut agents were warmly received. In April, Harrison put the Bawangas to work clearing brush for an airstrip two hundred miles from the coast. The field could provide an emergency landing site for Allied bombers. The going was painfully slow, despite the unceasing efforts of the Bawangas. They ripped out sturdy brush with their hands, poked at the ground with sticks, and trampled clods of mud with their bare feet.

To speed up the airstrip work—the Borneo invasion was scheduled to hit in a month—Harrison radioed for a parachute drop of tools. Two days later, two U.S. planes flew over the Bawanga village and dropped shovels, rakes, hoes, axes, spades, and mattocks. The airdrop scared the hell out of the Bawangas, and they refused to have anything to do with the modern tools. Instead, they went right on working with their primitive means and cleared the strip in time.

Amazingly, the three thousand Japanese in northern Borneo apparently had no inkling that an energetic Aussie named Tom Harrison was operating a large secret army of spies and killers right in their midst. However, the Semut leaders learned, Japanese officers had noticed that the flow into their posts of tobacco, salt, rice, and natives looking for work had virtually dried up. A native or two would drift into Japanese camps, ostensibly looking for paid labor, but these were Semut spies.

When the Japanese finally did sniff out the fact that something was out of kilter, they called in their longtime native procurement man, a Dayak tribesman named Bigar anak Debois, and demanded to know why the customary food and other supplies from the interior were not arriving as they had been during three years of occupation. What the Japanese did not know was that Debois had become a Semut spy. A cool operator, Debois lied that the supplies had been held up by important tribal ceremonies, floods, droughts, and plagues of rats. The Japanese seemed to buy that explanation, especially since it came from a collaborator as trustworthy as Bigar anak Debois.[5]

Early in May, a month before the Borneo invasion, Australian commanders (and the government in Canberra) voiced protests over the role assigned to the Aussie infantry. With the Allied momentum heading toward Japan, clearing the Japanese out of Borneo would be a bloody—and useless—affair, they declared. However, MacArthur pointed out that to cancel the invasion would upset his strategic plan and timetable for driving the Japanese out of the southwest Pacific.

On June 10, the Australian 9th Division stormed ashore on Labuan island, just off Borneo, and in Brunei Bay in Sarawak. Typically, the Supreme Commander "hit-'em-where-they-ain't," cutting off the Japanese in Borneo from their supplies and leaving them grouped in isolated cul-de-sacs.

In the Brunei region, the three thousand Japanese troops were under heavy naval bombardment and in danger of being isolated, so they pulled back several miles into the jungle to their rear area administrative installation. However, Major Tom Harrison, several of his Semut officers, and a large band of ferocious "wild men of Borneo" had gotten there first. When the Japanese infantrymen arrived, the rear facility, once a model of efficiency, was in shambles. Huts and buildings were wrecked or burned. Radio operators, supply sergeants, mechanics, clerks, and district government officers lay dead in their offices, outside their huts, or around the edges of the surrounding jungle. They had been shot, speared, knifed, or strangled by the Semut men and their native comrades.

Meanwhile, Douglas MacArthur went ashore at Brunei Bay just after the assault waves. While he strolled along a dirt road paralleling the beach, the sounds of rifle shots and machine-gun fire from both sides echoed stridently across the landscape. Inland a quarter of a mile, the general heard a burst of fire fifty yards to his front and walked forward to "see what's going on."

A pair of Aussies were hovering over two dead Japanese sprawled in a ditch. Suddenly, an Australian army combat photographer charged up, hoping to snap a picture of MacArthur and the enemy corpses. The general refused, so the photographer lifted his camera to take a picture of the two dead Japanese when a bullet intended for MacArthur plowed into the cameraman's shoulder.

Three weeks later at Balikpapen on the southeastern coast, MacArthur again landed shortly after the first waves and scrambled onto a low knoll less than two hundred yards from the Japanese. While the general stood upright and pored over a map, an Aussie major rushed up and told MacArthur and his entourage of brass to take cover, that there was a machine gun on a nearby hill. Moments later, there was an angry chatter from the automatic weapon and a stream of bullets whizzed past. Within a split second, the other generals and admirals (along with Lee Van Atta, a reporter for the International News Service) performed belly flops. Sheepishly, they glimpsed up to see MacArthur still upright and calmly inspecting the map.[6]

The Aussie diggers were startled to see the five-star Supreme Commander on the front line. One Aussie looked up, saw MacArthur, and called out to comrades, "Christ, it's the Messiah!"[7]

Japanese units that fled helter-skelter inland were repeatedly assaulted and hounded by Major Tom Harrison and his secret army of wild men of Borneo. For many weeks, the scattered bands of Japanese stumbled around in the trackless jungle. Many of them—starving, exhausted, demoralized, and terrorized by unseen pursuers—hanged themselves by belts from sturdy tree branches.[8]

In the meantime, hundreds of miles to the north, bitter fighting was raging on Luzon where General Tomoyuki Yamashita was trying desperately to hold back the American tidal wave.

A Close Call for **23**
Operation Giraffe

When General Tomoyuki Yamashita had fled Manila after the Lingayen Gulf landings, he brought with him to Baguio the head of the Philippine puppet government, José Laurel, along with cabinet ministers and other top officials. Two months later, when American forces began slugging their way through the green mountains of northern Luzon, Yamashita had Laurel and most of his key aides flown to Tokyo. Finding an excuse to remain in Baguio was Manuel Roxas, the masterspy who had refused to flee from Corregidor in early 1942, because MacArthur had asked him to stay behind and report on the activities and plans of the Japanese landlords.

Now, in mid-April 1945, elements of the U.S. 33rd Infantry Division were a short distance outside Baguio and preparing to launch an all-out attack on the peacetime summer resort. Manuel Roxas, three cabinet ministers, and the chief justice of the puppet Philippine Supreme Court stole out of Baguio under the cover of night and made contact with American troops.

When MacArthur was flashed word about Roxas, he promptly dispatched an airplane to bring the masterspy to Manila. There the Supreme Commander threw an arm around the Filipino's shoulders and greeted him warmly. MacArthur put his old friend back into uniform as a brigadier general in the Philippine Army and later awarded him the Distinguished Service Cross, America's second-highest decoration for valor.

While the red carpet was rolled out for Manuel Roxas, the four puppet government officials who had sneaked out of Baguio with him fared far worse—MacArthur had them thrown in jail. Then the Supreme Commander instructed the editors of the *Free Philippines*, a newspaper published in Manila by the U.S. Office of War Information, to print an article under the blaring headline:

ROXAS IS AMONG LIBERATED
4 CABINET AIDES CAUGHT

The article said that "four members of the Philippine collaborationist cabinet have been captured. They will be confined for the duration of the war as a matter of military security and then turned over to the government of the Philippines for trial and judgment."[1]

MacArthur, it was clear, was bent on making certain that any collaborationist stigma did not cling to Manuel Roxas, who had risked his life daily in order to provide the Supreme Commander with a direct pipeline into the highest councils of the Japanese regime in the Philippines.

Later, the Manila *Daily News*, which was owned by the Roxas family, resumed publication. Almost each day, it ran stories elaborating on the Supreme Commander's exoneration of him, although it would not be known for years the key undercover role that Manuel Roxas had played.[2]

Among those who had traveled northward from Manila with General Yamashita's headquarters was the American spy Richard Sakakida, who was now in the intelligence branch. At about the same time that Manuel Roxas had slipped away, Sakakida noticed that hostility among the Japanese staff toward him was growing more intense. So early in June, he stole away in the night and linked up with Filipino guerrillas in the nearby mountains.

A week later, it appeared that the Nisei's luck finally had run out. Japanese troops attacked the guerrilla band, and Sakakida was wounded by a shell burst and left alone as the others scattered. Fortunately for him, the Japanese withdrew before he was discovered. But within days, he was confronted by an implacable new enemy: malaria, dysentery, and beri-beri.

Although racked by pain, physically weak, nearly starving, and thought processes cloudy, Sakakida for many days struggled up one mountain and down another, always through thick forests and rugged terrain, hoping he was heading toward American lines to the south. Suddenly, he tensed and took cover in some brush. Walking toward him were eight armed soldiers. No doubt it was a Japanese patrol searching for him, he concluded. Then he heard the oncoming soldiers speaking English, and he noticed that they were not wearing Japanese uniforms.

Leaving his place of concealment, the emaciated Nisei, clad in his Japanese uniform, staggered toward the American soldiers, and called out in English. Rifles were aimed at him: Was this the common Japanese trick of yelling something in English so the Americans would let down their guard while the enemy soldier's comrades opened fire from the brush?

Sakakida explained that he was a sergeant in the U.S. Army and had been captured at Corregidor. The Americans didn't believe him; why was he wearing a Japanese uniform? Within hours, Sakakida was escorted to a U.S. command post where a radio inquiry was made to a Counter-intelligence Corps (CIC) office. Two CIC lieutenants hurried to the site and vouched for the suspect. Sergeant Richard Sakikida's four-year undercover war was over.

At the same time heavy fighting was going on in the Philippines, a secret little war-within-a-war was raging around the islands of Morotai and Halmahera, a few hundred miles to the south. When MacArthur had seized virtually undefended Morotai as a springboard to Leyte, he had purposely avoided assaulting Halmahera, which was separated from Morotai by twelve miles of water. There were 37,000 Japanese combat troops on Halmahera, and MacArthur left them to wither on the vine, powerless to contribute to the war effort. From their base on nearby Morotai, PT boats constantly harassed the enemy garrison on Halmahera, shooting up shore installations, sinking barges trying to sneak food and supplies, and keeping the large enemy force penned up on the island.[3]

Morotai was also an advance base for the AIB. Early in April, the AIB laid on Operation Giraffe, a secret mission to Tahoelandang, a small island in the large Sangir chain, located in the Celebes Sea west of Morotai. Giraffe would have a unique twist: Instead of the raiders going ashore from a PT boat, they would land nearby in a Catalina flying boat.

It was important to MacArthur's forces that Tahoelandang remain friendly because of its strategic perch right on the north-south shipping lanes between Japan and the Dutch East Indies. The native raja of Tahoelandang had been pro-Allies, but rumors had reached the AIB that indicated he was in ill health and his administration had been seized by an aide whose name was Manoppo. It was not known where Manoppo's loyalties, if any, lay.

While on Tahoelandang, the Giraffe party was to reconnoiter the island as a possible future Allied base and to gain intelligence from the

Sangirese natives and a few Europeans who had lived there for many years. The raiders were also to blow up an American bomber that had crashed on the beach to prevent the Japanese from retrieving secret instruments from the wreckage.

Shortly after Giraffe was conceived, R. K. Hardwick, a sixty-six-year-old British civilian, arrived at Morotai from AIB headquarters in Melbourne. On learning of the Giraffe mission, he began pestering British Major A. E. B. Trappes-Lomax, the leader of the party, to take him along. Wary about the older man playing a young man's game, Trappes-Lomax balked. But Hardwick finally convinced the major and AIB officers that his vast and intimate knowledge of the targeted region and its people would be of immense value.

In his youth, Hardwick had left England and moved to Borneo, "went native," and, clad only in a loincloth, roamed the big island and adjacent ones for four decades. During that time, he picked up most of the scores of dialects spoken in that part of the Pacific and became an expert in jungle survival. Proficient in the use of crude native weapons, the Brit had killed his own game food with blowpipes.

A year after war broke out in the Pacific, Hardwick learned about the AIB and, using a wide array of transportation modes, he reached Melbourne and offered his services to the cloak-and-dagger agency. Over the decades, Hardwick had been toasted a deep mahogany by the scorching tropical sun, so when he first entered the headquarters the AIB officers thought he was a native of the southwest Pacific.

Impressed by his resourcefulness and knowledge of his region of the southwest Pacific, the AIB accepted him into its ranks. In deference to his years, however, the bureau officials shunted him to a back room in Melbourne. There he fretted and fumed as he went about his desk-bound job—compiling extensive data on the remote regions that he knew so well.

At night over a few glasses of beer with AIB comrades, Hardwick ranted about his status and called himself a "Melbourne Commando." Ceaselessly, he plotted to change his sedentary role in the war. Perhaps because he had become a royal pain in the neck to authorities in Melbourne, Hardwick found himself bound for the AIB's base on Morotai early in 1945.

"I got transferred here because of illness," the delighted Hardwick quipped to his new Morotai comrades. "My officers in Melbourne got sick of me!"[4]

Giraffe could be perilous: No one knew if Japanese troops occupied Tahoelandang. It was known, however, that enemy units paid regular visits to the island. Rumors were that the raja was still loyal to the Allies but that some sort of skullduggery was taking place in his administration.

After a routine flight of two and a half hours, the Catalina carrying Major Trappes-Lomax, Hardwick, and the rest of the Giraffe party splashed down on a calm sea not far from the wreckage of the American bomber. From the air, a large number of natives had been seen gathering along the shoreline, but when the raiders began paddling dinghies to the island, the locals vanished into the jungle. Had they gone to notify the Japanese on the island? Or had they left to arm themselves to attack the intruders?

"Don't worry," the grizzled R. K. Hardwick reassured his comrades. "They're scared as hell. They'll come out soon—just don't force the matter!"[5]

Major Trappes-Lomax sent three demolition men to blow up the crashed bomber. Then he ordered three others with submachine guns and a radio to remain on the beach. In the event of big trouble, they were to radio Morotai for Royal Australian Air Force planes to dash to the rescue.

Pushing inland through the thick jungle for a half mile, the party came upon the raja's palace, which was empty. That was disturbing news. Where had he and his entourage gone? Inside, Hardwick found a note that had been written by the raja's assistant, Manoppo. Apparently, he had fled on the approach of the Giraffe party and had forgotten about the note.

Hardwick told Trappes-Lomax that the note was addressed to the Japanese commander on Siaoe, an island thirty miles away. It appealed for a force to be sent to wipe out the Tahoelandang "invaders." Now there was no doubt about Manoppo's allegiance. If the man were still on the island, Major Trappes-Lomax hoped to dig him out before he could dispatch a messenger with another note to the Japanese on Siaoe.

While the AIB party was scouring the island for Manoppo, Hardwick, using local dialect, talked with natives and confirmed the suspicions of the raiders. Not only was Manoppo pro-Japanese, but he had ruled Tahoelandang brutally, causing the natives to live in constant fear.

Hardwick returned to the shore near the bomber that had been blown to smithereens. An hour later, he saw a prahu skid onto the beach and four natives leaped out. They rushed up to the Brit and, panting for breath, said that two large vessels were being prepared at Siaoe, the island thirty miles distant. Standing by to board were some two hundred Japanese soldiers. Clearly, the Japanese were launching an expedition to Tahoelandang, so the treacherous Manoppo must have gotten a message through.

With Major Trappes-Lomax and his men roaming the island, Hardwick decided to take direct action himself. He ordered the radio man on the beach to break silence and request the Catalina to return immediately and fighter planes to take off from Morotai and attack the Japanese troop-laden vessels while they were sailing to Tahoelandang.

A short time later, Trappes-Lomax and his raiders returned to the beach. All eyes were on the sea horizon. It was not known if Hardwick's message had even reached Morotai. A storm had been raging over the Celebes Sea and the static had been so intense that the radio man on the beach could not tell if a reply had been sent.

Yet another haunting specter gripped the waiting men. Even had the request for fighter planes and the Catalina flying boat been received in Morotai, could the aircraft fly through the howling storm? Tomorrow could be too late. If the large Japanese force arrived from Siaoe, the raiders could expect no mercy.

The tension-packed hours slipped past. Two hours. Three. Five.

Unbeknownst to the Giraffe men, tension was also thick back at the AIB on Morotai. Even though the urgent message from Tahoelandang had been received and the planes dispatched, there was doubt that the aircraft could buck the shrieking winds or that the sea would be calm enough for the Catalina to land and pick up the raiders. Because radio silence was in effect, the AIB communications men could not contact the four Royal Australian Force Beaufighters or the flying boat, all of which were winging toward Tahoelandang. So the nervous officers at Morotai waited.

Just past 7:30 P.M., with dusk gathering, a radio man at the AIB called out, "They're coming—all of them!" Soon the four fighter planes and the Catalina landed.

Forty minutes later, Major Trappes-Lomax, exhausted but beaming, strode into the AIB center. Along with all of his party, he brought eight natives who had agreed to act as guides for future missions in the region and a close relative of the raja from whom valuable intelligence could be obtained about Japanese activities in the Tahoelandang area.

Minutes later, a telephone call from the nearby Beaufighter base reached the AIB. An Australian officer said that the Beaufighters had not sighted the Japanese vessels presumably heading for Tahoelandang, but the aircraft would take off again after dawn to continue the search. Sixteen hours later, Beaufighter planes sent back word that they had arrived over Tahoelandang just as the Japanese troops were unloading and that the enemy force had been heavily bombed and strafed and suffered an estimated one hundred casualties.

Meanwhile, the notorious Manoppo had disappeared; presumably he had taken a prahu to Siaoe and the protection of his Japanese friends.

R. K. Hardwick's crucial role in the hit-and-run raid was not lost on the AIB. The Englishman was appointed an honorary subaltern in the Netherlands East Indies Intelligence Service (a branch of the AIB), and would soon be going on another perilous mission.

On April 10, on the heels of Giraffe, AIB officers on Morotai received intelligence from native scouts that the Sultan of Ternate and his family were being brutalized by the Japanese and, with the advance of Allied troops, they were in danger of being executed. A small figure with sad eyes, the sultan had been the ruler of the entire area before the war in the days of Dutch sovereignty, including the nearby island of Hiri and a large number of islets. Thousands of Malays, most of whom were loyal to the Allies, looked to the sultan for divine guidance and protection. So it was essential that the sultan and his family be evacuated before the Japanese seized them, in which case the Malays would consider the Allies to be responsible for the royal family's demise.

With his two wives and beautiful fourteen-year-old daughter, Rene, the sultan had been living in exile on Ternate, a small, green island some two hundred miles southwest of Morotai. Ternate had been fought over by the Spanish, Portuguese, Dutch, and British before being turned over to the Dutch East India Company in the seventeenth century.

As a consequence of the sultan's peril, the AIB rapidly mounted Operation Opossum, a "snatch raid" to spirit away the Malay royal family and whisk it to safety. Most of the landing party belonged to the Netherlands East Indies Intelligence Service, including the honorary Dutch subaltern, R. K. Hardwick.

Shortly after dark on April 11, the AIB raiders scrambled aboard PT-178 (*Torpedo Junction*) and PT-364, and the American skippers set a course for Hiri island, one mile north of Ternate. It was an especially black night, a factor for which all of the rescuers were thankful. Just after 2:00 A.M., as the two boats neared Hiri, engines were muffled. Japanese were thought to be on the island, but there was no indication of their presence. A hundred yards offshore, the PTs lay to and put two rafts over the side. Silently, several raiders and native guides stole into each one and paddled ashore.[6]

Seemingly endless minutes later, the PT boaters glimpsed the squirt flash of light from the beach, the signal that the raiders had landed safely. Then, the PTs, according to plan, departed for Morotai. Promptly, the Opossum party pushed inland and soon reached a tiny village. When dawn broke, the raiders' eyes feasted on majestic Ternate Peak, just across the narrow strait.

Meanwhile, during the hours of darkness, a native guide had located a fifteen-foot prahu and paddled across a mile of black water to Ternate to deliver a message to the Sultan. In the guide's mouth was a small phial, inside of which was a terse note scrawled on the thinnest of tissue paper. Should the native messenger be seized by the Japanese on Ternate, he could unobtrusively swallow the phial and explain that he was walking through the dark jungle in search of medical help for an upset stomach.

Near to the Opossum party on Hiri was another village, whose leaders were thought to be loyal to the Japanese. If the suspect natives were not taken into custody, they no doubt would warn the Japanese on Ternate of the presence of the intruders. So the raiders stole noiselessly through the thick, green jungle after daybreak and stormed the hamlet before the inhabitants were aware of their presence. Without a shot being fired, some sixty males were rapidly rounded up, put in a group, and bound securely.

In the center of the hostile group and seething with fury was the man other villagers fingered as a pro-Japanese fanatic and one who had murdered numerous natives during his tyrannical rule of Hiri. Two armed men would remain to guard the bound suspects with orders to shoot to kill if any showed an inclination to escape.

In the meantime, along Hiri's south shore at 3:00 P.M., an Opossum lookout spotted a brown figure walking through the surf and onto the sandy beach. It was the native messenger, who had delivered the note to the sultan at his Ternate home and had swum back to Hiri. In the courier's mouth was the phial, which now contained a message from the sultan written on a tiny scrap of paper. R. K. Hardwick translated the dialect.

Spies and traitors were everywhere, the sultan said. So he planned to wait until darkness, come down from his mansion on the slope of Ternate Peak, bringing along his family and numerous close associates, climb into several prahus that had been concealed along the beach, and arrive on Hiri after daylight.

Hours later, as the sultan climbed from his prahu and waded onto the beach at Hiri, hundreds of his subjects, who had somehow learned of his anticipated arrival, virtually mobbed the ruler, trying to kiss his bare feet.

Speaking to the Opossum commander in fluent Dutch, his majesty explained that he was exhausted from the strain of his long exile on Ternate and the constant fear of his Malayan subjects being massacred by the Japanese. His health had declined and he took drugs in order to sleep. Although there were some thirty persons in the sultan's entourage, most raider eyes were cast toward his vivacious, shapely young daughter Rene, who was clad in a thin blue blouse and high-cut western-style shorts that left little to the imagination.

Despite the festive scenario, tension gripped the Opossums, especially after the sultan approached the Dutch commander and, without a trace of panic, declared, "We can expect a Japanese attack on Hiri late today or early tomorrow morning."

There was nothing the Dutchman could do other than to place his men on full alert: The PT boats were not scheduled to return until the next morning. Unbeknownst to the Opossum party, the Japanese commander on Ternate had learned of the royal flight and was throwing together a force to cross the narrow strait. But the gods of war were smiling on the raiders and the sultan: The waves were so high they would swamp the craft en route. So the assault against Hiri was postponed until the water calmed.

Just after daybreak, gunfire erupted from the Hiri coastline after Opossum men spotted several prahus loaded with dome-helmeted Japanese soldiers burrowing through the swells toward them. Machine guns were rushed to the site where the Japanese would try to land, and heavy bursts of fire tore into the fragile craft. A few prahus gurgled to the bottom of the sea. Still, the Japanese, brave soldiers all, continued paddling. Closer. And closer.

One by one, the prahus shuddered onto the sandy shore and the nimble Japanese soldiers leaped out and charged forward. Intense fusillades of machine-gun fire cut them down as would a gigantic scythe. A young Dutch lieutenant, on his first mission, leaped from the vegetation and rushed toward a Japanese soldier who was sprawled on the sand. Presumably, the Dutchman hoped to search the corpse for intelligence documents. Just as he neared the prone enemy soldier, the other, bleeding copiously from the stomach, raised an arm and shot the lieutenant through the head.

While the shootout raged along the Hiri shoreline, the Opossum commander ordered an urgent radio message to be sent to Morotai. "Under heavy attack. Casualties. Rush PT boats."

Neither the wily R. K. Hardwick nor the Dutch commander nor the sultan was under any illusions as to the fate of the Opossum men and the royal entourage should the PT boats fail to arrive soon—all would be killed in battle or captured and beheaded. The swift boats had several hours to go to reach Hiri while the Japanese commander could reinforce his initial assault wave from Ternate, only a mile away.

As the minutes ticked away into an hour and the furious firefight continued relentlessly, another haunting specter cast its shadow over Opossum: Not having anticipated an extended shootout, the raiders were nearly out of rifle and machine-gun ammunition. Consequently, a second message was radioed to the AIB on Morotai: "Ammo nearly gone. Situation desperate. Rush planes."

Suddenly, a hush descended over Hiri. The Japanese, leaving behind many dead comrades, had broken off the battle and apparently moved far up and down the shoreline to reorganize and assault the Opossum men from two directions. Most of the raiders felt they were goners.

Then a faint hum of engines could be heard in the distance. The commandos tensed: Were these the Japanese reinforcements from Ternate coming in motorized barges? Then a raider pointed toward the sky and shouted, "Beaufighters! Beaufighters!"

A cheer rang out as the sleek Australian planes zoomed in at treetop level, each craft waving its wings in a greeting. Climbing to several hundred feet, the Beaus circled overhead like mother hens protecting their brood. At noon, the PT boats arrived offshore.

Now the sultan, his family, and entourage were paddled in prahus to the waiting boats, where considerable difficulty was encountered by the royal women in climbing from the low-slung prahus up to the decks of the American craft. One of the sultan's wives, a heavy-set woman with an ample posterior, was struggling mightily to make the ascent. The young Opossum men in the prahu merely watched, but the wise old owl, R. K. Hardwick, who knew there was not a minute to be wasted, took matters into his own hands—literally. The Brit grabbed the woman by her buttocks and boosted her onto the PT-boat deck, where she landed with a resounding thud.

Soon the Opossum men, the sultan and his entourage, and the bodies of raiders killed in the shoreline battle were crammed into the pair of PT boats, which raced off for Morotai.[7]

Undergoing an exhaustive debriefing at the AIB base, the sultan proved to be a gold mine of information on Japanese installations, troop dispositions, and shipping in his region.

For his courage and leadership, R. K. Hardwick was formally commissioned as a major in the Australian army. As comrades congratulated him, Major Hardwick declared, "Hell, mates, that's nothing; you should have seen the bloody commendation I got from the United States Navy for the Opossum mission!"

"What did it say?" they eagerly demanded to know in unison.

Hardwick replied, "For the thoroughly efficient and entirely capable manner in which I handled her big royal ass in heaving the encumbered wife of the Sultan aboard a PT boat during a period of great peril."[8]

24 Covert Peace Feelers

On the afternoon of July 5, 1945, Douglas MacArthur called the press to his offices in the Manila City Hall. Filing into the building, the reporters were buzzing with conjecture: The Supreme Commander seldom held news conferences unless he had a major announcement to make. MacArthur got right to the point.

"The entire Philippine Islands are now liberated," he declared. "The Japanese during the operations employed twenty-three divisions, all of which were practically annihilated. Our forces comprised seventeen divisions."

As was the style of the master showman, MacArthur paused to let this disparity in numbers soak in. Then he continued, "This was one of the rare instances in the history of warfare when in a long campaign a ground force superior in numbers was entirely destroyed by a numerically inferior opponent."[1]

The Supreme Commander's "hit-'em-where-they-ain't" tactics and his undercover war had spared countless American lives. In operations elsewhere in the Philippines after the Luzon campaign, 821 GIs had been killed, while more than 21,000 Japanese troops had been slain and tens of thousands were hopelessly cut off and starving.

Meanwhile, MacArthur's undercover war south of the Philippines continued in full swing. During the first week of July, the AIB at Morotai learned of the existence of the South Seas Development Company, a civilian operation set up by the Japanese to distribute food to their scattered garrisons on Halmahera and the small islands off its west coast. As a civilian enterprise, the Japanese apparently hoped that the military-supply activities would not be interfered with by the Americans.

Further AIB probing by scouts revealed that the South Seas Development Company stole food from the natives, stored it in warehouses throughout Halmahera, and had the buildings guarded by native collaborators supervised by a few Japanese officers. When outposts needed food, the company hired (or forced) natives to haul it from warehouses in prahus, forty-foot-long craft that were able to carry more than a ton each.

A PT-boat raid was quickly organized. It would be led by U.S. Navy Lieutenant Joseph W. Burk, the holder of the world's record for single sculls (rowing) and a veteran of countless PT-boat actions. In his training days at Melville, Rhode Island, Burk's classmates had doubted if the soft-spoken, friendly skipper candidate would make the grade when the shooting started. They had had no idea that this mild-mannered pussycat would turn into a tiger in the southwest Pacific.[2]

As darkness began to fall on July 5, Tiger Joe Burk, a Dutch lieutenant, and thirty-seven native scouts climbed aboard Lieutenant E. F. Shaw's PT-348 (*Merry Mac*) and Lieutenant J. L. Grubb's PT-351 (*The Shadow*). Destination: Makian Island. Before casting off, Burk remarked to his crew, "Boys, the South Seas Development Company is about to hold an enforced going-out-of-business sale!"[3]

Approaching Makian, the raiders overtook a pair of food-laden prahus. Their native crews were petrified. They declared that the Japanese had forced them to man the boats and that they had orders to take the badly needed food to an isolated Japanese outpost on a nearby island. The troops there were starving, the prahu crews declared.

Lieutenant Burk ordered the native crewmen to climb aboard the PT boats, and several bursts of machine-gun fire sank the prahus.

Continuing onward under a veil of darkness, *Merry Mac* and *The Shadow* tied up at a wooden dock on Makian, and Burk led a party of Alamo Scouts and PT men to two warehouses belonging to the South Seas Development Company. They set the heavily stocked warehouses ablaze, ransacked a headquarters used part-time by the Japanese, removed bundles of military documents, and torched the structure.

Returning to the beach, Burk and his men discovered five prahus loaded with food partially concealed in the vegetation along the water's edge. Apparently, their crews had fled with the approach of the raiding party. Burk ordered the five craft towed to deep water where they were riddled by machine-gun fire and sank. Short on fuel and ammunition, the raiders returned to Morotai.

Forty-eight hours later, Tiger Joe Burk struck again to speed up the demise of the South Seas Development Company. This time, he took five PT boats for a barnstorming tour of the islands off Halmahera's west coast, where there was thought to be heavy activity by the Japanese food-supply operation. This jaunt would be a long one—two hundred miles one way—so decks were loaded with extra gasoline containers. Flying cover would be three Beaufighters of the Royal Australian Air Force.

Reaching Ohi Island off southwestern Halmahera, Burk led a landing party ashore, where they burned a South Seas Development Company warehouse stocked with food and a sago mill. Minutes later while patrolling the coast of Ohi, Lieutenant Steve L. Hudacek's PT-182 blew six beached prahus to smithereens with a forty-millimeter deck gun after a native crew and a few Japanese officers fled into the jungle.

Hardly had the last prahu been destroyed than a concealed machine gun on shore spat a necklace of bullets into Hudacek's PT boat, narrowly missing the skipper and several members of his crew. An urgent call for assistance was radioed to the circling Beaufighters, which zoomed in and raked the machine-gun locale with heavy bursts of fire, knocking out the weapon or discouraging those manning it.

Next, Joe Burk's rampaging PT boats headed south, and at the village of Amasing on Batjan Island, their guns sent broadsides of bullets and shells into a Japanese radio station and four warehouses used by the South Seas Development Company.

Now the PT boats reached the limit of their range, so they turned northward and divided: Three boats headed for Moti Island and two for Tidore Island. At Moti, a raiding party went ashore, set fire to a concealed Japanese warehouse, and returned to the boat in routine fashion.

It was a far different story at Tidore, where a party of ten men slipped ashore from Ensign William A. Klopman's PT-179 (*Betty Lou*) and Lieutenant C. C. Hamburger's PT-180 (*Marie*). No warehouses were found, but the raiders broke into an unmanned Japanese headquarters and scooped up several armloads of military documents, then set fire to the structure.

Trudging back through the jungle, the raiders did belly flops when a concealed machine gun sent a fusillade of bullets hissing past their heads. Then a second automatic weapon opened fire. The intruders had stumbled onto an ambush. Moments later, eight Japanese soldiers, brandishing bayonet-tipped rifles and screaming *banzai*, charged out of the thick vegetation.

Above the strident racket of chattering machine guns, an American voice called out, "Haul ass!" No one needed further encouragement. The raiders scrambled to their feet and began a mad dash for the beach, off which their PT boats were waiting. Huffing and puffing, the landing party reached the shore. The pursuing Japanese, still yelling *banzai* at the top of their lungs, were right on their heels.

On board *Marie*, Motor Machinist's Mate E. D. McKeever, manning the bow thirty-seven-millimeter gun, rapidly sized up the situation. When the Japanese riflemen broke out of the jungle and onto the beach, McKeever opened fire, cutting down all of the pursuers. Minutes later, the exhausted raiders, panting for breath, climbed aboard *Marie* and *Betty Lou*. Their work done and not wanting to press their good luck, the two PT boats abruptly departed Tidore Island and raced out to sea.[4]

Shortly afterward, the secret campaign to put the South Seas Development Company out of business resumed. PT-355 (*Hell's Cargo*), skippered by Lieutenant Kermit Montz, a former Franklin and Marshall University football star, and Lieutenant William D. Finan's PT-178 (*Torpedo Junction*) paid a call to Tidore Island and hit the jackpot. Gunners blasted forty-two prahus sitting on the beach, then the two boats sped to Halmahera's west coast and riddled nine more of the native craft. Two follow-up missions to the same region resulted in the destruction of a hundred more prahus, rigger canoes, sailboats, and barges—all important transportation units of the South Seas Development Company.

Then the AIB at Morotai learned that the food distribution firm had a large warehouse complex concealed in the jungle on Kajoa Island, near Ternate, the domain of the sultan. So on July 30, two PT boats, skippered by Lieutenant T. J. Lovvorn and Lieutenant R. C. Fisher, headed for Kajoa. On arrival, a landing party of six PT boaters and fourteen native scouts paddled ashore in rubber dinghies, stole through the jungle, and halted near five warehouses packed with food, copra oil, and clothing—vital supplies earmarked for the emperor's soldiers. Unaccountably, not a single Japanese guarded the valuable assets. The five warehouses were put to the torch, and the raiders hurried back to the PT boats. Crew members could still see towering plumes of black smoke when ten miles out to sea.[5]

As a result of this series of covert strikes by PT boaters, the South Seas Development Company, which had been sustaining tens of thousands of Japanese soldiers cut off by Douglas MacArthur's leapfrog tactics, was forced into bankruptcy and went out of business.[6]

In Japan, the people were still convinced that they were winning the war. Hundreds of villages continued to erect Churen Kensho-to (monuments to the victorious dead), as though Dai Nippon's enemies already had surrendered. Unaware that most of Japan's mightiest warships were resting on the bottom of the Pacific Ocean, the people thought the fleet was undamaged and intact. In the Philippines, the people were told that General Yamashita, who was trapped in northern Luzon, had conducted a brilliant maneuver to turn the tide in the Philippines.

The Japanese people had been told about the loss of Iwo Jima in March and then Saipan, but these were only insignificant islands, they were advised. Even when America's huge B-29 Flying Fortresses were taking off from Saipan to firebomb one Japanese city after the other, the homefront clung to its illusions that the United States was being defeated. In April, however, the people of Dai Nippon were worried by the American invasion of the large island of Okinawa, which was only one day's sailing distance from the southern Japanese islands. But their qualms were soothed when Imperial General Headquarters explained. A force of 180,000 U.S. Marines and GIs had been allowed to land so that kamikazes could sink their supporting ships and isolate the invaders on land, where they would be destroyed. Okinawa, not the Philippines, as the emperor's government had trumpeted earlier, would be the war's *sekigahara* (decisive battle).

When the U.S. commanders announced on June 21 that Okinawa had been captured, the invasion of the Japanese homeland was imminent.

Meanwhile, in Washington, the Pentagon, acting under the direction of President Roosevelt, reorganized the Pacific commands. Douglas MacArthur would be leader of all ground forces for the invasion of Japan, and Chester Nimitz would command all naval units. The general and the admiral, both holding five-star rank, were expected to work in the closest harmony.

The code name for the invasion of Dai Nippon was Downfall. It would be launched on November 1, 1945, with Operation Olympic, a frontal assault on Kyushu by 766,701 men under General Walter Krueger. Kyushu would provide airfields to cover Operation Coronet, the main landing on Honshu, which was set for March 1, 1946.

MacArthur held no illusions about the savagery that lay ahead. He told Secretary of War Henry Stimson that Downfall would "cost over a million casualties to American forces alone."[7]

With the overall command in the Pacific now split between army and navy, William "Wild Bill" Donovan's cloak-and-dagger agency, the OSS, tried once again to get a piece of the action. In North Africa, Europe, Burma, and elsewhere around the world, Wild Bill's organization had been performing with great distinction and producing untold results. Now, a branch of the OSS, Research and Development (known in-house as the "dirty tricks department"), sent an emissary to see Douglas MacArthur in Manila. The OSS man brought with him a top secret scheme for paving the way in the Japanese homeland invasion— phosphorescent foxes.

Appealing to MacArthur's well-known bent for undercover and psychological warfare, the OSS representative suggested that just before American troops hit the beaches at Dai Nippon, several hundred foxes daubed with phosphorescent paint would first be let loose offshore and swim to the land at night. This would help spread consternation and panic among the superstitious Japanese who believed "a ghostly fox seen at night carries an evil spirit," the visitor declared enthusiastically. Mac-Arthur was far from impressed, pointing out that the short swim ashore would wash off most of the phosphorus.

Undaunted, the OSS man returned to Washington where an effort was made to prove the Supreme Commander wrong. At Rock Creek Park, in nearby Maryland, eight or ten foxes glowing with phosphorus were dropped over the side of a boat a short distance from shore one night. When the animals reached the beach, most of the paint was gone, just as MacArthur had predicted. What the foxes succeeded in doing was frightening several couples engaged in amorous endeavors in the backseats of parked automobiles. No surrenders were reported from Rock Creek Park.[8]

With each passing day, General MacArthur felt surer that peace was near, that Downfall never would have to be launched. In late July, he told George Kenney, his air force chief, that he believed the Japanese would surrender "by September 1 at the latest and perhaps even sooner." A day later, the Supreme Commander called an off-the-record press briefing at Manila City Hall and predicted to astonished reporters, "The war may end sooner than some think."

What neither Kenney, many other U.S. commanders in the southwest Pacific, and newspaper correspondents could not be told was that MacArthur was privy to an ongoing litany of cloak-and-dagger peace negotiations that were taking place halfway around the world in Europe. Key figure in these covert activities was Allen W. Dulles, OSS chief for southern Europe, with headquarters in Berne, Switzerland.

The first peace effort was launched by a mysterious Dr. Fritz Hack, who might have come out of a whodunit spy novel. Hack, a German and longtime friend of Japan, enlisted the aid of Commander Yoshiro Fujimura, the Japanese naval attaché in Berne, who realized that his country had lost the war and felt it was his duty to bring peace no matter what the personal risk. Hack and Fujimura were joined in the conspiracy by two like-minded Japanese—Shintaro Ryu, the European correspondent of *Asahi Shimbun,* and Shigeyoshi Tsuyama, the European representative of the Osaka Shipping Line.[9]

In a secluded inn outside Berne, the four conspirators held a series of meetings with Allen Dulles's representatives and convinced the Americans of their own political reliability and sincerity. They pointed out to the OSS agents that they had access to a Navy Type 94 code machine with which they could communicate directly with Imperial Navy Headquarters outside Tokyo without having to go through government channels.

Allen Dulles sent a report on the meetings to Washington, and orders came back to commence direct peace negotiations with the Hack and Fujimura conspirators. After being informed of this development, the four self-appointed peacemakers sent a top secret message addressed to Navy Minister Mitsumasa Yonai and the commander of the Combined Fleet, Admiral Soemu Toyoda (who had been appointed to that post after the death of Admiral Mineichi Koga in the briefcase episode on Cebu). The communication informed the two Japanese leaders in Tokyo that Dulles had offered to act as mediator and described him as "a leading political figure of America who has long associated with and enjoys the confidence of [Secretary of State] Stettinius . . . and is directly connected to President Roosevelt."[10]

The conspirators had confused the OSS station chief in Berne with his brother John Foster Dulles, the Assistant Secretary of State, but did accurately say that Allen Dulles had been "guiding the American political warfare for nearly all of Europe." Also correctly, the message went on to state that Allen Dulles was "largely responsible for the separate peace [with Nazi Germany]" that had been obtained in northern Italy in early May.

Emboldened by the positive response from Washington, the four peacemakers now took another audacious step. Near midnight, Fujimura and Tsuyama cautiously stole into the darkened Japanese legation building in Berne. It was risky business. Should they be caught, no doubt they would be sent back to Tokyo, tried as traitors, and beheaded. With flashlight in hand, they stealthily climbed to the third floor and entered the code room. Tsuyama set the machine for the proper date and hour and then began typing the message in romanized Japanese. The machine automatically transmitted this in code. All the while, Fujimura remained outside the door, alert for any approaching danger.

During the next eight nights, the episode was repeated six times. The secret telegrams told about American and British plans for moving huge numbers of troops and accoutrements of war from Europe to the Far East, along with urging peace be sought before a catastrophe hit Dai Nippon.

For two weeks, there was only silence from Imperial Navy Headquarters. Then Yonai and Toyoda replied (although the message was signed by a lower-level functionary), "The principal point of your negotiations with Dulles fully understood. But there are certain points which indicate an enemy plot. Therefore we advise you to be very cautious."[11]

Fujimura and his peacemakers were furious. They felt that the two navy bigwigs in Tokyo were engaged in a subterfuge to protect their own hides should the unauthorized negotiations with the United States suddenly blow up and scapegoats were sought by the emperor's government. In another message, Fujimura requested "concrete evidence" that Dulles was engaged in a plot since it was the four peacemakers who had approached the OSS station chief. The message to Tokyo added, "Mr. Dulles is expecting a sincere reply from Japan. Even if we concede . . . it to be an enemy plot, would it not be more advantageous to avoid the sad plight of Germany which lost everything?"[12]

Imperial Navy Headquarters did not reply. But the series of secret messages from the midnight halls of the legation building in Berne touched off acrimonious debates among naval leaders in Tokyo. Three top officers were strongly for accepting the Dulles position as a reliable high-level contact between the two sides, and they even offered to fly incognito to Switzerland to open peace negotiations. But Admiral Toyoda and the remainder of his staff were strongly opposed. The Dulles proposal was merely "a plot to lower Japanese morale," they held.

The failure of Tokyo to respond to his urgent messages frustrated Fujimura. He told Dulles that he intended to fly to Japan to explain in person the enormous significance of the Dulles proposal. However, the OSS boss talked him out of that drastic action, no doubt fearing that Fujimura would be signing his own death warrant. Instead, Dulles suggested that Tokyo send an authorized emissary to Switzerland, and that the United States would guarantee safe air transportation. Fujimura transmitted this offer to Navy Minister Yonai in words so strong that they fell just short of insubordination.

Yonai was goaded into action and he took the Dulles proposal to Foreign Minister Shigenori Togo. A member of a samurai family, Togo was a heavyset, tough-minded career diplomat who had an understanding of European ways. Years earlier, he had scandalized his family by marrying a German woman. Unlike most diplomats, Togo said what he meant with a bluntness that many construed as rudeness.

Togo was leery about the Fujimura telegrams from Berne. He knew nothing about Allen Dulles. Covering all bets, however, he suggested that Yonai explore the peace feelers more thoroughly, so the navy minister dispatched a vaguely worded message to Berne, "Your point is fully understood. . . . You are requested to take proper measures in close cooperation with [Dulles] and the other persons concerned at your place."[13]

Commander Fujimura and his co-conspirators were elated at this seeming encouragement from Tokyo. But their enthusiasm dulled as time passed and not a peep on how to proceed was heard from Togo or Yonai. This absence of word from Tokyo also caused Allen Dulles and his American cohorts to lose interest. What those involved in Berne did not know was that Admiral Toyoda had become convinced that Fujimura, who was "only a commander," had been suckered into an American plot.

A month later, in early July, a second clandestine maneuver to negotiate a "just peace" for Dai Nippon was triggered in Switzerland. It was inspired by an offhand remark made by Lieutenant General Seigo Okamoto, the military attaché, to Kojiro Kitamura and Kan Yosimura, officials of the Bank for International Settlements in Basel.

"Japan intends to fight to the end," the general told the bankers. "However, if there is any peace move on the part of the Americans, I would like to negotiate with them."[14]

These words from a Japanese general elated the two bankers. They had seen with their own eyes the destruction that had been heaped on Germany by the awesome Allied military machine, and they were determined to save their native Japan from extinction. But how could the ruling military clique in Tokyo be persuaded to approve these covert peace negotiations?

General Okamoto replied that army Chief of Staff Yoshijiro Umezu had formerly been his commander and was a close friend. "He'll listen to what I have to say," the military attaché declared.

The two Japanese bankers decided to send peace feelers to the Americans, but who had the significant prestige to act as go-between?

They decided on Per Jacobsson, a Swede, a director of their bank, and a man known for his skill in mediating international disputes. What's more, Jacobsson was highly regarded by the Americans and, as a neutral, he would not be held in suspicion by the Japanese.

Jacobsson readily agreed to accept the crucial role, and he quickly made contact with one of Allen Dulles's operatives in Berne. Within a week, the Swede reported back to the two Japanese bankers: The conditions for peace talks would be unconditional surrender. The bankers balked—that would mean dethroning the emperor, who was regarded as a god by most Japanese.

It was agreed that Jacobsson would continue with his clandestine negotiations. So on July 10, the Swede was talking to Gero von Schulze Gaevernitz, Dulles's number two man, at an isolated hotel on the outskirts of Berne. Gaevernitz, a German-born naturalized American, had first come to the United States in 1934 at the age of twenty-nine to launch a career in international banking. Later, he returned to Germany and established a high niche in elite circles of banking and industry. Adolf Hitler came to power and Gaevernitz's father, who had been a prominent German legislator, fled to Switzerland with his Jewish wife. When war broke out, their son, Gero, joined them in Berne. After Allen Dulles set up his OSS station in Switzerland in late 1942, Gero volunteered his services and performed with such distinction that he was made top assistant to Dulles.

Now Gaevernitz, acting on instructions from Washington, stressed that Japan's unconditional surrender would be demanded, but he also mentioned that the Japanese might be able to retain their emperor.

"Will you put that in writing?" Jacobsson asked.

"No, only President [Harry S] Truman and Prime Minister Winston Churchill could do that—and it could take weeks."

Instead, Gaevernitz, speaking in his thick Teutonic accent, suggested that Jacobsson "exaggerate a bit" and tell the Japanese that he was "in direct contact with the Americans responsible for peace negotiations."[15]

Now the ball was in the Tokyo court. However, General Okamoto, the military attaché in Switzerland who had instigated the conspiracy, seemed to have gotten cold feet. He told Jacobsson that he would not urge his old friend, Chief of Staff Umezu, to get involved until he was sure of the fate of the emperor and his family.

Undaunted, Per Jacobsson set up a personal meeting with Allen Dulles at the OSS chief's new headquarters in Wiesbaden, Germany. For his part, Dulles was mainly concerned over the sincerity—or lack of it—of the Japanese negotiators. The Swede assured Dulles that they were sincere and that the "peace group" in Tokyo was doing its best to bring about a surrender. Dulles, whose rimless glasses, smoking pipe, and tweed jackets gave him a professorial appearance, was suspicious.

"Isn't this perhaps a trick of the Japanese warlords to strengthen morale, to try to show how unreasonable the Americans are?" he asked.[16]

An argument erupted that lasted for several hours. Jacobsson resented the implication that he was a stooge for a diabolical deception scheme hatched by the Japanese. When the meeting broke up, nothing was resolved. But now, Washington—and Douglas MacArthur—knew that there was a considerable peace movement active inside the high circles of Dai Nippon.

On Sunday, August 5, a courier arrived from Washington to call on General MacArthur in Manila. He brought word that a device known as an atomic bomb would be dropped on an industrial city south of Tokyo on the following day. It was the first inkling the Supreme Commander had that the United States had developed this awesome weapon of mass destruction.

At the same time MacArthur was learning about the revolutionary bomb, sixteen hundred miles to the north, the citizens of the city of Hiroshima, which was unscarred by the heavy B-29 firebomb assaults of recent weeks, were going about their routine activities. Located on the southeast coast of Honshu, Japan's main island, Hiroshima was the empire's eighth largest city. Already 125,000 civilians had been evacuated to the countryside, but 245,000 remained.

Although Hiroshima was a manufacturing center, the headquarters of the 2nd General Army, and an important military port of embarkation to the battle zones, the citizens felt confident that their city would be spared. Many of their reasons for immunity were preposterous: President Truman's mother lived nearby; the city was so beautiful that the Americans wanted it for a recreation area after the war; many citizens had relatives in the United States.

Few of Hiroshima's citizens had paid any attention to the 750,000 leaflets that high-flying B-29s had dropped two days earlier, warning them to leave, that their city among others would be wiped off the map unless Japan surrendered immediately. American propaganda, they assured one another.

High Drama in Tokyo 25

I n a building outside Tokyo, members of the Yamatoda Signal Corps, expert radiomen from the Japanese Navy, were keeping a round-the-clock vigil over a room crammed with 178 powerful wireless receivers. Their job was to monitor and record all radio signals coming from American transmitters in the Pacific.

Early on the morning of August 6, 1945, the monitors picked up a call sign they had heard almost three weeks earlier. The signal was traced to Tinian Island and was tagged the "New Task Company" for quick reference. To the signal corps men, it was just another of thousands of items that had been reported and logged. They had no way of knowing that the New Task Company was actually the elite and highly secret U.S. 509th Bomb Group, whose mission was to conclude the war.

Near Tinian, the U.S. Third Fleet, one of the most powerful naval strike forces ever assembled, was steaming hell-bent to pound predesignated targets in southern Japan. Suddenly, the fleet's admirals received orders to retrace its course and head back out to sea. The men with the gold braid were puzzled.

On the USS *Ticonderoga*, Rear Admiral Clifton A. "Ziggy" Sprague, a veteran of many sea battles in the Pacific, called his combat intelligence officers to the flag cabin. Waving the pullback order, Sprague thundered, "This is a hell of a way to run a war! What's it all about, anyhow?"

The order stated, "It is imperative that there be non-interference with operations of the 509th Bomb Group. It is directed that you send no planes over [the Japanese islands of] Kyushu or Honshu."

A lengthy discussion about the reason for the pullback order ended with Sprague's intelligence officers putting a dollar bill and a slip of sealed paper on which each had written his guess into a pool. The guesses would be opened later, and the man coming the closest would win the money in the pool.

Lieutenant Edwin P. Stevens of New York City was as mystified as the others. However, his mind flashed back to 1941, when a physicist friend remarked briefly that certain scientists were trying to release colossal amounts of energy by breaking the nuclei of atoms. Stevens had only the foggiest notion of what the friend had been talking about, but, on a hunch, he scribbled some mention of "nuclear energy" on his piece of paper.

Almost at the same moment Ed Stevens was dropping his guess in the *Ticonderoga*'s pool, Professor Yoshitaka Mimura, an eloquent and popular teacher at Hiroshima Bunri University, was mesmerizing a group of over five hundred young and eager Japanese Army officers who were posted in and around the city. Mimura, a theoretical physicist, was telling his class about the possibility of Dai Nippon's developing a revolutionary new weapon that could result in a dramatic outcome of the war. Both the professor and the army officers knew that the Americans were massing forces in the Philippines and elsewhere in the western Pacific for an invasion of the Japanese homeland.

A lieutenant colonel asked, "Sir, can you tell us what is an atomic bomb?"

Researchers at Tokyo University had theoretically penetrated the secrets of nuclear fission, Professor Mimura explained. "If they could apply their theories practically, an atomic bomb, if exploded above a large city, could possibly destroy 200,000 lives," he added.

A hush fell over the room. However, the army officers realized that an atomic bomb was only a "scientific theory."

A few hours later, an American B-29 Superfort, piloted by thirty-year-old Colonel Paul W. Tibbets and named *Enola Gay*, winged high over Hiroshima. Moments later, a brilliant pinkish light burst over the bustling city like a gigantic flashbulb on some huge supernatural camera. Clocks all over Hiroshima were fixed forever at 8:15.

Among the thousands who died, conceivably, were large numbers of the army officers who had been assured that an atomic bomb was only a scientific theory.

In Tokyo the next morning, high-ranking Japanese military officers and government leaders convened to discuss the awesome new development. Some of the army brass attached no great significance to the fact that a lone bomb virtually had blasted Hiroshima off the map. Foreign Minister Shigenori Togo, however, pointed out with logic that the A-bomb "drastically alters the whole military situation and offers [us] ample grounds for ending the war." When he suggested that they accept the Allies' unconditional surrender demand, he was all but shouted down by the military men.

"Such a move is uncalled for," War Minister Korechika Anami, who held the rank of general, responded. "We don't yet know if the bomb was atomic." They had only President Truman's word for it. It might be a diabolical American trick. Before any decision was reached, Dr. Yoshio Nishina, the nation's leading nuclear scientist who had been working to create an atomic bomb, would be sent to investigate Hiroshima.

Nishina's plane flew over Hiroshima the next afternoon. He concluded instantly that only an atomic bomb could have wreaked such widespread destruction. He returned to Tokyo and informed Japanese officials that it had been a uranium-type bomb similar to the one he had been trying to develop.

When the Japanese warlords ignored another surrender ultimatum from Washington, a second A-bomb mission was prepared on the island of Guam. But first, 16 million leaflets were printed in Japanese and widely scattered over the home islands by B-29s. Aimed at public morale, the leaflets said in part:

> Before using a second atomic bomb . . . we ask that you now petition the emperor to end this useless war. . . . You should take steps now to cease military resistance. Otherwise we shall resolutely employ this bomb . . . to promptly and forcefully end the war. . . . Evacuate your cities now.

On the morning of August 9, a giant ball of fire, belching forth enormous white smoke rings, rose from Nagasaki, an industrial city of two hundred thousand people. Much of the ancient city was incinerated. It was 9:01 A.M.

Learning through clandestine sources that the emperor was determined to surrender, President Truman suspended B-29 raids on Japan. Three days after that, on August 15, Hirohito took to Radio Tokyo to announce that the empire was surrendering. "We must endure the unendurable and suffer the insufferable," he told his people.

The emperor's declaration stunned his subjects. They had never heard even his recorded voice. It also set off a flurry of ceremonial *hara-kiri* suicides by generals and admirals. A day later, thirty-two die-hard young Japanese junior officers broke into the emperor's palace and tried to murder him, claiming that he was not really Hirohito and that the radio announcement was a fake, a devious American scheme to gain victory. All of the militants were slain on the grounds of and inside the palace by the emperor's bodyguards.

President Truman—with the approval of political leaders in England, the Soviet Union, and China—appointed Douglas MacArthur to the new post of Supreme Commander for the Allied Powers. A few days later, Joseph Stalin, the Soviet dictator, had second thoughts. The Soviet Union had declared war on Japan two days before the Bomb was dropped, and now Stalin was demanding that a Soviet field marshal should be named a full partner to MacArthur in ruling over defeated Japan. Truman, with the use of the earthy vocabulary for which he was noted, rejected the Soviet demand.

Meanwhile, in Manila, these were among the most hectic days of Douglas MacArthur's long career. Every Allied general, admiral, government official, and exalted nabob in the Far East insisted on calling on the Supreme Commander. He took time out, however, when a few hundred GIs gathered under the window of his second-story office to cheer him.

Struggling to conceal his emotions, MacArthur told them, "I hope from the bottom of my heart that this is the end of the war. If it is, it is largely due to your own efforts. Very soon, I hope, we will all be going home."[1]

There was, even after the emperor's surrender announcement, a lurking suspicion among MacArthur's staff officers that the Japanese might be baiting a trap. The treachery of Pearl Harbor still loomed in the minds of many. What's more, there were more than 2 million armed and organized Japanese soldiers in the homeland, most of whom would be willing to fight to the death should they be given the order. There were scores—perhaps hundreds—of kamikaze planes whose pilots might plunge into Allied ships approaching Japan. Word that army hotheads had tried to murder Hirohito added to the nervousness.

Under this ominous cloud of uncertainty and looming danger in Japan, MacArthur's aides urged him not to fly to Atsugi near Tokyo as planned. They pointed out the peril for an American five-star general, unarmed and without bodyguards, to drop out of the sky into the midst of 70 million people who, until two weeks earlier, had been pledged to his annihilation.[2]

Chief of Staff Dick Sutherland told MacArthur, "My God, general, the emperor is worshipped as a real god, yet they still tried to assassinate him. What kind of target will that make you?"[3]

MacArthur shrugged and replied, "I'm going."

At dawn on August 28, Colonel Charles Tench, a member of Mac-Arthur's staff, made history. Japan was the only major power whose soil had never been sullied by the boot of an enemy soldier. Now Tench stepped from a C-47 and set foot on Atsugi Airport. Instantly, a mob of Japanese rushed toward him. Tench reached for his pistol, but they suddenly halted, beaming and smiling, and offered him orange juice. "No hostile action encountered," Colonel Tench radioed Manila.

Two days later, big transport planes, flying from Okinawa, landed at Atsugi with 500 paratroopers of the U.S. 11th Airborne Division. In one of the first aircraft was twenty-year-old Corporal George Doherty. Clad in jungle greens, Doherty and the others climbed out of the C-54s and looked around. With a few hours marching time, there were twenty Japanese divisions, some 300,000 fully armed men.

"If the Japs are going to pull a second Pearl Harbor, this is the time and place to do it," Doherty told his comrades. "If they're so inclined, they can wipe out General MacArthur when he arrives and all the Pacific brass—and us paratroopers—in one blow!"[4]

Hardly had the airborne men reached the ground than a C-54—the *Bataan*—touched down on the bomb-pocked runway. Nearly all of the American brass in the Pacific advanced to the aircraft ramp. After what seemed to be an interminable time, the door of the *Bataan* opened, and there stood the great general, corncob pipe in mouth, eyes shielded by oversized sunglasses.

"Wow!" Corporal Doherty whispered to a gawking trooper. "This is one of history's most momentous occasions!"[5]

Just inside the *Bataan* and waiting for the Supreme Commander to descend the portable ramp, General Bonner Fellers, a longtime aide, heard MacArthur mutter, "This is the payoff!" Fellers thought, "I agree. But what kind of a payoff—an assault on the *Bataan* by masses of fanatical Japanese troops?"

Once on the tarmac, MacArthur was in high good humor. Nearby was a large group of GIs, and he strolled over to talk with them. A young sergeant, flustered on seeing the legendary general coming toward him, reached for his rifle to present arms (the customary salute when a soldier has a weapon). Instead, the GI grabbed a bamboo pole. Standing in front of the sergeant presenting arms with the pole, MacArthur said softly, "Son, I think you're in the wrong army." Chuckling, he moved on.[6]

On September 2, Colonel Sidney Mashbir, who, as chief of the ATIS, had played a key role in MacArthur's undercover war, was at the pier in Yokohama when the Japanese surrender delegation rolled up in spiffy limousines. Mashbir led the group up the gangplank of the destroyer *Lansdowne* and into a wardroom. With Mashbir was Captain Henry H. Smith-Hutton, a former naval attaché in Tokyo, who had been interned there when war broke out.

After the emissaries were ensconced, Mashbir and Smith-Hutton went up on deck. The colonel sensed that the navy officer was upset about something, and finally he came out with it.

"Colonel, I am in a very embarrassing position," Smith-Hutton declared. "I was flown out here directly from Washington by Admiral Nimitz's order to conduct the Japanese delegation aboard the [battleship] *Missouri*."[7]

Mashbir was astonished. Clearly, the U.S. Navy and Army were continuing their wartime rivalry even up to and including the surrender ceremonies. To Mashbir, it appeared that the navy bigwigs had launched a last-minute offensive to try to deprive General MacArthur of his rightful place as Supreme Commander. The colonel's mind flashed back twenty-four hours to when he had seen a press release distributed by the U.S. Navy. It described how the *Missouri* had been prepared for the surrender ceremonies, with a specially built platform for the photographers and moving picture cameras, awnings in the event of rain, and concluded with these words. "Everything has been arranged by the Navy for stylish [media] coverage." No mention was made of the Supreme Commander in the Pacific, Douglas MacArthur.

Now Sid Mashbir pulled out the order under which MacArthur had designated him to lead the Japanese delegation aboard the battleship. Smith-Hutton had been put on the spot by jockeying for position by Washington bigwigs. Finally, Smith-Hutton came up with a proposal that would permit both officers to carry out their orders from on high: Mashbir would lead the surrender delegation, and Hutton-Smith would bring up the tail end.

It was 8:55 A.M. when Colonel Mashbir started up the gangway of the *Missouri*, anchored in Tokyo Bay. Trailing was the sixteen-member Japanese delegation headed by Foreign Minister Mamoru Shigemitsu, whose left leg had been blown off by an assassin's bomb in Shanghai before the war.

Earlier, Mashbir had given the Japanese delegation the protocol to be followed once they were aboard the *Missouri:* The military officers were to salute when MacArthur appeared, the civilians were to take off their hats and bow. "And I suggest that all of you wear a *shiran kao* [nonchalant face]," Mashbir advised.[8]

Once the Japanese were in place on the deck, they came to attention for the playing of the "Star-Spangled Banner." Then General MacArthur appeared with five-star Admirals Chester Nimitz and Bull Halsey and walked briskly to a battered mess table covered with a coffee-stained green felt cloth. On it were a batch of documents arranged to hide the stains.

"We are gathered here, representatives of the major warring powers, to conclude a solemn agreement whereby peace may be restored," said MacArthur, speaking in stentorian tones. "The issues, involving divergent ideals and ideologies, have been determined on the battlefields . . . and hence are not for our discussion or our debate."

MacArthur continued, "It is my earnest hope—indeed the hope of all mankind—that from this solemn occasion a better world shall emerge out of the blood and carnage of the past, a world founded upon faith and understanding, a world dedicated to the dignity of man and the fulfillment of his most cherished wish for freedom, tolerance and justice."

At that moment, almost as if on cue from some supernatural body, the gray clouds parted, and in the distance the peak of Mount Fuji sparkled in the sun. Minutes later, the documents of surrender were signed by the Japanese and the Allied commanders.

"Let us pray," the Supreme Commander said, "that peace now be restored to the world and that God will always preserve it. These proceedings are now closed."[9]

Notes and Sources

Chapter 1. *Manila: Hotbed of Intrigue*

1. Dr. José Rizal led an uprising against the Spanish rulers of the Philippines and was executed by them on December 30, 1896.

2. John Toland. *But Not in Shame* (New York: Random House, 1961), p. 94.

3. Lewis H. Brereton. *The Brereton Diaries* (New York: Norton, 1946), pp. 24–25.

4. At 8:00 A.M. on December 7, 1941, at Pearl Harbor, Hawaii, it was 3:00 A.M. on December 8 in the Philippines.

5. Some background and details about the activities of Richard Sakakida and Arthur Komori came from *Military Intelligence*, a booklet compiled by Diane L. Hamm, U.S. Army Intelligence and Security Command, Arlington, Virginia. Also, information to author from U.S. Senator Daniel Inouye of Hawaii, a Nisei who was badly wounded fighting in Europe in World War II.

6. A few months after Yay Panlillio joined the guerrillas, she married their leader, a man named Marking.

Chapter 2. *Kidnapping a President*

1. Sidney L. Huff. *My Fifteen Years with General MacArthur* (New York: Harper, 1964), p. 79.

2. John S. Beck, *MacArthur and Wainwright* (Albuquerque: University of New Mexico Press, 1974), p. 125.

3. Huff, p. 80.

4. Vice Admiral John D. Bulkeley (Ret.) told the author that one of his main recollections in the long and hazardous dash to Mindanao was Jean MacArthur's courage.

5. Author interview with Vice Admiral John D. Bulkeley (Ret.).

6. Ibid.

7. Carlos Romulo. *I See the Philippines Rise* (Garden City, N.Y.: Doubleday, 1946), p. 113.

8. Author interview with Vice Admiral John D. Bulkeley (Ret.).

9. Ibid.

10. A few days later, President Manuel Quezon awarded Philippine decorations for valor to torpedomen James Light and John Houlilhan.

11. Author interview with Vice Admiral John D. Bulkeley (Ret.). Bulkeley was awarded the Congressional Medal of Honor, the Navy Cross, and two U.S. Army Distinguished Service Crosses for his actions in the Philippines during the first four months of the war in the Pacific.

12. Ibid.

13. When MacArthur returned to the Philippines in fall 1944, he did not land on Mindanao, but rather on the island of Leyte, to the north of Mindanao.

14. Allison Ind. *Allied Intelligence Bureau* (New York: David McKay, 1956), p. 58.

15. After General MacArthur took command in Australia, Lieutenant General George H. Brett and Vice Admiral Herbert F. Leary were relieved of their posts.

16. Huff, p. 72.

Chapter 3. *Thumbs Down on Wild Bill's OSS*

1. *St. Louis Post-Dispatch,* March 22, 1942.

2. Some criticism arose because General MacArthur brought Ah Cheu on the trek from Corregidor. It was explained that as a Filipina she would have been tortured and perhaps killed by the Japanese once they learned of her connection with the MacArthurs.

3. Author interview with Vice Admiral John D. Bulkeley (Ret.).

4. In August 1945, when a Japanese delegation asked to see MacArthur about surrender terms, the general ordered it to radio Bataan as to its identification code. The Japanese balked but finally complied when MacArthur insisted.

5. Huff, p. 102.

6. George C. Kenney. *General Kenney Reports* (New York: Duell, Sloan & Pearce, 1949), p. 47.

7. To mask its true clandestine function, the OSS was originally called the Coordinator of Information, or COI.

8. Breckenridge Long. *The War Diary of Breckenridge Long* (New York: Harper, 1951), p. 234.

9. Bradley F. Smith, *The Shadow Warriors* (New York: Basic Books, 1983), p. 104.

10. Ibid., p. 105.

11. Richard Dunlop. *Donovan* (Chicago: Rand McNally, 1982), pp. 301–2.

Chapter 4. *A Clandestine Agency Is Born*

1. A talented major league baseball player of the early 1900's, Wee Willie Keeler, was asked the reason for his great success as a batter. He replied: "Because I hit-'em-where-they-ain't."

2. Charles A. Willoughby. *MacArthur* (New York: McGraw-Hill, 1954), p. 76.

3. Ansin Bulu was eventually released by the Japanese and survived the war.

4. Frazier Hunt. *The Untold Story of Douglas MacArthur* (New York: Harper, 1954), pp. 82–83.

5. George C. Kenney. *The MacArthur I Know* (New York: Random House, 1953), p. 53.

6. Ibid., p. 54.

Chapter 5. *Sneaking Back into the Philippines*

1. Courtney Whitney. *MacArthur: His Rendezvous with History* (New York: Knopf, 1956), p. 128.

2. Ibid., p. 129.

3. Arch Whitehouse. *Espionage and Counterespionage* (New York: Doubleday, 1964), p. 147.

4. Whitney, p. 130.

5. Willoughby. *The Guerrilla Resistance Movement in the Philippines* (New York: Vantage, 1972), p. 76.

6. Frank Jones and his sister, Helen Jones, managed to survive the war while under the noses of the Kempei Tai.

Chapter 6. *Ferdinand's Pistol-Packing Padre*

1. Walter Lord. *Lonely Vigil* (New York: Viking, 1977), p. 58.

2. Ibid., p. 58.

3. Ibid., p. 60.

4. After the Japanese were driven from Guadalcanal in early 1943, U.S. Major General Alexander M. Patch pinned second lieutenant's bars on Father Emery de Klerk, even though the padre was a Dutch national.

5. Father de Klerk survived the war and continued with his missionary work on Guadalcanal for many years.

6. Willoughby, *MacArthur*, p. 155.

7. Ibid., p. 157.

Chapter 7. *The Great Manila Bay Silver Heist*

1. Earlier, $2 million in gold bullion belonging to the Philippine Commonwealth had been shipped to the United States on the submarine *Trout*.

2. Readers Digest Association, *Secrets and Spies* (Pleasantville, N.Y.: Readers Digest Associations, 1962), p. 165.

3. Ibid., p. 166.

4. Ibid., p. 170.

5. All but one of the American sea divers survived the war.

6. After the war, the U.S. Navy raised $2.5 million from the bottom of Manila Bay, then quit trying because the boxes kept crumbling from rot and damage inflicted on them by the GI divers. It was costing more to bring up the silver than the value of the silver.

7. Although General MacArthur and Admiral Nimitz cooperated closely during the Guadalcanal campaign, the island was actually in Nimitz's area. Guadalcanal had originally been in MacArthur's Southwest Pacific Area, but the demarcation line with Nimitz had been moved to the western end of Guadalcanal because the navy had the ships and Marines available to invade the island.

8. Captain Robert J. Bulkley, Jr. *At Close Quarters* (Washington: Naval History Division, 1962), p. 180.

9. Ibid., p. 181.

10. *Chicago Tribune*, June 7, 1942.

Chapter 8. *A Spectacular Prison Break*

1. Major Nelson Raymond, the counterintelligence officer, was captured on Corregidor and later was killed or drowned when an unmarked POW ship was torpedoed while on the way to Japan.
2. Richard Sakakida retired years later as a lieutenant colonel in the U.S. Army and was living in the western United States in 1994.
3. Hamm, *Military Intelligence*, pp. 40–41.
4. *Popular Aviation*, April 1967.
5. Ibid., p. 43.

Chapter 9. *The Cat with Nine Lives*

1. Author interview with Mrs. Helge Janson (1988).
2. Willoughby, *Guerrilla Resistance*, p. 87.
3. Cat's-eyes was the term used for the narrow slits that remained when vehicle headlights were masked with tape or painted.
4. Willoughby, *Guerrilla Resistance*, p. 102.
5. After the war, Ruperto K. Kangleon became minister of defense for the new, independent Republic of the Philippines and later a senator.
6. Some fourteen thousand Japanese POWs were interrogated by the ATIS during the war. None were harmed or brutalized.
7. Sidney F. Mashbir. *I Was an American Spy* (New York: Vantage, 1952), pp. 227–28.
8. Ibid., p. 339.

Chapter 10. *"Fan the Peacock's Tail!"*

1. At the same time the Japanese "battleship admirals" were feuding with the "aircraft admirals," an identical fuss was raging in Washington.
2. Edwin P. Hoyt. *How They Won the War in the Pacific* (New York: Weybright and Talley, 1970), p. 252.
3. Henderson Field was named after a heroic U.S. Marine pilot who was killed in the crucial naval battle of Midway in early June 1942.
4. *Popular Aviation*, April 1967.
5. Edward Jablonski. *America in the Air War* (Alexandria, Va.: Time/Life Books, 1982), p. 154.
6. On September 11, 1945, the War Department officially credited Tom Lanphier with shooting down Admiral Yamamoto's bomber.
7. *Popular Aviation*, April 1967.
8. William Manchester. *American Caesar* (Boston: Little Brown, 1978), p. 320.
9. After the war, American investigators thought that Yamamoto was piloting the bomber when it was ambushed, but there was only circumstantial evidence.
10. *New York Times*, May 25, 1943.
11. Marine Lieutenant Charles Lanphier died at Rabaul only two weeks before his POW camp was liberated. Apparently, he never knew that his brother Tom had shot down Yamamoto's bomber.

Chapter 11.   *Boom and Bang in Singapore Harbor*

1. After the war, the Japanese admitted that five thousand Singapore civilians had been executed by the conquerors.

2. Ronald McKie. *The Heroes* (New York: Harcourt Brace, 1963), p. 31.

3. Ibid., p. 33.

4. Frogmen were specially trained and equipped underwater swimmers used by most of the warring military forces.

5. McKie, p. 112.

6. Ibid., p. 179.

7. Don Congdon, ed., *Combat World War II* (New York: Arbor House, 1958), p. 358.

Chapter 12.   *An All-Out Propaganda Blitz*

1. Douglas MacArthur. *Reminiscences* (New York: Norton, 1964), p. 271.

2. Whitney, p. 92.

3. Ibid., p. 134.

4. Ibid., p. 141.

5. Ibid., p. 142.

6. Willoughby, *MacArthur*, p. 219.

7. Ibid., p. 221.

8. Russell W. Volckmann. *We Remained* (New York: Norton, 1954), p. 132.

9. Ibid., p. 133.

Chapter 13.   *Rendezvous with MacArthur's Master Spy*

1. Willoughby, *MacArthur*, p. 222.

2. After the war, Jorge Vargas was cleared of collaboration with the Japanese.

3. José Laurel was cleared of collaboration after the war, and he became leader of the Nacionalista political party.

4. Willoughby, *MacArthur*, p. 231.

5. John Toland. *The Rising Sun* (New York: Random House, 1961), p. 319.

6. In August 1946, Manuel Roxas learned that the man who had saved his life, Colonel Nobuhiko Jimbo, was a prisoner in China awaiting trial as a war criminal. Roxas wrote a personal letter to Chiang Kai-shek, the head of state in China, pleading for amnesty for Jimbo. He was released and returned to Tokyo, where he lived for many years and maintained periodic contact with Manuel Roxas.

7. Willoughby, *MacArthur*, p. 246.

8. Ibid., p. 255.

9. Ibid., p. 261.

10. When the Philippines was granted independence by the United States in 1946, Manuel Roxas barely defeated Sergio Osmeña to become the first president of the new republic.

Chapter 14.   *Spying on the Conquerors*

1. Whitney, p. 146.

2. The Geneva Convention (or Treaty) provides for the humane treatment of prisoners and wounded men in wartime. It was first written in 1864 and new provisions were added in 1906, 1929, and 1949. Its terms were accepted by the United States, all European countries, and some of the nations of Asia (excluding Japan) and South America.

3. Whitehouse, pp. 138–39.

4. After Bataan fell, some sixty-five thousand American and Filipino soldiers, sailors, and airmen (and about forty U.S. Marines) were forced to march under horrendous treatment in the blazing sun for sixty miles to a POW enclosure called Camp O'Donnell. Thousands died or were murdered by the Japanese along the route.

5. After the war, High Pockets (Claire Fuentes) returned to the United States and was awarded the Medal of Freedom—the highest decoration for a civilian—by the federal government.

Chapter 15. *Raid on a Hidden Japanese Base*

1. The U.S. 503rd Parachute Infantry Regiment was the first unit to make a combat jump in the Pacific. However, the Marine 1st Parachute Battalion was the first American airborne outfit to fight in World War II when it made an amphibious landing on Tulagi, in the Solomons, on August 7, 1942.

2. Author provided background and some details of the Pulie River operation by Alyce Mary Guthrie, Executive Director of PT Boats, Inc., an association of some ten thousand PT-boat veterans.

3. William F. Halsey. *Admiral Halsey's Story* (New York: McGraw-Hill, 1947), p. 170.

4. Author interview with former PT-boat skipper Edward I. Farley (1990).

5. Walkie-talkies were hand-held, lightweight radios used to communicate over relatively short distances.

6. Author interview with Edward I. Farley (1990).

7. Author was unable to dig out names of American and Australian AIB men at Gloucester, but their efforts no doubt saved many GI lives.

Chapter 16. *An Intelligence Bonanza in a Briefcase*

1. Author correspondence with Colonel Gibson Niles (Ret.).

2. Ibid.

3. Kenney, *Know*, p. 359.

4. Walter Krueger, *From Down Under to Nippon* (Washington: Combat Forces Press, 1953), p. 49.

5. Manchester, p. 343.

6. Krueger, p. 50.

7. Kenney, *Know*, p. 360.

8. D. Clayton James, *The Years of MacArthur*, vol. I (Boston: Houghton Mifflin, 1975), p. 387.

9. Toland, *The Rising Sun*, p. 479.

10. Negros Island in the Philippines is not to be confused with Los Negros Island in the Admiralties.

11. After the war, James Cushing's difficulties with General MacArthur were resolved, due largely to the AIB officials. Cushing was reinstated as a lieutenant colonel and awarded a hefty cash bonus for his guerrilla work on Cebu. He died in the Philippines twenty years later, still beloved by the guerrillas who had fought under him.

12. Toland, *The Rising Sun*, p. 481.

13. Ibid., p. 482.

14. Several theories about Admiral Mineichi Koga's death were advanced for many years in the Philippines. One held that he was ambushed, like Yamamoto, and shot down and the dying Koga was picked up by a U.S. submarine and grilled by the skipper. Another theory was that he had crash-landed on a remote island and remained there the rest of his life, ashamed to return home.

Chapter 17. *Hoodwinking the Enemy*

1. Whitney, p. 175.

2. Ibid., p. 176.

3. Jean de Bruijn and Victor Gout were evacuated by submarine from Hollandia and survived the war.

4. Author correspondence with Colonel John M. Dove (Ret.).

5. A great deal of publicity in books and a movie was generated by the Allied use of dummy paratroopers in the D-Day invasion of Normandy, but MacArthur was the first to use the hoax.

6. The handful of ambush escapees eventually reached AIB stations, where they told the story.

7. Whitney, p. 183.

8. *New York Times*, May 2, 1944.

9. Interrogated after the war, Colonel Kazuo Horiba, a staff officer of the Japanese Southern Armies, declared, "Hollandia was a surprise.... When the enemy came when he did, far before the time expected, our defense preparations were not yet completed."

Chapter 18. *The Mysterious Mister X*

1. Not even Neil Armstrong, the first man to set foot on the moon, received the enormous worldwide adulation as did Charles Lindbergh for his solo flight across the Atlantic.

2. Lindbergh had been an Army Air Corps reserve captain. After his cross-Atlantic feat, he was promptly promoted to full colonel at age twenty-five.

3. Charles A. Lindbergh, *The Wartime Journals of Charles A. Lindbergh* (New York: Harcourt Brace Jovanovich, 1970), p. 871.

4. Ibid.

5. Leonard Mosley. *Lindbergh* (Garden City, N.Y.: Doubleday, 1976), p. 323.

6. Author interview with former PT-boat skipper Rumsey Ewing.

7. Robert L. Eichelberger. *Our Jungle Road to Tokyo* (New York: Viking, 1950), p. 213.

8. *New York Times,* July 30, 1944.

9. Eichelberger, p. 221.

Chapter 19. *"They're Waiting for Me Up There!"*

1. Halsey, p. 199.

2. Manchester, p. 376.

3. W. J. Holmes. *Double-Edged Secrets* (Annapolis: Naval Institute Press, 1979), pp. 188–90.

4. Willoughby, *MacArthur,* p. 172.

5. Army engineers threw up a prefabricated, white-washed house on the side of a green mountain for Douglas MacArthur to live and work in at Hollandia. From far below, the structure looked like a "white mansion," as one reporter falsely put it. Out of those reports grew outlandish rumors, including one that GIs were garbed in tuxedos and serving as butlers. Actually, the "white mansion" was primitive in nature.

6. Kenney, *Reports,* p. 156.

7. Mashbir, p. 256.

Chapter 20. *Rescuing the Philippines' First Family*

1. The Russian aim in tipping off the Japanese about the Philippines invasion apparently was that dictator Josef Stalin wanted to prolong the Pacific war until he decided the time was right to leap in and stake out postwar territorial claims.

2. Mashbir, p. 269.

3. David J. Steinberg. *Philippine Collaboration in World War II* (Ann Arbor: University of Michigan Press, 1967), p. 103.

4. Volckmann, pp. 175–76.

5. Manchester, p. 398.

6. After the war, Lieutenant Colonel Russell W. Volckmann tried to get faithful old Mr. Saito excepted from forced repatriation to Japan. His efforts were in vain. After living in the Philippines for more than forty years, Mr. Saito was sent back.

7. Holmes, pp. 193–94.

8. Volckmann, pp. 179–80.

9. Even in the early 1990s the name of Douglas MacArthur evokes reverence among thousands of World War II-era Philippine citizens.

Chapter 21. *Joey's Password Was Courage*

1. James, vol. II, p. 641.

2. *Readers Digest,* August 1951.

3. Readers Digest Association, p. 181.

4. A few days later, Captain Manuel Colayco was killed during fighting in the suburbs of Manila.

5. Josefina "Joey" Guerrero survived the war, and friends, who knew of her guerrilla role, arranged for her to become a patient at a leprosy hospital in the United States. She eventually regained much of her strength, her health greatly improved,

and her sores healed. Meanwhile, the U.S. government awarded Joey the Medal of Freedom, the nation's highest decoration for a civilian.

6. *New York Times,* February 7, 1945.

7. Author interview with Colonel Edward H. Lahti (Ret.), who led a regiment of the U.S. 11th Airborne Division in the Manila fighting. Also: James, vol. II, p. 644; Jay Luvaas, *Dear Miss Em: General Eichelberger's War in the Pacific* (Westport, Conn.: Greenwood, 1972), p. 225; Bertram C. Wright, *The First Cavalry Division in World War II* (Tokyo: privately printed, 1947), pp. 133–34; David Bernstein, *The Philippine Story* (New York: Dial, 1947), p. 217.

Chapter 22. *The Wild Men of Borneo*

1. For one of the few times it erred, the AIB missed the mark by far in estimating the number of Japanese the American invaders would face on Corregidor. AIB had estimated six hundred, but six thousand Japanese were hidden in caves and tunnels.

2. Author interview with Vice Admiral John D. Bulkeley (Ret.).

3. Author interview with Brigadier General George M. Jones (Ret.).

4. Daniel E. Barbey. *MacArthur's Amphibious Navy* (Annapolis: Naval Institute Press, 1969), p. 320.

5. Tom Harrisson. *World Within* (London: Crescent, 1959), p. 231.

6. Kenney, *Know,* pp. 132–33.

7. Ibid., p. 136.

8. On October 29, 1945—nearly two months after Japan surrendered officially—the last organized Japanese combat unit on Borneo capitulated.

Chapter 23. *A Close Call for Operation Giraffe*

1. *Free Philippines,* April 21, 1945.

2. *Manila Daily News,* August 26, 1945.

3. Although Morotai was a major U.S. base, a large number of armed Japanese units remained on the island until after Japan surrendered.

4. Ind, p. 169.

5. Ibid., p. 174.

6. Bulkley, p. 374.

7. Ibid., p. 376.

8. Rumors spread through the PT-boat squadrons based at Morotai that the Sultan of Ternate, in appreciation for his rescue, offered the PT men on the mission the choice of his harem for the night. There apparently was no foundation to the report.

Chapter 24. *Covert Peace Feelers*

1. *Washington Star,* July 6, 1945.

2. Author interviews with former PT-boat skippers Rumsey Ewing and Rear Admiral John Harllee (Ret.).

3. Ibid.

4. Bulkley, p. 389.

5. Ibid.

6. At the end of the war, all of the mahogany-and-plywood PT boats in the Pacific were collected on the island of Samar in the Philippines and burned in a gigantic "funeral pyre."

7. MacArthur, p. 261.

8. Jules Archer. *Frontline General* (New York: Julian Messner, 1963), p. 140.

9. "The Mysterious Dr. Hack," *Frankfurter Allgemeine Zeitung*, August 31, 1965.

10. Ibid.

11. Ibid.

12. Ibid.

13. Ibid.

14. Erin E. Jucker-Fleetwood, ed., "The Per Jacobsson Mediation," 1947. National Archives.

15. Ibid.

16. Ibid.

Chapter 25. *High Drama in Tokyo*

1. Hunt, p. 412.

2. Later, British Prime Minister Winston Churchill wrote, "Of all the amazing deeds in the global war, I regard General MacArthur's landing at Atsugi [Airport] as the bravest of the lot."

3. James, vol. II, p. 785.

4. Author interview with George Doherty.

5. Ibid.

6. William Craig. *The Fall of Japan* (New York: Harper, 1967), pp. 292–93.

7. Mashbir, p. 321.

8. A year later, Foreign Minister Mamoru Shigemitsu was convicted as a war criminal by an Allied tribunal. His sentence was commuted to life imprisonment, and after serving a couple of years, he was released. Soon he was again foreign minister, with the blessings of the Allies.

9. *New York Times*, September 3, 1945.

Index